SACRED MATTERS

SACRED MATTERS

Material Religion in South Asian Traditions

Edited by
Tracy Pintchman
and
Corinne G. Dempsey

SUNY PRESS

Published by State University of New York Press, Albany

Printed in the United States of America

For information, contact State University of New York Press, Albany, NY
www.sunypress.edu

Production, Diane Ganeles
Marketing, Kate R. Seburyamo

Library of Congress Cataloging-in-Publication Data

Sacred matters : material religion in South Asian traditions / edited by Tracy Pintchman and Corinne G. Dempsey.
pages cm
Includes bibliographical references and index.
ISBN 978-1-4384-5943-1 (hardcover : alk. paper)
ISBN 978-1-4384-5942-4 (paperback : alk. paper)
ISBN 978-1-4384-5944-8 (e-book)
1. Southeast Asia—Religious life and customs. 2. Religious articles—Southeast Asia. 3. Southeast Asians—Material culture. I. Pintchman, Tracy. II. Dempsey, Corinne G.

BL1055.S328 2016
200.954—dc23 2015008210

10 9 8 7 6 5 4 3 2 1

Contents

List of Illustrations vii

Acknowledgments xi

Introduction 1
Tracy Pintchman

1. The Icon of Yoga: Patañjali as Nāgarāja in Modern Yoga 15
Stuart Ray Sarbacker

2. God's Eyes: The Manufacture, Installation, and Experience of External Eyes on Jain Icons 39
John E. Cort

3. North Indian Materialities of Jesus 67
Mathew N. Schmalz

4. Celebrating Materiality: *Garbo*, a Festival Image of the Goddess in Gujarat 89
Neelima Shukla-Bhatt

5. The Goddess's Shaligrams 115
Tracy Pintchman

6. The Camphor Flame in an Age of Mechanical Reproduction 135
James McHugh

7. Metal Hands, Cotton Threads, and Color Flags: Materializing Islamic Devotion in South India 153
Afsar Mohammad

8. Monastic Matters: Bowls, Robes, and the Middle Way in South Asian Theravāda Buddhism 173
Bradley Clough

9. Letting Holy Water and Coconuts Speak for Themselves: Tamil Catholicism and the Work of Selva Raj 195
Selva J. Raj and Corinne Dempsey

List of Contributors 219

Index 223

Illustrations

Figure 1.1	Modern image of Patañjali as King of the Serpents (Nāgarāja).	16
Figure 1.2	Patañjali as Nāgarāja image at Krishnamacharya Yoga Mandiram.	21
Figure 1.3	Patañjali as Nāgarāja image at the Ramamani Iyengar Memorial Yoga Institute in Pune, Maharashtra.	22
Figure 1.4	Patañjali as Nāgarāja image from Cidambaram Temple, Tamil Nadu.	29
Figure 2.1	Ornamented Śvetāmbara icon of Ādeśvara (Ādinātha), Śāmḷājī Pārśvanātha temple, Patan, North 7 Gujarat, July 18, 1996.	41
Figure 2.2	Digambara icon of Ādinātha, Baṛā Terāpanth temple, Jaipur, July 24, 2013.	41
Figure 2.3	Glass *cakṣu* in workshop of Haricharan Manekchand Jadiya, Ahmedabad, November 9, 1995.	43
Figure 2.4	Glass *cakṣu* in collection of author.	44
Figure 2.5	Enamel *cakṣu* in collection of author.	44
Figure 2.6	Śvetāmbara icon of Pārśvanātha, dated 988. Originally from Broach, now in the collection of the Los Angeles County Museum of Art	

(M.71.26.38). Gilt copper inlaid with silver and gemstones. 46

Figure 2.7 Śvetāmbara icon of Ādeśvara (Ādinātha), Aṣṭāpad temple, Patan, North Gujarat, August 13, 1996. 52

Figure 2.8 Ornamented Śvetāmbara icon of Pañcāsar Pārśvanātha, Pañcāsar Pārśvanātha temple, Patan, North Gujarat, August 13, 1996. 58

Figure 3.1 Catholics hang a picture of Jesus as Guru at the Mission. 71

Figure 3.2 A worshipper prostrates himself before an image of Jesus in the Ashram's chapel. 76

Figure 3.3 Jesus as charismatic healer at the Ashram. 79

Figure 3.4 The resurrection of Jesus depicted in an aluminum grille at the Varanasi Cathedral. 81

Figure 3.5 Jesus depicted in the Jeevan-Darshan exhibit at the Varanasi Cathedral. 84

Figure 4.1 *Garbo* arena in Naranpura Village, October 2004. 95

Figure 5.1 Shaligram stones at the Parashakthi Temple. 129

Figure 7.1 The Metal Battle Standards of the Martyrs. 157

Figure 7.2 Metal battle standards in a procession. 160

Figure 7.3 Red sacred threads for sale. 161

Figure 7.4 Holy staff displayed inside the *dargah* of the Baba Fakhruddin. 165

Figure 9.1 Coconut sapling carried in St. Antony festival procession in Puliampatti. 203

Figure 9.2 Sandalwood paste is applied to a newly shaved head at St. John de Britto Shrine in Oriyur. 207

Figure 9.3 St. Antony festival procession on the beach. 209

Figure 9.4 Selva Raj interviewing pilgrims outside St. John de Britto shrine. 215

Acknowledgments

We offer our deepest gratitude to the colleagues whose contributions appear in this volume. Several of the chapters were initially prepared as papers for the June 2006 Conference on the Study of Religions of India, held at Loyola University of Chicago. Our colleague Selva Raj was at the time president of the conference organizing committee and was the individual responsible for suggesting we put together a collaborative volume around the theme of material religion. Several colleagues who could not attend the conference in 2006 agreed to contribute chapters to fill out the book. We wish also to offer our most heartfelt thanks to the editorial and production staff at State University of New York Press, especially Nancy Ellegate, Diane Ganeles, and Eileen Nizer for their support of this project. Finally, many thanks to Elspeth Tupelo of Twin Oaks Indexing, who prepared the index to the book with funding provided by Loyola University of Chicago.

Introduction

Tracy Pintchman[1]

There has been a tendency in many forms of religious discourse to associate religion primarily with the nonmaterial realm of extramundane considerations and experiences, especially beliefs about God or "the Ultimate" variously understood, timeless truths about eternal realities, and experiences that lie beyond the realm of ordinary human awareness. This tendency has remained remarkably tenacious despite numerous attempts by religious studies scholars to unseat it. It can be traced to the origins of contemporary religious studies in Enlightenment-era Protestant theology with its emphasis on belief and doctrine as the defining elements of religion. The field of religious studies continues also to be influenced by early phenomenological categories and approaches to religion scholarship, with their emphases on, for example, "the Holy" or "the Sacred" as categories that reside, ultimately, outside of history and the material realm. As Dick Houtman and Birgit Meyer have recently observed about the origins of the academic study of religion,

> Wasn't the opposition between spirituality and materiality the defining characteristic of religion, understood as geared to a transcendental "beyond" that was "immaterial" by definition? Grounded in the rise of religion as a modern category, with Protestantism as its main exponent, this conceptualization entails the devaluation of religious material culture—and materiality at large—as lacking serious empirical, let alone theoretical interest. (Houtman and Meyer 2012, 1)

An overriding emphasis on ideas, beliefs, theologies, and doctrines as the essence of religion persists in a widespread discursive practice of equating "religion" with "faith" and speaking of individuals as "members of the (Buddhist, Jewish, Hindu, and so forth) faith" and promoting "interfaith dialogue" as a means of bridging differences among religiously diverging groups.

The devaluation of the material realm in the study of religion is reinforced within critical academic religious studies scholarship by approaches that elevate texts and the ideas contained therein as the most favored objects of serious scholarly inquiry. This kind of textualism has now extended beyond the written word to include approaches to various nonliterary religious phenomena as, metaphorically speaking, simply other kinds of texts to be deciphered using the same methods of textual interpretation in which earlier generations of religion scholars indulged uncritically and unproblematically (c.f. Vaquez 2011, 15). Thomas Csordas observes that textualism

> has become, if you will, a hungry metaphor, swallowing all of culture to the point where it becomes possible and even convincing to hear the deconstructionist motto that there is nothing outside the text. It has come to the point where the text metaphor has virtually . . . gobbled up the body itself. . . . I would go so far as to assert that for many contemporary scholars the text metaphor has ceased to be a metaphor at all and is taken quite literally. (Csordas 1999, 146, quoted in Vasquez 2011, 15)

It is not at all our intention in this book to argue that there is anything inherently problematic with studying religious texts, doctrines, or ideas, or with approaching non-textual phenomena as metaphoric texts. But it is our intention to call into question the normativity of such approaches in the academic study of religion, moving to the margins of religious studies to focus our attention squarely not on ideas, beliefs, texts, or words, but instead on stuff. Here we join a growing movement of scholarly interest in material religion, a movement that fixes its gaze on visuality, materiality, and embodiment as vital religious categories. Focusing on materiality in the study of religions "signals the need to pay urgent attention to a real, material world of objects and a texture of lived, embodied experience" (Houtman and Meyer 2012, 4). Methodologically, moving beyond a textual approach to religious phenomena requires also engaging a more practice-centered approach to religion, one that demands placing the objects of our inquiry "in their contexts of production, circulation, and consumption" (Vasquez 2011, 255).

A move toward taking "the material" seriously in humanistic and social scientific scholarship was given an enormous boost by trends in culture studies, beginning primarily in the 1980s, that called for more sustained academic consideration of the cultural dynamics surrounding material objects. Works like Arjun Appadurai's seminal edited volume *The Social Life of Things: Commodities in Cultural Perspective* (1988) or Mihaly Csikszentmihaly and Eugene Rochberg-Halton's *The Meaning of Things: Domestic Symbols and the Self* (1981) helped focus attention on the nature of "things" as highly significant, and often shifting or complex, loci of meaning, identity, and culture. The idea that "objects have 'social lives'" helped engender new hermeneutical possibilities based on the premise that "in modern societies, where meanings and interpretations attached to images are relatively flexible and fluid, objects have careers or trajectories whereby their meaning for consumers changes over time and space" (Woodward 2007, 29). Thus emerged a newly invigorated, interdisciplinary field of material culture studies that has generated interest over the last few decades across a wide swath of disciplines in the humanities and social sciences. Ian Woodward notes of this "material turn":

> The fundamental conviction of material culture studies is that objects do matter for culture and society. . . . Not only do we constantly engage with objects in a direct, material way, we also live in a world where objects are represented as images and have global mobility. This means that understanding the 'social lives' (Appadurai, 1986; Kopytoff, 1986) of objects is one of the keys to understanding culture. (Woodward 2007, 28)

Religious studies as a field of academic inquiry has begun to be marked by this material turn. Books like Colleen McDannell's *Material Christianity* (1998), David Morgan's *Piety: A History and Theory of Popular Religious Images* (1998), Elisabeth Arweck and William Keenen's *Materializing Religion* (2006), Manuel Vasquez's *More Than Belief: A Materialist Theory of Religion* (2011), and Houtman and Meyer's *Things: Religion and the Question of Materiality* (2012), for example, have helped establish both the importance and the legitimacy of focusing scholarly attention on religious objects, highlighting the role they play in religious life. The creation of a journal in 2005 called *Material Religion* is a further indication of the extent to which the academic study of religion has in the last ten years come to take material culture increasingly seriously (see http://www.bergpublishers.com/us/material/material_about.htm).

The study of Asian religions has also turned its gaze toward the material realm. In the first half of the twentieth century, there was a penchant in American and European cultures for representing the religions of Asia, especially Hinduism and Buddhism, as contemplative, otherworldly religions concerned primarily with spiritual matters. The rising popularity in the United States since the 1960s of meditation and yogic practices—which engage the body but do so largely as a way of involving the whole self in processes that are ultimately about spiritual transformation—has often helped perpetuate this stereotype; and popular culture and media have sometimes tended to juxtapose, crudely, Western materialism with Eastern spiritualism. During the last few decades, however, changes in the academic study of religion in general and the study of South Asian religions in particular have helped draw more attention to forms of religiosity, including South Asian religiosity, that are concretely embodied in temples, pilgrimage practices, icons, amulets, religious objects, works of art, clothing, and so forth. In his book, *The Impact of Buddhism on Chinese Material Culture* (2003), for example, John Kieschnick argues that Asian religious material culture has been overlooked, and he devotes his efforts in this book to examining and analyzing the impact of Buddhism on material religious culture in China. In the study of Indian religions in particular, books like Diana Eck's *Darśan: Seeing the Divine Image in India* (1998), Richard Davis's *The Lives of Indian Images* (1999), and Jacob Kinnard's *Imaging Wisdom: Seeing and Knowing in the Art of Indian Buddhism* (1999) have done the same kind of thing, especially in relation to icons and other kinds of visual images employed in Indian religious practices.

In keeping with this growing interest in the complex and multivalent significances of things, this book examines material objects in South Asian religions in their regional, institutional, and ritual diversity. The chapters explore how, within the context of South Asian religious and cultural pluralism, objects embody, influence, create, exemplify, and shape the worlds of religious participants. Our focus here is on objects that have come to play vital roles in contexts we consider to be self-evidently religious in some way: these objects are, for example, worshiped, used, or displayed in religious buildings, settings, and practices, or for purposes that one typically recognizes as religious. Objects are not removed from cultural, historical, social, or political processes and trends but instead are deeply embedded and implicated in them, residing at the crossroads of cultural and religious vectors. Objects also have agency. They do not function simply as passive repositories of cultural meanings; instead, they may actively shape meaning, human activity, and social relations in diverse contexts depending on the varying ways they are engaged, manipulated, and interpreted.

Houtman and Meyer note the existence of a gap between "the promise of concreteness that makes the turn to 'things' and the notion of 'materiality' appear so attractive, on the one hand, and our still rather meager understanding of and lack of agreement about what we mean by 'matter' and 'materiality on the other" (4). Rather than venture too deeply into this quagmire about definitions, I note here that we agree with Arthur Asa Berger who observes, "Scholars may argue about definitions of material culture. Generally speaking, we can say that if you can photograph it and it isn't too large and complicated, we can consider it to be an example of material culture" (Berger 2009, 16). For purposes of this volume, to speak of material *religion* is to speak of particular, photographical (following Berger) objects that are deployed in some way in religious contexts. We explore collectively a range of traditions, including Hinduism (including yoga and diaspora Hinduism), Buddhism, Islam, Jainism, and Catholicism. We readily acknowledge the limitations of the term "religion" and the constructed nature of the "isms" named above and yet use these terms as useful starting points from which to launch our analyses. By examining material culture across a variety of South Asian religions, this volume helps highlight which aspects of material religious culture might seem to be shared and which might be distinctive to particular contexts and hence not necessarily part of a shared cultural base.

The first five chapters of this book focus on objects that serve as either iconic or non-iconic forms of deity or divine power across religious lines as dynamic embodiments of (sometimes conflicting) spheres of meaning and social relations. In chapter 1, "The Icon of Yoga: Patañjali as Nāgarāja in Modern Yoga," Stuart Ray Sarbacker focuses on an increasingly ubiquitous image (*mūrti*) of the sage Patañjali, the semi-mythical founder of yoga, found in yoga centers and yoga studios throughout the international yoga community. Although this icon has several key variations, the most commonly found image is of Patañjali in a half-human, half-serpent (*nāga*) form. This form is often said to represent the conception of Patañjali as an incarnation of Ādiśeṣa, the auspicious "Serpent-King" associated with the Hindu deity Viṣṇu. What is striking about this icon is its recent rise to international prominence despite being relatively uncommon in India. Sarbacker argues that this image demonstrates the transformation or transfiguration of a particular element of South Indian Hindu culture into a symbol for the international phenomenon of yoga through the vehicle of the "yoga diaspora." He examines the broader culture of the icon and the religious narratives that inform how it is interpreted in its native context in comparison to that of contemporary yoga movements. He further argues that the Patañjali icon resides at intersections between narratives that are at times in competition and at other times mutually interwoven.

While Sarbacker's chapter examines the icon of Patañjali in a global context, the second chapter, John E. Cort's "God's Eyes: The Manufacture, Installation, and Experience of Eternal Eyes on Jain Icons," focuses on the ornamentation of Jain icons in temple settings in Gujarat, North India. There are two main divisions of Indian Jainism: Śvetāmbara and Digambara. Śvetāmbara icons of Jinas, Jain "saints," have external eyes of glass, crystal, or enamel affixed to their faces, whereas Digambara icons do not. Exploring this material difference leads Cort to a consideration of central issues in Jain sectarian identity concerning the definition of the Jina and the relationship of Jains to icons of the Jina. Śvetāmbara Jains have criticized external eyes on the grounds that they harm icons, detract from religio-aesthetic experience of the icon, or signify a wrong understanding of the nature of the liberated Jina. Cort's essay focuses on the ways that the production and display of Jain icon eyes intersect with issues of community formation and identity in North India with respect to not only Śvetāmbara and Digambara Jains, but also the producers of the eyes (who happen to be Hindus and Muslims) and the "consumers" (Śvetāmbara Jains).

Chapter 3, Mathew N. Schmalz's "North Indian Materialities of Jesus," explores the ways images of Jesus are deployed at the Catholic Mission at Shantinagar in Eastern Uttar Pradesh (North India), an institution that is now fifty years old. During the 1960s, a new picture of Jesus was placed at the entrance to the mission's church in which Jesus is in the full lotus position, wearing the ochre robe of a traditional Hindu renunciant. The picture was designed to reflect Catholic adaptation to North Indian culture, but for the indigenous Catholic population, which consisted largely of untouchable manual laborers, this image of Jesus seemed disengaged from the world and stood in sharp contrast to the material concerns of the mission itself. Indigenous Catholics favored instead two other images of Jesus. The first was a light-skinned Jesus who was often presented as a larger-than-life cardboard cutout and placed on the stage for Catholic charismatic healing services. This Jesus spoke the language of the charismatic movement, a language that emphasizes not only the embodied nature of human being, but also the material prosperity brought by faith in Christ. The second image was a colorized version of the negative photo of the shroud of Turin—often taken to be an image of Jesus Christ himself. This image is housed in a chapel at a Catholic ashram in Varanasi to which Catholics of the Shantinagar mission often make pilgrimage. They bring offerings such as fruit, rice, and money and place them before the image, often bowing in reverence. Materiality thus is the primary medium through which these Catholics engage Jesus, not only to obtain favor but also to rid themselves of inauspiciousness. This chapter examines these different modes of "materiality" and what they reflect about the dynamics of Catholicism, inculturation, and untouchability in North India.

The next two chapters explore not icons per se, but rather aniconic representations of deities as they come to life in specific devotional contexts.

Chapter 4, Neelima Shukla-Bhatt's "Celebrating Materiality: *Garbo,* a Festival Image of the Goddess in Gujarat," explores material dimensions of the *garbo* ritual dance. In the lunar month of Ashvin (September/October), the Hindu festival of Navarātri or "nine nights" is celebrated with much fanfare in honor of the great goddess of the Hindu tradition. In the state of Gujarat, in western India, the chief component of the celebration is a worship dance, *garbo,* that has been prevalent in the region since at least the seventeenth century CE. It is traditionally performed by women at night around a festival icon of the goddess, a round, perforated clay pitcher in which a lamp is kept lit for the duration of the festival. The image is called *garbo,* a word linked to Sanskrit *garbha* ("fetus" or "womb"), and represents the cosmic womb of the goddess containing the divine light of life. But songs for the dance are also called *garbo,* as is the dance itself. Due to its popularity, *garbo* is now a part of popular culture even as it continues to be a religious form and performance. Since the female body is closely linked to materiality in Hindu cultures, and since popular culture is often expressed through material objects, *garbo* serves as a lens through which one may examine materiality in South Asian religions. This chapter examines the links among the materials used in *garbo,* the goddess as the cosmic mother, and the dancing bodies of women. It draws on symbolic meanings of clay pitchers in Indic traditions, Hindu theological concepts that identify the goddess with matter, and theories of dance in which "kinetic qualities of movement" convey knowledge.

My chapter, "The Goddess's Shaligrams," explores understandings of two special shaligram stones and the role they play in the context of an American temple called the Parashakthi, or Eternal Mother, Temple. Established in 1999, the Parashakthi Temple sits on sixteen acres of wooded land in Pontiac, Michigan. The Divine Mother worshipped in this temple is the Tamil goddess Karumariamman, "Black Mariamman," who, it is claimed, has manifested herself both in the village of

Thiruverkadu, just outside Chennai in Tamil Nadu, and at the Parashakthi temple in Pontiac. A beautiful icon of Divine Mother occupies center stage at the temple, yet since the temple's founding in 1999, many additional deities have been installed. In 2008, the spiritual director of the Parashakthi Temple, Dr. Krishna Kumar, brought to the temple from India two shaligram stones. Shaligram stones are understood broadly in the Hindu tradition as natural manifestations of Viṣṇu, but they play a different role at the Parashakthi Temple. According to Kumar, these particular shaligram stones are extraordinary, mystical, powerful objects whose arrival at the temple was orchestrated by Divine Mother herself for a specific purpose. This chapter asks a series of questions about the stones: How did shaligram stones, normally associated with devotion to Vishnu, come to play an important role at a temple nominally dedicated to the Divine Mother? What significance is normally attached to shaligram stones, and how is this meaning reconstituted in the context of the Parashakthi temple in Michigan? And by exploring these questions, what might we learn about the religious significance of materiality and material objects at this particular Hindu goddess temple?

The last four chapters of the book shift away from iconic and aniconic embodiments of divinity to focus on other religious objects, especially as they are deployed in contexts of ritual practice. James McHugh explores the shifting meaning of camphor in his chapter, "The Camphor Flame in an Age of Mechanical Production." Camphor, a white, pungently fragrant, crystalline substance, has long been a highly valued material in South Asian culture. It is used in traditional Indian medicine (Āyurveda) and is also an important ingredient in traditional perfumes and incenses. References to camphor abound in Sanskrit literature. But for many people, the context most strongly associated with the use of camphor in South Asia is religion, since one of the most conspicuous uses of camphor in India (as well as in Hindu religious contexts outside India) is in *pūjā* rituals of worship. McHugh explores the ways that camphor's religious and cultural significance, as well as its social meanings and uses, served as powerful forces in changing the mode of production of camphor from a system of forest production and trade to an industrial chemical process. What camphor is at any place and time is conditioned by a network of social, technological, institutional, discursive, economic, and, in this case, even theological factors.

In chapter 7, "Metal Hands, Cotton Threads, and Color Flags: Materializing Islamic Devotion in South India," Afsar Mohammad observes that normative versions of Islam strictly prohibit all types of external markers or objects that signify devotion. However, various public ritual performances of living Islam in South Asia highlight the use of metal icons, flags, and materials like sacred red threads. These objects are deeply implicated in the construction of local Islamic devotion as they produce and sustain context-specific meanings, narratives, and ritual practices among Muslims in Andhra Pradesh, South India. This chapter explores the multiple uses and meanings of ritual objects within the ritual settings of Muharram and *'urs* and in the ritual practices of *faqīri* and offerings of rags, flags, and cradles. The very use of these objects has become contentious throughout South Asia as a new wave of Islamic reformism strives aggressively to remove these kinds of Islamic objects from public spaces.

Bradley Clough's chapter, "Monastic Matters: Bowls, Robes, and the Middle Way in South Asian Theravāda Buddhism," explores the role that monks' bowls and robes have played in the religious lives of Theravāda Buddhists in South Asia. Looking primarily at the monastic code of Theravāda Buddhism, the Vinaya Piṭaka of the Pāli Canon, Clough examines the greater meanings that these items have had in this tradition, meanings that go well beyond ideas concerning the well-being of monastics' bodies and stomachs. Among the Vinaya's minutiae regarding the use of the robes and bowls one finds rules applied to their usage that address many of Buddhism's central values. Clough argues that Theravāda Buddhism has employed regulations concerning the use of the robes and bowls in order to inculcate in monks many central principles of the religion's "middle way," such as equanimity, mindfulness, detachment, and generosity.

The final chapter of the book, Selva J. Raj and Corinne Dempsey's "Letting Holy Water and Coconuts Speak for Themselves: Tamil Catholicism and the Work of Selva Raj," is co-authored because Raj, who was originally to be a co-editor on this volume, died very suddenly of a heart attack in March of 2008, and Dempsey graciously volunteered to step in and finish his chapter. Lay devotional religion in South Indian Catholicism centers around ritual actions and performances executed with the aid of material objects at pilgrimage sites and popular shrines. While these actions may be carried out throughout the year, lay involvement is particularly prominent during religious festivals. The material objects used at such occasions include a wide variety of votive objects, such as coconut, sandal paste, *neem* tree leaves, fruits, flowers, and body facsimiles in silver, aluminum, and gold. Even a cursory look would convince one of the striking uniformity in the votive objects used by South Asian religious practitioners, whether Hindu, Christian, or Muslim. This essay explores the patterns, logic, and grammar of a shared material religious culture that serves as a metaphor for the culture of dialogue that defines South Indian religious practice. Raj and Dempsey argue that the spontaneous, grassroots dialogue, manifest in the ritual lives of ordinary lay practitioners, emerges organically from their material culture and lived experiences. This is qualitatively different than the more orchestrated forms of interreligious ritual dialogue advocated by the religious elite.

What do we learn by reading these essays in conjunction with one another as a collective scholarly effort? What themes and patterns seem to emerge, and what larger issues for further consideration do these varied chapters seem to raise? Here I would like to conclude by highlighting three themes I glean from these pages as they pertain to what, in the contexts we explore, religious objects *mean*, what they *do*, and what they *embody*.

First, together these chapters expose a dynamic between continuity and discontinuity of discursive meaning that religious objects may carry from context to context. Shukla-Bhatt argues in her chapter, for instance, that the *garbo*'s core meaning, equating the universe with the divine, serves as an important and stable "point of departure" for the varied and divergent additional meanings it engenders across a diversity of ritual arenas. Sarbacker, similarly, argues that the image of Patañjali as Nāgarāja or "Serpent-King" in modern forms of yoga, while a modern image strongly tied to the Krishnamacharya yoga tradition of Southern India and its prominent disciples, nonetheless "serves as a vehicle for drawing the various threads of yoga tradition together with modern intellectual and bodily cultures." Other authors, however, emphasize the dynamic, contingent, and often shifting meanings that objects assume in relationship to particular contexts, be they geographical, historical, social, devotional, representational, or economic. McHugh, for example, notes of camphor that "the changing mode of production of camphor is closely tied to its changing religious significance," and that these changes have profound economic implications concerning camphor's value. And I note in my essay that in Michigan, shaligram stones become the province of the Goddess, not Vishnu, as they most often tend to be in more traditional Hindu contexts. Exploring what objects mean entails exposing and probing both continuities and divergences across time and space. Meaning can and does change, although it is not necessarily categorically unstable.

In addition to *meaning* things, however, religious objects also *do* things. Religious objects have power to shape the worlds they inhabit. Read together, these chapters offer a range of insights about what objects in South Asian religions are capable of doing, especially with respect to human relationships. Schmalz observes that the images of Jesus he explores in his chapter, for example, instantiate "particular relationships of giving, receiving, and exchange," and Cort probes "the role of material culture in the formation, maintenance and division" of North Indian Jain communities. In this regard, objects function in some contexts to help build social cohesion and solidarity between different religious or social groups; in other contexts, however, they can instigate or promote social or political conflict between or among groups. Hence Dempsey and Raj observe that, in South India, the use of religious objects in Catholic ritual indicates that "the power and flexibility of a range of ritual objects, whether traditionally Hindu or Catholic, potentially used by an array of practitioners, is foundational to the interreligious exchanges—and intra-religious tensions—that structure lay Catholic rituals at rural shrines." Raj observes how slivers of coconut blessed by a Hindu deity but consumed gleefully by a South Indian Catholic boy can serve as a site of exchange that transcends religious difference. Mohammad, on the other hand, highlights the nature of objects like battle standards, flags, and ritual threads as sites of identity conflict and differentiation among different Muslim groups. Objects can help produce a sense of collective identity or tradition even as innovation occurs, as McHugh and Sarbacker argue about camphor and Patañjali icons, respectively. Or they can generate anxiety as sites of potential conflict, like the robes and bowls that Clough describes as carrying the potential to materialize feelings of attachment and greed, or the eyes on Jain icons that Cort notes as a mark of distinction between Digambara and Śvetāmbara Jains.

Finally, in addition to meaning and doing, objects in South Asian religions—like other examples of material culture—*embody* histories. They evince the marks of past worlds. As Igor Kopytoff famously noted in "The Cultural Biography of Things"—and as other scholars have since emphasized—objects have biographies (Kopytoff 1986; c.f. Davis 1999), and exploring an object's biography "can make salient what might otherwise remain obscure" (Kopytoff 1986, 67). Kopytoff observes:

> In doing the biography of a thing, one would ask questions similar to those one asks about people: What, sociologically, are the biographical possibilities inherent in its 'status' and in the period and culture, and how are these possibilities realized? Where does the thing come from and who made it? What has been its career so far and what do people consider to be an ideal career for such things? What are the recognized 'ages' or periods in a thing's 'life,' and what are the cultural markers for them? How does the thing's use change with its age, and what happens to it when it reaches the end of its usefulness? (Kopytoff 1986, 66–67)

Hence, for example, Clough explores the multiple "biographical possibilities" inherent in Buddhist monks' bowls and robes by delineating their changing religious status over time. With regard to where things come from and who makes them, Cort and Mohammad document how the objects they examine in their chapters are sometimes not even made by Jains and Muslims, respectively, complicating their identity as religious objects. My chapter examines the biography of the Goddess's shaligrams to make sense of their significance at the Parashakthi Temple, observing that their unique biography gives them a unique form of power not shared by similar shaligram stones. Regarding different "ages" or "periods" in a thing's life, McHugh examines how camphor's story changes over time in response to changes in use and market demand, for example, and Sarbacker traces the development of the "Serpent-King" icon of Patañjali. As Sarbacker notes, religious objects can exemplify "the complexity and multidimensionality of cultural flow." Digging into the stories of religious objects often unearths social vectors beyond the realm of what we ordinarily think of as religion.

Almost all of the chapters in this volume address in some way different opinions—within and between traditions, cultures, and locations—about the "ideal" career of the highlighted objects. By way of contrast, none addresses directly the question that Kopytoff raises about what happens to an object when it comes to the end of its usefulness. Perhaps our lack of concern with "endings" signals our collective sense that the serious study of material religion in South Asian traditions is really just at the beginning stages. The deployment of material items in a plethora of South Asian religious, cultural, regional contexts shows no sign of waning. It is worth our while to begin paying closer attention.

Note

1. I am deeply grateful to Corinne Dempsey for her help in revising and refining this introduction.

References

Appadurai, Arjun, ed. 1986. *The Social Life of Things: Commodities in a Cultural Perspective*. Cambridge: Cambridge University Press.

Arweck, Elisabeth, and William Keenen. 2006. *Materializing Religion: Expression, Performance and Ritual*. Burlington, VT: Ashgate.

Berger, Arthur Asa. 2009. *What Objects Mean: An Introduction to Material Culture*. Walnut Creek, CA: Left Coast Press.

Csikszentmihaly, Mihaly, and Eugene Rochberg-Halton. 1981. *The Meaning of Things: Domestic Symbols and the Self.* Cambridge: Cambridge University Press.

Csordas, Thomas. 1999. "Embodiment and Cultural Phenomenology." In *Perspectives on Embodiment: The Intersection of Nature and Culture,* edited by Gail Weiss and Honi Fern Haber, 143–62. New York: Routledge.

Davis, Richard. 1999. *The Lives of Indian Images*. Princeton, NJ: Princeton University Press.

Eck, Diana. 1998. *Darśan: Seeing the Divine Image in India.* 3rd ed. New York: Columbia University Press.

Hautman, Dick, and Birgit Meyer. 2012. *Things: Religion and the Question of Materiality.* New York: Fordham University Press.

Kieschnick, John. 2003. *The Impact of Buddhism on Chinese Material Culture.* Princeton, NJ: Princeton University Press.

Kinnard, Jacob. 1999. *Imaging Wisdom: Seeing and Knowing in the Art of Indian Buddhism*. New York: Routledge.

Kopytoff, Igor. 1986. "The Cultural Biography of Things: Commoditization as Process. In *The Social Life of Things: Commodities in Cultural Perspective,* edited by Arjun Appadurai, 64–91. Cambridge: Cambridge University Press.

McDannell, Colleen. 1998. *Material Christianity: Religion and Popular Culture in America.* New Haven, CT: Yale University Press.

Morgan, David. 1998. *Visual Piety: A History and Theory of Popular Religious Images.* Berkeley: University of California Press.

Vasquez, Manuel. 2011. *More than Belief: A Materialist Theory of Religion.* New York: Oxford University Press.

Woodward, Ian. 2007. *Understanding Material Culture*. London: Sage.

1

The Icon of Yoga

Patañjali as Nāgarāja in Modern Yoga

Stuart Ray Sarbacker

Introduction

The display and use of the *mūrti*, an icon or "statue" of a deity of Indian or of broadly Asian origin, is a common phenomenon in the material culture of contemporary yoga traditions. Upon entering contemporary yoga studios, a visitor is often greeted with a display of icons native to the Hindu and Buddhist traditions of South, Southeast, and East Asia, most notably images of Śiva, Viṣṇu, Gaṇeśa, Devī (often in the form of the Goddess Lakṣmī), and Gotama Buddha (the "historical" Buddha). The use of such images, along with framed popular representations of such deities, is an important aspect of the material culture of the Hindu and Buddhist religious diaspora and of a larger and more amorphous spiritual and physical culture of yoga that is not anchored in a particular sectarian identity or geographical location.

One particular image that conveys the complexity of this negotiation of religious identity and authority in the contemporary context is that of Patañjali, a Hindu scholar and sage. Patañjali is the reputed compiler of the *Yogasūtra* (third to fifth century CE), one of the most authoritative textual representations of yoga philosophy. The use of the Patañjali image is only on the fringes of popular Hindu devotion but prominent within contemporary European and American yoga circles. In this form, Patañjali is the embodiment of yogic authority. He is portrayed as a *nāga*, the upper part of his body being human, with four arms, and the lower portion of his body the coils of a snake, wound two or three times and bearing the imprint of reptilian scales. The arms of the image bear a conch (*śaṅkha*) and a discus (*cakra*), along with either the combination of a sword (*asi*) and a no-fear gesture (*abhaya mudrā*) or the two hands folded together in a gesture of reverence (*añjali* or *namaskāra mudrā*). Patañjali is, in this form, identified as the king of serpents, Nāgarāja, Ādiśeṣa, or Ananta, a deity associated with the god Viṣṇu and with accounts of Hindu cosmogony and cosmology found in the Hindu Purāṇa literature. Patañjali is also, in this form, viewed as the author of important treatises on medicine and grammar as well as yoga.

Figure 1.1. Modern image of Patañjali as King of the Serpents (Nāgarāja). Photo courtesy of Mina Carson.

What will be argued in this chapter is that this *mūrti*, or image, of Patañjali exemplifies the complexity and multidimensionality of cultural flow, especially that of material culture, within the Indian and transnational contexts in which yoga has been propagated. The symbol of Patañjali embodies the multivalent and polysemic character of yoga itself, key factors in its propagation on an international scale. The attempt to bring together practices of yoga under a unified rubric is demonstrated on a textual level by the appeal to the authority of the *Yogasūtra* and on the level of visual culture through the representation of Patañjali as embodying the numinous power of yoga as an archetypal *yogī* or *guru*. What will be argued is that the constructed and malleable nature of the symbols and practice of yoga should not be seen as a mark of inauthenticity, as contextuality and universality are in a dynamic relationship with one another in a process of negotiation that is cyclical and multidirectional. To illustrate this, we will examine the material culture of the image of Patañjali in three interconnected contexts—within the "modern" traditions of yoga represented by Krishnamacharya and his disciples such as B. K. S. Iyengar, K. Pattabhi Jois, T. K. V. Desikachar, and Srivatsa Ramaswami; in the historical and textual world of Hindu and Buddhist asceticism and theism; and in the context of cosmopolitan forms of contemporary yoga that extend out of, but also diverge from, these precursors. It will be demonstrated that the theriomorphic form of Patañjali as Nāgarāja is a nexus of symbolism drawn from textual and material modalities, and its hybrid nature is the basis for its fluidity in crossing cultural, linguistic, and geographic boundaries.

Patañjali and the Modern Yoga Traditions

The emergence of yoga as a touchstone for Hindu spirituality in the late nineteenth and early twentieth century was in great part due to the championing of yoga by the Hindu missionary Swami Vivekananda, whose address at the Parliament of the World's Religions in 1893 is often viewed as a watershed moment in the modern history of Hinduism. In his numerous publications, Vivekananda formulated his vision of the Hindu religious path into different "yogas," and this championing of yoga as representative of the Hindu tradition helped to bring Pātañjala yoga to the center of Hindu orthodoxy with respect to yoga. Following the examples of other Hindu reformers, Vivekananda formulated a vision of yoga as a generic path that could be seen to have four primary permutations—action, devotion, meditation, and knowledge—and could be seen as universal within Hinduism and across the span of religious traditions (DeMichelis 2004, 124). The culmination of Vivekananda's work on yoga was his authorship of a series of books on yoga on each of the four themes mentioned above (two published posthumously) (124–25). Among these, the most important and influential was his *Rāja Yoga* (1896), a set of discourses on and a translation of Patañjali's *Yogasūtra*, which sought to integrate Pātañjala Yoga with concepts of *haṭhayoga*, Neo-Vedānta, modern science, and occultism (149–50). Elizabeth DeMichelis argues that this work is the root source in the formation of modern yoga, drawing multiple threads of narrative about yoga and various interpretations of yoga under the "eight-limbed yoga" (*aṣṭāṅgayoga*) rubric (151). Mark Singleton argues, similarly, that Orientalist scholarship in the late nineteenth and early twentieth centuries provided a solid foundation for consolidation of the plurality of yoga practices under one authoritative rubric (Singleton 1998, 37–39). These factors contributed to the modern conception of the "eight-limbed yoga" as a rubric into which all forms of yoga can be subsumed, a conception that is often at the heart of contemporary attempts to define yoga in a coherent and authoritative manner. It is no surprise, then, that the representation of the persona of Patañjali himself would emerge as a prominent emblem of authority with respect to yoga in the modern era. What might not be expected is the manner in which Patañjali is represented—as "Serpent-King" or Nāgarāja.

The proliferation of this type of icon can be tied to the influential tradition of modern yoga associated with the so-called "Father of Modern Yoga," Tirumalai Krishnamacharya (1888–1989). The authority of Patañjali and the *Yogasūtra* was a hallmark of Krishnamacharya's teachings on yoga, and quite notably of his disciples, many of whom are key figures in the development of modern yoga, such as B. K. S. Iyengar, K. Pattabhi Jois, T. K. V. Desikachar, and Srivatsa Ramaswami. According to the biography of Krishnamacharya, written by his son T. K. V. Desikachar, Krishnamacharya's yoga was the product of years of study and travel in which Krishnamacharya sought out prominent teachers of yoga and Indian philosophy in Southern and Northern India, culminating in a period of study with a prominent guru in Tibet, Ramamohan Brahmacharya (Desikachar 1998, 37–39). Having left his family in what Desikachar refers to as a "rupture," Krishnamacharya found his way ultimately to Lake Mansarovar at the foot of Mount Kailash, one of the most important pilgrimage sites in the Himalayas for both Hindus and Buddhists, where Ramamohan Brahmacharya lived in a cave ashram (37–39). Krishnamacharya is said to have studied with Sri Ramamohan for seven years, in which he learned some 3,000 of the 7,000 postures (*āsana*) that his guru knew, mastering yoga as a philosophy and a "science" and gaining the ability to arrest his respiration and heartbeat (43). Krishnamacharya is said to have committed Patañjali's *Yogasūtra* to memory and to have learned to chant it with "exactness of pronunciation" (43).

Upon the completion of his studies, Krishnamacharya is said to have been told by his guru to return to the householder life and teach yoga (44). This gave way to the next stage of Krishnamacharya's career, namely his career in the Mysore Palace, where, under the patronage of the Maharaja Krishna Wodeyar, he formulated and systematized his theory and practice of yoga, especially in the 1930s and 40s (Singleton 2010, 184–90). This phase came to fruition in the establishment of his *yogaśālā* or yoga studio in the Mysore Palace gymnasium, the attraction and training of numerous important disciples (including B. K. S. Iyengar and K. Pattabhi Jois) and noteworthy public figures, and in his authorship of two works on yoga, *Yogamakaranda* and *Yogāsanagaḷu*. Following independence and the subsequent diminishing of the Maharaja's political and economic power in Mysore in the shift toward secular governance, Krishnamacharya moved to Madras (Chennai), where his teaching continued to evolve. Ultimately, the Krishnamacharya Yoga Mandiram was founded in Chennai to celebrate his legacy and to provide for the ongoing dissemination of Krishnamacharya's teachings.

The recent work of scholars such as Norman Sjoman, Joseph Alter, Elliott Goldberg, and Mark Singleton has helped to clarify the emergence of modern forms of yoga, especially the influential traditions of Krishnamacharya. What each of them have argued, with respect to different but interrelated spheres, is that "modern yoga," i.e., the form of yoga that emerges in the late nineteenth to early twentieth century, is a composite entity, distinct in a number of ways from its historical precursors. As such, modern forms of yoga bring together a broad range of physical, intellectual, and religious cultures—from Indian Pātañjala Yoga, *haṭhayoga* and other traditions to European physical culturalist thought, Indian and European wrestling, calisthenic, and gymnastics training systems and metaphysical and occultist systems. Though it might be argued that this integration of various intellectual and physical cultures is somehow disingenuous, it might also be looked at as an authentic attempt to represent the traditions of yoga in a manner that is relevant to its audience. Modern yoga systems have to be understood as cosmopolitan in nature, as they are the product of a historical moment of exchange.[1] One of the great appeals of modern yoga practices is that they are, on a verbal and somatic level, simultaneously exotic and familiar to a broad global and cosmopolitan audience.

This is why the model of Patañjali is so compelling—the *aṣṭāṅgayoga* or "eight limbed yoga" rubric serves to weave the various threads of culture into a fabric that has unity and integrity, purpose and value. It is authoritatively representative of yoga, and yet flexible enough to incorporate "modern" ideas and practices. Patañjali was a systematizer and synthesizer of his own time, integrating philosophical ideas and ascetic practices from a broad spectrum of Hindu, Buddhist, and Jaina traditions. As such, Patañjali serves as a model for the scholar or practitioner of yoga who can masterfully present a coherent worldview and practice. We might look at Krishnamacharya as a sort of "latter-day Patañjali," who sought to codify and embody the integrity and coherence of a modern practice of yoga.

Lastly, Patañjali is often invoked, via mantra, at the beginning of the practice of yoga in the Krishnamacharya lineage, including in the traditions of his disciples K. Pattabhi Jois and B. K. S. Iyengar. Such invocations situate the practice of modern and contemporary traditions within the overarching rubric of Pātañjala yoga and within an understood lineage or sectarian tradition of yoga. Though they are rarely translated, such verses refer to Patañjali in his half-human, half-serpent form, wielding the discus, mace, and sword, with a 1,000-headed radiant cobra-hood. In some cases, these verses are connected to another set of verses that invoke Patañjali as a sage (*muni*) who cures diseases of body, speech, and mind by means of teaching medicine, grammar, and yoga. Patañjali is thus the "patron saint" or patron deity of the practice of yoga, and the invocation of Patañjali is presented as both validating the teachings of the lineage and as setting up an auspicious environment for the practice of yoga.

The Krishnamacharya Tradition and the Icon of Patañjali

This focus on Patañjali and his teachings as authoritative and worthy of veneration takes its most concrete form in the iconic representation of Patañjali in modern yoga. One of the most important examples is the iconic representation of Patañjali as Nāgarāja that is found at the Krishnamacharya Yoga Mandiram in Chennai, Tamil Nadu, in the heart of the institutional home of the Krishnamacharya tradition, and the "home base" for Krishnamacharya's son, Desikachar. This image represents Patañjali in the half-human, half-serpent form, with a human head sheltered by a five-headed *nāga* hood, hands in *añjali mudrā* with a set of *mālā* beads between the hands, and with two-and-a-half serpent coils beneath. Another image of great importance is that of Patañjali at the Sage Patañjali Temple in Bellur, Karnataka, a temple built by B. K. S. Iyengar and lauded by the Iyengar association as the first temple in

Figure 1.2. Patañjali as Nāgarāja image at Krishnamacharya Yoga Mandiram in Chennai, Tamil Nadu. Photo courtesy of Krishnamacharya Yoga Mandiram.

India dedicated specifically to Patañjali. It is no surprise, then, that it is among the disciples of Desikachar and Iyengar that we find the icon of Patañjali becoming a prominent symbol of authority and orthodoxy. Just as Krishnamacharya had systematized and popularized yoga for his generation in Southern India, Iyengar brought yoga to an international community through his high-profile publications (most notably *Light on Yoga*) and through demonstrations around the globe. Iyengar websites and practice-halls are adorned with the image of Patañjali as Nāgarāja, linking these local traditions to the source of their authority in the teachings of their guru B. K. S. Iyengar and his representation of Patañjali's tradition of yoga.

Figure 1.3. Patañjali as Nāgarāja image at the Ramamani Iyengar Memorial Yoga Institute in Pune, Maharashtra. Photo courtesy of Jayne Jonas.

Iyengar's temple of Patañjali, perhaps the first of its kind, demonstrates how the concretization of the authority of Patañjali has resulted in the propagation of a Patañjali "cult" that probably did not exist in an independent manner in the premodern context. This is not to say that traditions surrounding Patañjali or of *nāga*-worship did not exist prior to Iyengar's innovations. Rather, the modern representation of Patañjali in this particular form represents a transformation of existing Indian traditions in the cosmopolitan currents of the twentieth and twenty-first centuries. In order to understand this, it makes sense to examine where this image has come from, how Patañjali and Ādiśeṣa are connected, and how such conceptions filtered into modern and contemporary yoga. In order to explore these issues, we will turn to a discussion of the historical and literary roots of the connection between the *nāga*, the *nāgarāja*, yoga, and ultimately, Patañjali.

Patañjali and the Nāga Traditions

In key works of Hindu narrative, such as the Mahābhārata and the Purāṇa literature, the *nāga* is a representative of a "race" of beings that are cosmologically linked to the creation of the world (via Brahmā or Viṣṇu), human society, and the underworld of the cosmic order. Much like the theriomorphic image of the *kentauros* or *centaur* in the Greco-Roman tradition, it might be speculated that the *nāga* as a mythical being is symbolic of an ethnic or cultural group allied to snakes with regard to their livelihood (such as snake charming) or through particular religious practices (such as snake worship and handling) (Nash 1984, 273–91). This is, in fact, argued by some with respect to the tribal groups that continue to exist under the rubric of the designation of *nāga* (Handa 2004, 80–106). The *nāga* as such can be understood as a symbolic representation of a type of social identity that is woven into narrative through the medium of genealogy, and connected through elemental associations and regional geography, bridging the gap between translocal (or even pan-Indian) and local traditions. The *nāga* is strongly associated with the forces of nature, such as water, and particular places (such as termite mounds or a particular pond) which are the locus of snakes or serpents. As regional forms of the village deity (*grāmadevatā*) or chosen deity (*iṣṭadevatā*), the *nāga* represents a unique permutation of a larger, overarching motif of the spirit-cult, akin to the traditions of other nature spirits such as those of the *yakṣa* and *yakṣī*.

Nāga traditions were particularly important in the early Indian Buddhist tradition as well, with the Buddha himself understood as a descendent of a *nāga* lineage, and the spirit-cult of the *nāga* playing an important part in the Buddhist tradition as testified in scripture and in art (Panda 1986, 36–37). This connection continues to play an important role in Theravāda Buddhism and Tibetan Buddhism, where the *nāga* (Pali *naga*, Tibetan *lü*) remains an important force to be reckoned with in the contemporary practice of Buddhism (Baker and Laird 2000; DeCaroli 2004). For Mahāyāna Buddhists, the realm of the *nāga* world is the place where esoteric teachings are stored or originate, exemplified by the connection with the philosopher-*siddha* Nāgārjuna, who gains his heroic appellation through his retrieval of texts from this subterranean world (Dowman 1985, 117–18). *Nāgas* are viewed as keepers and protectors of hidden knowledge and treasure and may be understood to become aggressive when human beings upset the natural order of things (Panda 1986, 26–28).

Among the *nāga* figures of Hindu narrative, the one that stands out most clearly in classical narratives is that of Ādiśeṣa, Śeṣa or Ananta, understood to be "the" *Nāgarāja*, "King of the Serpents." This particular *nāga* is identified in the Mahābhārata as a Prajāpati, who, following the emergence of Brahmā from Mahāviṣṇu, and through Brahmā's son Kaśyapa and his consort Kadrū, was born as Ananta (Mani 1975, 34). Ananta, initially given to ascetic austerities, was asked by Brahmā to support the world from its base in the underworld, Pātāla, and he does so in rapturous splendor as a 1,000-hooded cobra that is crowned with gems (Mani 1975, 34–35; Vogel 1926, 75, 190–98). In this capacity, Ananta is the firmament of the world, and thus Śeṣa, "remainder," or Ādiśeṣa, the "primordial remainder."

Perhaps the most well-known form in both classical and modern art and literature, however, is of Ādiśeṣa serving as the bed upon which Viṣṇu reclines in his heavenly repose (Vogel 1926, 192–94). The "crowning" of Viṣṇu by the serpent, as a mark of royal ease and protective shelter, is the most prominent example of a long-standing association between sacred figures and the "sheltering" or ornamentation by serpents or specifically the *nāga*. The figure of Viṣṇu reclining on Śeṣa is represented in another permutation in which Viṣṇu sits upon the coils of Śeṣa and is covered by the hoods of the *nāga* (Vogel 1926, 194; Desai 1973, 24–30). Likewise, Śiva in his anthropomorphic form is often adorned with serpents; in iconic form as the *liṅga*, he is often sheltered by the hood of a *nāga*.

The representation of Patañjali as Nāgarāja also bears resemblance to the Indian motif of the seated ascetic sheltered by a *nāga* (Huntington 1993, 22). Examples of this motif include the example from the Indus Valley Civilization and, most importantly, images of Tīrthaṃkara Pārśvanātha and Gotama Buddha. In the cases of the Jina and the Buddha, the representation is of the *nāga*, or *nāgarāja*, as a protector of an ascetic, sheltering him from anti-ascetic spiritual forces and the assault of the elements. Pārśva or Pārśvanātha, the 23rd Tīrthaṃkara, or "crossing maker" and fully enlightened sage of Jainism, is commonly represented as a naked seated figure, with crossed legs, in the posture of meditation (*dhyānamudrā*) sheltered under the hood of a many-headed *nāga*. This representation is tied into a narrative in which the *nāgarāja* Dharaṇendra protects Pārśva from the attacks of the god Meghamālin or Saṃvara, who showers Pārśva with torrential rain and floods, and sends minions to hurl rocks after the sage's enlightenment (Shah 1987, 3). Dharaṇendra shields the Tīrthaṃkara with his hood and coils from the attacks of Meghamālin, which resemble closely the attacks on Gotama Buddha by Māra, the so-called "lord of death," who attempts to prevent Gotama from achieving enlightenment. In the case of Gotama Buddha, we see a similar representation in which Gotama Buddha is seated in *dhyānamudrā* upon the coils of the *nāgarāja* Mucilinda, whose hood protects Gotama from a driving wind and rainstorm after the Buddha's awakening (3). This iconography of the ascetic that is protected by the *nāga* parallels the Patañjali image, though in the case of Patañjali, the two figures (ascetic and *nāga*) are unified, as the figure of Patañjali is of a half-human, half-serpent figure. There is thus a thematic if not genealogical relationship between these figures—Pārśva, Gotama, and Patañjali—who embody the ascetic or yogic principles within the respective traditions of Jainism, Buddhism, and Hinduism. The link between Patañjali as *yogin* and *nāga* is consistent with the identification of Śeṣa the *nāgarāja* as an ascetic, and the overarching theme in Indian literature of the link between ascetic practice and the powers of the *nāga*. It is also consistent with the theme of the homologizing of the powers of the *nāga*—specifically control over the elements—with the powers of the *yogin* or *yoginī*, which Cozad has argued is key to understanding the relationship between the Buddha and Mucilinda (Cozad 2004, 81–106).

This process, which validates *nāga* worship and subsumes it under the overarching rubric of a sectarian tradition of asceticism, makes great sense from the viewpoint of the nature of yogic practice and its effects. The renunciatory (liberative or cessative) element of yoga, which emphasizes withdrawal from worldly life and concerns, is tied into a reconnection with nature and especially the forest, the *locus classicus* of ascetic practice in the Indian tradition. Trees are particularly significant as being the abode of ascetics and the seat of their practice. Gotama's and Mahāvīra's enlightenment experiences are represented as happening at the base of a tree. The situation of the *nāga* within the realm of the wilderness, and at specific locations within that wilderness, parallels the locus of asceticism. The powers of the *nāga* over the elements parallel the power that ascetics gain through *tapas* or austerities. The physical disciplines and contemplative practices of yoga are understood in Indian philosophical and narrative literature to lead to both power and liberation (Sarbacker 2005; 2008). The powers are "numinous" or akin to those of a deity, and can also be referred to as "elemental" powers because they represent the ascetic's control over the morally ambivalent forces of nature (Sarbacker 2008, 171–72). The *nāga* thus acts as a powerful symbol for the connection between asceticism and nature, and for the connection between yogic practices and the attainment of power over the environment.

The Many Faces of Patañjali

The importance of Patañjali as an authority on the practice of yoga in the Hindu tradition is rooted in his authorship or compilation of the

Yogasūtra, or "thread of yoga," which is a Sanskrit text dated to approximately third to fifth century CE. The *Yogasūtra* consists of 195 verses that lay out the foundational principles of what is referred to as the *yoga darśana*, or "yoga view," a philosophical system that is often referred to as one of the "orthodox" (*āstika*) systems of Indian philosophy. This type of scholarly narrative is typically augmented by either an oral or written commentary by a guru or scholar who can, in principle, explicate the full meaning of the text by means of his experiential and intellectual knowledge on the topic. In the case of the *Yogasūtra*, the primary resource for interpretation is the *Yogabhāṣya* commentary, attributed to Vyāsa (fifth to seventh century CE). Other important commentaries include those of Vācaspatimiśra (ninth to tenth century CE), Śaṃkara (tenth to fourteenth century CE), and Vijñānabhikṣu (sixteenth century CE) (Larson 2008, 50–52). One of the most influential concepts in the *Yogasūtra* is that of the "eight-limbed yoga" (*aṣṭāṅgayoga*), which encapsulates yoga as being composed of eight parts: restrictions (*yama*), observances (*niyama*), posture (*āsana*), breath-control (*prāṇāyāma*), sense-withdrawal (*pratyāhāra*), mental fixation (*dhāraṇā*), meditation (*dhyāna*), and contemplation (*samādhi*). Yoga is represented as a means to obtain magical powers over worldly phenomena (*siddhi* and *vibhūti*) and separation (*kaivalya*) from the world and ultimately the process of birth and rebirth (*saṃsāra*). These concepts and principles bear great resemblance to ascetic and yogic disciplines in Buddhism and Jainism, which Patañjali was clearly drawing upon.

As the author of the *Yogasūtra*, Patañjali thus represents the embodiment of authority with respect to the yoga tradition. Numerous theories have been ventured as to his identity, with one of the key dynamics being between envisioning Patañjali as first and foremost a philosopher (in some cases identified with the Sāṃkhya philosopher Vindhyavāsin) and envisioning Patañjali as first and foremost a *yogin*, or practitioner of yoga (Larson 2008, 54–70; Bronkhorst 2005, 62–76; Whicher 1998, 42–45). Gerald Larson has argued strongly that the *Yogasūtra* represents the emergence of a "neo-Sāṃkhya" philosophy in response to the development of Buddhist philosophy (Larson 2008, 21–52). Dasgupta goes as far as referring to the "Pātañjala school of Sāṃkhya" (Dasgupta 1922, 229). However, the roots of the yoga tradition are clearly deep within the ascetic traditions of ancient India, and strong arguments can be made that the *Yogasūtra* reflects an attempt to present the discipline of yoga in a coherent and integral fashion (Whicher 1998, 45). In this spirit, Whicher argues for an image of Patañjali as a scholar-*yogī* and likely the head of a lineage of practitioners (43). However, there are also questions as to whether Patañjali can be thought of as an author at all, and even some questions as to whether the name Patañjali was ascribed to the text as an author or composer at a later date (Bronkhorst 2005, 71). The issues of

Patañjali as a scholar or as a practitioner and the nature of his "authorship" of the text are brought to greater complexity by the traditional identification of Patañjali as the author of works on grammar and medicine as well as yoga. Patañjali as the author of the *Yogasūtra* has been traditionally identified with the author of the Mahābhāṣya, a commentary on Pāṇini's grammar, and the author of the *Carakapratisaṃskṛta*, a commentary on Caraka's work on medicine (Larson 2008, 54–61). Likewise, Woods has pointed out how this connection is made in manuscripts of the *Mahābhāṣya* (Woods 1914, xiv). Thus, Patañjali is seen as a key commentator or codifier of the traditions of knowledge regarding mind (*citta*), language (*śabda*), and medicine (*cikitsā*). Larson argues that these connections are important in that they reify the authority of Patañjali as the master over the Hindu "sciences" in the early centuries of the Common Era (Larson 2008, 54–61).

Patañjali, as the master of these three domains, is further represented in important literary invocations as Nāgarāja or Ādiśeṣa himself having taken on human form. Phillip Maas has argued that such invocations have a clear genealogical history on the manuscripts of the *Yogasūtra*, and that this identification begins in Northern recensions of the *Yogasūtra* and finds its way throughout the tradition over time (Maas 2008, 97–119).[2] Deshpande argues that it may have been connected to the linguistic conflation of Patañjali as Ādiśiṣṭa, "foundational scholar," with Patañjali as Ādiśeṣa (Deshpande 1992, 113n7; 1997, 453). One of the clearest links between Pātañjala Yoga and Ananta or Śeṣa is made in an invocation (*maṅgala*) to Vyāsa's *Yogabhāṣya*. In this passage, Vyāsa is represented as providing an invocation to Śeṣa, who is portrayed as one that has "abandoned his primal form" as a hooded serpent with attendant serpents, and is asked for protection as the giver of yoga who is himself immersed in yoga (Woods 1914, 3–4). Vyāsa's invocation appears to be a reference to the incarnation (*avatāra*) doctrine, which is central to Vaiṣṇava theology, and importantly provides grounds for the theological link between Patañjali and Ādiśeṣa. Vijñānabhikṣu makes this association transparent, articulating an understanding that Śeṣa has given up his original serpent-form and taken the form of Patañjali in order to transmit yoga. Ananta or Śeṣa thus becomes the "patron deity" or "chosen deity" (*iṣṭadevatā*) of yoga and Patañjali and Ananta come to be viewed as one and the same being.[3]

The Link to the Temple Tradition

Deshpande has argued that the origins of the iconographic representation of Patañjali as Ādiśeṣa probably began in southern India at the

Naṭarāja temple at Cidambaram in the thirteenth century CE (Deshpande 1992, 95–116). He notes that one of the earliest literary references to Patañjali as an incarnation of Śeṣa appears in the Kashmirian poet Rājānaka Jayaratha's *Haracaritacintāmaṇi* (113n7). Another source for the development of the Patañjali-Śeṣa connection is the *Patañjalicarita* of Rāmabhadra Dīkṣita (seventeenth century CE), perhaps the most elaborate source with respect to the narrative of Patañjali, his connection with Cidambaram, and the identification of Patañjali as Śeṣa or Nāgarāja. In the *Patañjalicarita*, the narratives of Patañjali as *yogī*, grammarian, and divine being come together in an explicit fashion. One of the key narratives in the *Patañjalicarita* is of the birth of Patañjali, in which Goṇikā, a daughter of a sage, prayed to the sun god for a son, at which point Ananta fell into (or out of) her hands in the form of a sage (following the "folk" etymology of *pat* + *añjali*, "fallen into/from the folded hands [of Goṇikā]") (Younger 1995, 171). Goṇikā raised the young sage, went on worship Śiva at the Cidambaram temple, who in turn blessed Patañjali with the capacity to write his grammatical work (Mani 1975, 583). Another narrative is told of how Patañjali taught from behind a curtain and at one point "cursed" all of his students except for one, an ancestor of the great grammarian Bhartṛhari (583). The narrative of Patañjali is represented from a different angle in the *Citamparamāhātmya*, a twelfth- or thirteenth-century South Indian Sanskrit text that may have served as a pilgrim guidebook for North Indian visitors (Younger 1995, 171). This story of Patañjali is centered upon the story of the sages of the Tārukā forest, in which Śiva and Viṣṇu appear in disguised form in order to test and charm the ascetic sages. The height of this narrative is a sequence in which Śiva dances and mesmerizes the entirety of his audience, including Viṣṇu, with his "Dance of Bliss" (*ānanda tāṇḍava*). Later, Viṣṇu, having returned to his heavenly abode, relates this story to Ananta, who swoons at the thought of witnessing such a dance (171). Śiva promises to perform the dance again, but asks Ananta to find his way to Cidambaram and take on a human birth (171). Ananta does so by first traveling a subterranean path, and then is born to human parents in his half-human, half-serpent form. In this variation of the narrative he falls (*paṭ*) from the hand (*añcali*) of his surprised mother (171). This narrative has the effect of placing Ananta, and by extension Viṣṇu, in a position secondary to that of Śiva, which is not surprising given the strong Śaiva sectarian tradition associated with the Cidambaram temple and the larger influence of Āḻvār Vaiṣṇava traditions (Palaniappan 2007). This also coincides with a common theme in south Indian temples in which Ananta is represented as a tutelary deity (Shulman 1980, 122).[4]

What is clear is that Cidambaram is at the hub of a nexus of narrative and art that establishes connections between Patañjali as grammarian, *yogī*, and as an incarnation of the *nāgarāja* Adiśeṣa, Śeṣa, or Ananta. As grammarian, Patañjali is at the heart of the priestly (*brāhmaṇa*) liturgical and educational life of the temple. As a *yogī*, Patañjali represents the connection between Śiva, ascetic traditions, and the authoritative literature on yoga. As Nāgarāja, Patañjali is an integral part of the cosmogony and cosmology of the Hindu universe, an agent of, if not an incarnation of, the god Viṣṇu, and representative of the power of the *nāga* on the level of localized grassroots religiosity. These factors all come together at Cidambaram, in that Patañjali is represented as both *yogī* and grammarian and parallels the connection between the local *nāga* cult and the practice of asceticism. The oldest image of Patañjali at Cidambaram, perhaps twelfth or thirteenth century CE, represents Patañjali as a half-human and half-serpent, with a human head, two arms with hands in *añjali mudrā* and holding a *mālā*, with a five-headed *nāga*-hood, and a serpentine lower body with two-and-a-half coils.

Figure 1.4. Patañjali as Nāgarāja image from Cidambaram Temple, Tamil Nadu. Photo courtesy of David Smith.

The Icon of Patañjali: Past and Present

This is where our discussion comes full circle. The image at Cidambaram is a visual and material link to the contemporary image of Patañjali at the Krishnamacharya Yoga Mandiram in Chennai. It provides a tangible link between the traditions of Patañjali at that temple and the Yoga tradition of Krishnamacharya as centered in Chennai. Iconographically, the two images are a near perfect match, with the exception that the image at Cidambaram has fangs and the Krishnamacharya Yoga Mandiram image does not—perhaps representing a softening of the image (Staal 1972, xvi, frontispiece, plates 1–2; Desikachar 1998, 196, plate 1). In the Patañjali tradition of Cidambaram, the image is at the hub of the merging of various threads of tradition, including grammar, philosophy, asceticism, devotion, sectarian traditions of Viṣṇu and Śiva, Northern and Southern Indian traditions, grassroots traditions of *nāga* worship, and regional sectarian competition. As such, Patañjali is the archetype for the scholar-*yogī*, a figuration that Krishnamacharya and his disciples (especially Iyengar and Jois) have clearly striven toward, if not fully realized, in their lifetimes. Patañjali serves as the model for the yoga *guru* and scholar, or polyglot, and arguably in a broader sense for the collective self-perception of the community itself, to put it in Durkheimian terms. As an originator or founder of the lineage, Patañjali represents the ultimate source of authority that is to be respected and emulated by scholars and practitioners of yoga.

The archetypal nature of the representation of Patañjali is furthermore supported by the use of Patañjali's *aṣṭāṅgayoga* rubric and the scope of the *Yogasūtra*, which becomes a framework for drawing together the threads of the plurality of yoga methods with modern and cosmopolitan physical and intellectual culture in a holistic fashion. As Klas Nevrin has argued, the *Yogasūtra* itself also becomes virtually *śruti* (literally "heard," but implying "revealed") literature in the Hindu tradition, part of a yogic liturgy that has power in its recitation as well as in its discursive capacity (Nevrin forthcoming). In addition to this, for Krishnamacharya, who was a Vaiṣṇava *brāhmaṇa*, the association of Patañjali with Ananta resonated with the symbolic content of his religious worldview. The principal deity of Krishnamacharya's Śrī Vaiṣṇava tradition was the Viṣṇu incarnation (*avatāra*) of the "horse necked" Hayagrīva, a deity with a human body and a horse's head, often portrayed with the hood of a *nāga* above it. Reverence toward a theriomorphic figure, including the figuration of the *nāga* hood above the deity, was part of Krishnamacharya's liturgical life. To the degree that Śeṣa is seen as a manifestation or incarnation (*avatāra*) of Viṣṇu or his attendant Adiśeṣa, the theriomorphic Vaiṣṇava figure is a familiar concept and form.

As discussed earlier, the figure of the *nāga* can be linked to the mastery of elements, the powers of yoga being comparable to the elemental powers of the *nāga*. The *nāga* realm of the underworld could be said to represent that which lies outside the boundaries of the visible and familiar world, and the numinous power of the unknown, mysterious, and dangerous. To the degree that Patañjali as a model represents both the elemental power of the *nāga* and the institutional authority of scriptural, philosophical, grammatical, and liturgical connections, Patañjali would seem to draw on both elemental authority and institutional authority. With respect to elemental authority, it can be pointed out that Krishnamacharya and his disciples won over a greater public through their demonstration of mastery over their bodies, primarily through their demonstration of complex postural (*āsana*) practice, involving a high level of strength, stamina, and mobility (Desikachar 1998, 85–91). Krishnamacharya was also well known for his ability to stop his heart from beating (27–28). These extraordinary abilities conferred upon Krishnamacharya an authority as a sort of wonder-worker that was instrumental in his institutional success, and established a paradigm that would be followed by his prominent disciples, including B. K. S. Iyengar and K. Pattabhi Jois. This aspect was augmented by Krishnamacharya's association with powerful patrons and celebrities, whose authority and virtuosity complemented his own, an association that continues in contemporary yoga traditions between prominent teachers and celebrity patrons (23–24, 85–97).[5]

Patañjali as Nāgarāja in Contemporary Yoga

The representation of Patañjali as Nāgarāja in contemporary yoga is part of a larger material culture of yoga that exploded in popularity and visibility in the global context in the late twentieth century. Popular publications have used symbols and representations of yoga as a basis to sell products for the practice of yoga and the yoga "lifestyle." The government of India has run advertising campaigns for tourism in India, including one entitled "Incredible India," that portray figures in various yoga *āsana* positions, with regional backdrops of various Indian destinations—implicitly suggesting that yoga is the underlying spiritual unity behind India's diversity. These advertisements highlight the exotic, with emphasis on the beauty of India's natural resources and little attention to the urban sphere. Yoga has filtered into the mainstream of global, and especially European and North American, consciousness, facilitated by the celebrity culture of yoga, which includes such notable twenty-first-century figures in popular European and American musical culture as Madonna, Sting, and Russell Simmons. The market for yoga "goods" has expanded tremendously, spurred on by publications such as *Yoga Journal*, which has become a clearinghouse for yoga products and services. The market for such goods revolves around yoga apparel and yoga "props," items such as yoga mats, blocks, bolsters, straps, and other materials that facilitate the primarily posture-driven practice of popular yoga. Religious goods such as icons and images of deities and ritual implements, such as incense burners and bells, serve to inform the atmosphere of the practice of yoga and, in some cases, connect the practice of yoga to its sectarian or spiritual roots. The attire, various props, and the material culture of yoga more broadly can be seen as a permutation of "amulet" culture, in that these objects are charged with symbolic power, having the ability to evoke a particular set of emotions that are inspirational to the practitioner of yoga (Sarbacker 2008, 176–77).

Traditions such as Sivananda Yoga, which has retained a strong sectarian identity, are often the most orthodox with respect to having a dedicated image—such as Viṣṇu or his incarnation as Kṛṣṇa—as part of their practice space. In many studios in North America, sectarian affiliation or identity is less apparent, but there is some consistency with respect to the use of images, in that many, if not most, studios contain images that are a permutation of Śaiva, Vaiṣṇava, Śākta, and Buddhist images. Images are rarely formally consecrated (*prāṇapratiṣṭha*) or used ceremonially for worship (*pūjā*), though they may be venerated and given "offerings" of incense and fruit. McDannell's concept of "kitsch culture" is a good fit for this creation of a spiritual atmosphere that icons and images of Hindu and Buddhist deities provide in many contemporary yoga studios (McDannell 1995, 163–97).[6] These icons and other materials provide for the creation of an atmosphere that is intended to inspire and set apart the space of the yoga studio. Stepping into the yoga studio means stepping into another world, or stepping out of one type of space (often urban) into another.

There is an interesting dynamic between the exoteric and esoteric nature of these symbols. Experienced practitioners in Europe and America, particularly those who have traveled in India or formally studied Hinduism or Buddhism, often develop an understanding of the contextual meaning of such symbols in their native environments. The use of the image of Patañjali as Nāgarāja, which is most prominent in studios dedicated to the Iyengar tradition, exemplifies this dynamic. Iyengar yoga is in some ways the most secularized of contemporary yoga traditions, known especially for its therapeutic application to musculoskeletal conditions, especially injuries. However, there is a great dedication in many Iyengar-yoga communities to the study of Iyengar's scholarly works and the philosophical and religious underpinnings of yoga as he has represented them. The exotic, for some, gives way to the esoteric knowledge of the meaning of the representation of Patañjali as Nāgarāja, and the narrative context of Hinduism in which this representation is situated. The icon functions as a symbol of the exotic, esoteric, or both, to the degree to which it is an element of the foreground or background, or figure and ground, of yoga. The demand for such icons translates economically into higher production and prestige for the producers of such crafts in India and into the expanding visibility of Patañjali as an iconic figure in contemporary Hinduism. In this respect, the theriomorphic form of Patañjali can be also seen as symbol of the transnational and globalized culture of yoga, one that in its malleability is able to cross the fluid boundaries between national and religious identities on a global scale.

Conclusion

The utilization of the icon of Patañjali as Nāgarāja or "Serpent-King" in modern forms of yoga has its roots in the representation of Patañjali and the *Yogasūtra* as the embodiments of authority and orthodoxy in yoga. This form of representation is strongly tied to the Krishnamacharya yoga tradition of Southern India and its prominent disciples. As such, the icon encapsulates the many ways in which Patañjali and his tradition serves as a vehicle for drawing together the various threads of yoga tradition together with modern intellectual and bodily cultures in an integral and holistic fashion. The image of Patañjali represents simultaneously the ideal of the polyglot scholar-*guru* who is able to bring together these threads and the community that is built around the exoteric images and esoteric principles that are associated with yoga. It carries the implication that synthesizing and harmonizing various traditions is not disingenuous, but rather is the opposite—it is the way that the "classical" authority on yoga, Patañjali himself, sought to unify yoga during his own era. The image has its roots in many different facets of the popular, philosophical, and literary traditions of Hinduism, including *nāga* worship, narrative literature such as the Mahābhārata and Purāṇas, grammatical works, philosophical treatises, and asceticism and its narratives in Hindu, Buddhist, and Jaina contexts. It is illustrated in the temple culture of Southern India, especially that of the temple of Cidambaram and the integrative work of its priestly (*brāhmaṇa*) scholars. These examples all point to the shifting cultural and geographic contexts in which traditions of yoga and the narrative representation of Patañjali have been situated. They also demonstrate the malleability of yoga and its polysemic and multivalent nature with respect to contemplative practices and bodily disciplines. The hybridity of the theriomorphic figure of Patañjali as Nāgarāja extends across various planes of discourse, culture, and geography. It represents both the exotic and esoteric facets of yoga and the multidirectionality of cultural flow, being transformed by its new symbolic environment as it moves, and likewise transforming the symbolic world around it. It also represents how for some contemporary practitioners, yoga is simply a temporary excursus from ordinary life, while for others it offers a radical transformation of worldview and lifestyle.

Notes

1. For a range of discussions of concepts of cosmopolitanism, see Breckenridge, Pollock, and Bhabha 2002.

2. Maas indicates that the earliest source that he is aware of regarding the Patañjali-Ananta identification is the *Sarvasiddhāntasaṃgraha* of a pseudo-Śaṃkara from the second millennium CE. See Maas 2008, 114.

3. It should also be mentioned that the conception that the practice of yoga should be initiated by an invocation to Śeṣa or Nāgarāja is evident as well in the later Haṭhayoga tradition, as exemplified in a passage of Brahmānanda's *Jyotsnā* commentary (possibly eighteenth century CE) to the *Haṭhayogapradīpikā* of Svātmārāma (fourteenth century CE), in which salutations of Ananta are proscribed as a preliminary to yoga practice *sādhana*. A translation of these verses, which follow verse 2.48 on *sūryabhedana*, can be found in *The Haṭhayogapradīpikā of Svātmārāma*, see Tatya 2000, 30–31. Ananta is also mentioned in verse 3.1. This particular passage is extremely useful in that it clearly connects Ananta to the practice of Haṭhayoga and provides explicit details as how yoga was to be pragmatically and systematically applied on a daily basis in order to achieve yogic *samādhi*. *Samādhi* is identified in the *Haṭhayogapradīpikā* as the definitive practice of Pātañjala Yoga or *rājayoga* tradition, and is seen as the ultimate goal of the practice of yoga from the viewpoint offered in the text. *Haṭhayogapradīpikā* I.1, IV.1–8. Bhāratī has argued more broadly that the invocation of Ananta in yoga (particularly at the beginning of practice) is coextensive with the invocation of Ananta in other ritual contexts. See Bhāratī 2004, 576–586.

4. According to Palaniappan, this tradition identifies Patañjali as both grammarian and *yogī*, a theme developed to make the role of Naṭarāja at Chidambaram competitive with the role of Dākṣiṇāmūrti at Madurai. See Palaniappan 2007; Younger 1995, 117n11; Smith 2003, 131–34.

5. One reason for this may be that yoga serves to support the physical and psychic demands of a virtuoso or high-stress lifestyle, whether it is of a world-class musician or a political leader. Yoga adds to the mystique, glamour, and idiosyncrasy of the celebrity practitioner. Likewise, the manner in which politicians and celebrities become symbolic or archetypal of the concerns and aspirations of their constituents or followers mirrors the manner in which practitioners of yoga have traditionally been seen to become "gods on earth" and objects of popular devotion through their mastery of yoga methods. See McKean 1996; Van Der Veer 1988. As such, the celebrity, *yogī/yoginī*, and politician all "embody" authority and can mobilize communities in unique ways.

6. McDannell's work focuses on the negative interpretations of the term "kitsch," whereas the usage here is intended to be less evaluative in nature.

References

Alter, Joseph. 2000. *Gandhi's Body: Sex, Diet, and the Politics of Nationalism*. Philadelphia: University of Philadelphia Press, 2000.

———. 2004. *Yoga in Modern India: The Body Between Science and Philosophy*. Princeton: Princeton University Press, 2004.

Baker, Ian A., and Thomas Laird. 2000. *Dalai Lama's Secret Temple: Tantric Wall Paintings from Tibet*. New York: Thames and Hudson.

Bhāratī, Swami Veda. 2004. *The Yoga Sūtras of Patañjali with the Exposition of Vyāsa: A Translation and Commentary*, vol. 2, *Sādhana-Pāda*. Delhi: Motilal Banarsidass Publishers.

Breckenridge, Carol A., Sheldon Pollock, and Homi K. Bhabha. 2002. *Cosmopolitanism*. Durham, NC: Duke University Press.

Bronkhorst, Johannes. 2005. "The Reliability of Tradition." In *Boundaries, Dynamics and Construction of Traditions in South Asia*, edited by Federico Squarcini, 62–76. Firenze, Italy: Firenze University Press.

Bühnemann, Gudrun. 2007. *Eighty-four Āsanas in Yoga: A Survey of Traditions*. New Delhi: D. K. Printworld.

Cozad, Laurie. 2004. *Sacred Snakes: Orthodox Images of Indian Snake Worship*. Aurora, CO: The Davies Group.

Dasgupta, Surendranath. 1922. *A History of Indian Philosophy*, vol. 1. Cambridge: Cambridge University Press.

DeCaroli, Robert. 2004. *Haunting the Buddha: Indian Popular Religions and the Formation of Buddhism*. New York: Oxford University Press.

De Michelis, Elizabeth E. 2004. *A History of Modern Yoga: Patañjali and Western Esoterism*. London: Continuum.

Desai, Kalpan S. 1973. *Iconography of Viṣṇu: In Northern India, Up to the Medieval Period*. New Delhi: Abhinav Publications.

Deshpande, Madhav M. 1992. "The Changing Notion of Śiṣṭa from Patañjali to Bhartṛhari." In *Bhartṛhari: Philosopher and Grammarian: Proceedings of the First International Conference on Bhartṛhati*, edited by Saroja Bhate and Johannes Bronkhorst, 95–114. Delhi: Motilal Banarsidass.

———. 1997. "Who Inspired Pāṇini? Reconstructing the Hindu and Buddhist Counter-Claims." *Journal of the American Oriental Society*, 117, no. 3: 444–66.

Desikachar, T. K. V., and R. H. Cravens. 1998. *Health, Healing, and Beyond: Yoga and the Living Tradition of Krishnamacharya*. New York: Aperture.

Desikachar, T. K. V. 1997. *Patañjali's Yogasūtras: An Introduction*. New Delhi: Affiliated East-West Press in association with Rupa & Co.

Desikachar, T. K. V., ed. 1985. *Patañjalayogadarśanam: Text with chant-notation in Sanskrit and Roman Script and Ādiśeṣāṣṭakam of Sri. T. Krishnamacharya*. Chennai: Krishnamacharya Yoga Mandiram.

Dowman, Keith. 1985. *Masters of Mahamudra: Songs and Histories of the Eighty-Four Buddhist Siddhas*. Albany: State University of New York Press.

Handa, O. C. 2004. *Nāga Cults and Traditions in the Western Himalaya*, New Delhi: Indus Publishing Company.

Huntington, Susan. 1993. *The Art of Ancient India: Buddhist, Hindu, Jain*. New York: Weatherhill.

Iyengar, B. K. S. 1979. *Light on Yoga: Yoga Dipika*. New York: Schocken.

———. 1993. *Light on the Yoga Sūtras of Patañjali: Patañjala Yoga Pradīpikā*. London: Aquarian Press.

Jois, K. Pattabhi. 2002. *Yoga Mala*. New York: North Point Press.

Larson, Gerald James, and Ram Shankar Bhattacharya. 2008. *Yoga: India's Philosophy of Meditation*, Encyclopedia of Indian Philosophies, Volume XII. Delhi: Motilal Banarsidass.

Maas, Phillip. 2008. "'Descent With Modification': The Opening of the *Pātañjalayogaśāstra*." In *Śāstrārambha: Inquiries into the Preamble in Sanskrit*, edited by Walter Slaje, 97–119. Wiesbaden: Harrassowitz Verlag.

Mani, Vettam. 1975. *Purāṇic Encyclopedia: A Comprehensive Dictionary with Special Reference to the the Epic and Purāṇa Literature*. Delhi: Motilal Banarsidass.

McDannell, Colleen. 1995. *Material Christianity: Religion and Popular Culture in America*. New Haven: Yale University Press.

McKean, Lise. 1996. *Divine Enterprise: Gurus and the Hindu Nationalist Movement*. Chicago: University of Chicago Press.

Mundukur, Balaji. 1983. *The Cult of the Serpent: An Interdisciplinary Survey of Its Manifestations and Origins*. Albany: State University of New York Press.

Nash, Harvey. 1984. "The Centaur's Origin: A Psychological Perspective." *The Classical World* 77, no. 5: 273–291.

Nevrin, Klas. Forthcoming. "Performing the Yogasutra: Towards a Methodology for Studying Recitation in Modern Hatha Yoga." *Chakra: Tidskrift för Indiska Religioner*.

Palaniappan, S. 2007. "Madurai and Chidambaram: The Tamil Cities that Created Important Sanskrit Myths," *Indology: Resources for Indological Scholarship*. http://indology.info/email/members/palaniappan/patanjali.shtml.

Panda, Sadhu Charan. 1986. *Nāga Cult in Orissa*. Delhi: B. R. Publishing Corporation.

Rukmani, T. S. 1981. *Yogavārttika of Vijñānabhikṣu: Text with English Translation and Critical Notes along with the Text and English Translation of the Pātañjala*

Yogasūtras and Vyāsabhāṣya, vol. 1–4. New Delhi: Mushiram Manoharlal Publishers.

Sarbacker, Stuart Ray. 2005. *Sāmadhi: The Numinous and Cessative in Indo-Tibetan Yoga*. Albany: State University of New York Press.

———. 2008. "The Numinous and Cessative in Modern Yoga," in *Yoga in the Modern World: Contemporary Perspectives*, edited by Mark Singleton and Jean Byrne, 161–83. London: Routledge.

Shah, Umakant Premanand. 1987. *Jaina-rūpa-maṇḍana: Jaina Iconography*. New Delhi: Abhinav Publications.

Shulman, David Dean. 1980. *Tamil Temple Myths: Sacrifice and Divine Marriage in the South Indian Śaiva Tradition*. Princeton, NJ: Princeton University Press.

Singleton, Mark. 2008. "The Classical Reveries of Modern Yoga: Patañjali and Constructive Orientalism." In *Yoga in the Modern World: Contemporary Perspectives*, edited by Mark Singleton and Jean Byrne, 77–99. London: Routledge.

———. 2010. *Yoga Body: The Origins of Modern Posture Practice*. New York: Oxford University Press.

Sjoman, Norman E. 1996. *The Yoga Tradition of the Mysore Palace*. New Delhi: Abhinav.

Smith, David. 2003. *The Dance of Śiva: Religion, Art, and Poetry in South India*. Cambridge: Cambridge University Press.

Staal, Frits. 1972. *A Reader on the Sanskrit Grammarians*. Cambridge, MA: MIT Press.

Svātmārāma. 2000. *The Haṭhayogapradīpikā of Svātmārāma*. Trans. Tookaram Tatya. Chennai: Adyar Library and Research Center.

Van Der Veer, Peter. 1988. *Gods on Earth: The Management of Religious Experience and Identity in a North Indian Pilgrimage Center*. London: The Athlone Press.

Vogel, J. 1926. *Indian Serpent-Lore, or The Nāgas in Hindu Legend and Art*. London: Arthur Probstain.

Whicher, Ian. 1998. *Integrity of the Yoga Darśana: A Reconsideration of Classical Yoga*. Albany: State University of New York Press.

Woods, James Haughton. 2007 (1914). *The Yoga System of Patañjali: Or the Ancient Hindu Doctrine of Concentration of Mind*. Delhi: Motilal Banarsidass.

Younger, Paul. 1995. *The Home of Dancing Śivaṉ: The Traditions of the Hindu Temple in Citamparam*. New York: Oxford University Press.

2

God's Eyes

The Manufacture, Installation, and Experience of External Eyes on Jain Icons

JOHN E. CORT

What is the role of material culture in the formation, maintenance and division of religious communities? When considering the causes of internal sectarian divisions within religious traditions, many scholars of religion have tended to look first at the arena of doctrine. One thinks of the disputes over the authority of the Pope and the definition of the trinity that have divided the Eastern Orthodox and Western Catholic traditions for a millennium, or the disputes over the cause of salvation that split the Western Christian tradition into Catholic and Protestant wings. In Islam, one thinks of the disagreement concerning the nature of Muhammad and prophethood that led to the Sunni-Shi'i split. Profound differences concerning the nature of *nirvāṇa,* and therefore the status of the Buddha after his bodily liberation, led to the division of Buddhism into Theravāda and Mahāyāna branches. Nor have the Jains been immune from such developments. The gradual split in the early centuries of the first millennium CE into the Śvetāmbara ("White Clad") and Digambara ("Sky Clad") branches was based on disagreement concerning the sartorial requirements for truly engaging in mendicant conduct, and therefore the very meaning of world renunciation. The two also have disagreed strenuously over whether or not women are capable of attaining liberation, and the ontological status of the Jinas—the enlightened and liberated beings who teach the Jain doctrine and establish the Jain community—between the time of their embodied enlightenment and their final liberation from the body and all karmic bondage at the time of physical death (Dundas 2002, 45–59).

Further, when looking for materials to study these doctrinal differences, scholars often turn primarily to the rich textual traditions produced by the relevant religious communities, in which doctrines are vigorously defended and opposing doctrines criticized with equal vigor. Scholars of religion tend to be rooted in what I have elsewhere described as a "text-centered logocentrism" (Cort 1996a, 614).

Doctrines are not the only things that can divide religious communities, however, and divide them deeply. Nor are texts the only places we can go to study sectarian divisions. Material culture plays an important role as well. Even a casual visitor to a baroque Catholic cathedral and a white clapboard Baptist meeting house can see that the Catholic-Protestant divide is as much a matter of the different visual and material cultures of the two as it is a matter of doctrines and texts.

The situation in Jainism is not all that different. The disagreements concerning mendicant conduct are obvious, as they are visually signaled by the difference between whether monks are clothed in white or totally naked. Śvetāmbara and Digambara authors have argued about this and other sectarian differences for over one thousand years, and Jain (and academic) libraries are full of texts articulating their arguments. Most Jains, however, interact with monks only on special ritual occasions, and many Jains go years without seeing a single monk. Nor do the other doctrinal differences impinge in any significant way upon the daily lives of most Jains. The sectarian difference that will first strike the casual observer—and the casual visitor to both Śvetāmbara and Digambara temples, of which there are tens of thousands in India and increasingly in Europe and North America—is one not of philosophy, theology, or monastic practice, but rather of material culture.

Most Śvetāmbara icons in temple settings have extra, external eyes affixed to their faces (Figure 2.1).[1] External eyes are not found on Digambara icons (Figure 2.2).[2] This material difference between the forms of temple icons in the two traditions is quite readily noticeable by any visitor to a Jain temple. Temples are central to the ritual and material cultures of the Śvetāmbara and Digambara traditions. A temple, however, is not important in itself as much as it is meaningful due to the Jina icons that it houses. The simple, visible difference between the form of the eyes on Śvetāmbara and Digambara icons, therefore, signals theological differences between the two traditions about the meaning of icons in temples.

When a Jain enters a temple, he or she engages in the ritual of visual interaction with the icon known as *darśana*. This ritual is deeply informed by inherited practices of how to look upon an icon, an inheri-

Figure 2.1. Ornamented Śvetāmbara icon of Ādeśvara (Ādinātha), Śāmḷājī Pārśvanātha temple, Patan, North Gujarat, July 18, 1996. Photo © the author.

Figure 2.2. Digambara icon of Ādinātha, Baṛā Terāpanth temple, Jaipur, July 24, 2013. Photo © the author.

tance that I call the "Jain devotional gaze." Investigating the Jain devotional gaze allows us to see how the Jain experience of the Jina icon, and therefore the very basics of Jain theology, are profoundly shaped by the presence or absence of the external eyes. Humans are embodied, so understanding is also an embodied act, mediated by the senses. Sight in particular is a powerful sense, and analyzing the Jain material culture that shapes and creates Jain visual experience gives us access to the inner world of the Jain devotee as he or she stands in a temple and gazes lovingly upon a Jina icon.

In this essay I discuss three aspects of what I term "God's eyes."[3] First, I describe how, and by whom, the eyes are made. Second, I discuss when, historically, Śvetāmbaras probably started to affix eyes to icons. Third, I consider both criticisms and defenses of the external eyes. This last aspect of my essay also falls into three parts. There is an internal criticism of the external eyes found within the Śvetāmbara Mūrtipūjaka ("Icon-Worshiping") sect. According to this criticism, the external eyes are harmful to the icons themselves. This is what we might call an indigenous conservator's argument. Second, there is an aesthetic criticism from both inside and outside the Śvetāmbara tradition that external eyes are garish ornamentation. The criticism is that the eyes are so large in comparison to the rest of the icon that they disrupt its natural symmetry and proportion. Finally, there is a sectarian Digambara criticism that external eyes signal a mistaken understanding of the theological meaning of the icon. According to the Digambaras, the external eyes transform the inward focused, world-renouncing Jina into an outward focused, world-ruling king.

My discussion here pertains solely to icons of Jinas. Śvetāmbaras affix external eyes to icons of other deities, and the practice is widespread in western India among Vaiṣṇavas, as well as worshipers of Śiva, the goddess, and various "folk" deities. The affixing of external eyes to Jina icons is therefore part of a much larger regional ritual, visual, and material culture. In the interest of concision and focus, I choose to limit my discussion in this essay to the Jains and the icons of the Jinas.

The Production of External Eyes

In 1995, when I conducted my initial fieldwork on this topic, there were two workshops in Ahmedabad that manufactured the external eyes (*cakṣu*) that are affixed to Śvetāmbara icons. They were both still in operation as of 2007. One was headed by a man from a northern Indian Vaiṣṇava jeweler caste (*jaḍiyā*). He was the first generation in his family to work in Ahmedabad. He himself was born in Mathura, and his father had been born in Murshidabad.

The other workshop was headed by a Muslim, who said his family had been in the business in Ahmedabad for a century. One of his sons had shifted to Cambay, where the son manufactured tools for cutting and polishing ornamental stones. While the Ahmedabad workshop was clearly that of a Muslim, as there were posters on the wall with writing in Urdu script, the craftsman's appearance was no different from that of a traditional Hindu, Jain, or Muslim Ahmedabadi merchant. I asked another son if the family felt any tension in providing the material ornamentation for Jain idols.[4] This son gave what was probably a predictable answer: what he did was simply a matter of work (*kām*), and only after Jains bought the eyes and affixed them to the idols did they become part of worship (*pūjā*). The orthodox Muslim prohibition of idol-worship did not pertain to his occupation.[5]

The two craftsmen knew each other, and their relationship was one of professional rivalry. Both sold eyes to temples throughout western and northern India, and even in North America. Neither sold eyes off the shelf, nor were eyes available through the large Jain shop in Ahmedabad that sells all sorts of ritual paraphernalia (*upkaraṇ*). When an icon, either a new one or an old one in need of repair, required eyes, the trustees of the temple placed a special order for them. They then either returned to the workshop to pick up the eyes or arranged for the craftsman to deliver them himself. Both workshops made eyes only for Jain icons, not Hindu ones. The simple reason they gave for this sectarian specialization was that Jains were willing to pay more for eyes, and therefore working with Jains was more profitable.[6]

The workshops manufactured three types of eyes: quartz crystal (*sphatik*), glass (*kāc*), and enamel (*mīnā*).

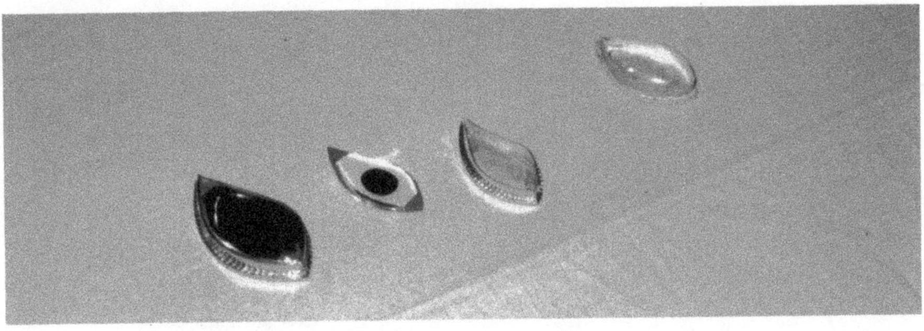

Figure 2.3. Glass *cakṣu* in workshop of Haricharan Manekchand Jadiya, Ahmedabad, November 9, 1995. Photo © the author.

There are three layers to a crystal or glass eye. At its flat base is a silver plate. The crystal or glass is affixed to the plate and then further held in place by a silver frame. Gold leaf (*varak*) is often laid onto the outside of the silver frame. Paint is applied to give the features of the eye: a black circle in the center, and red at either end to fill out the ocular shape:

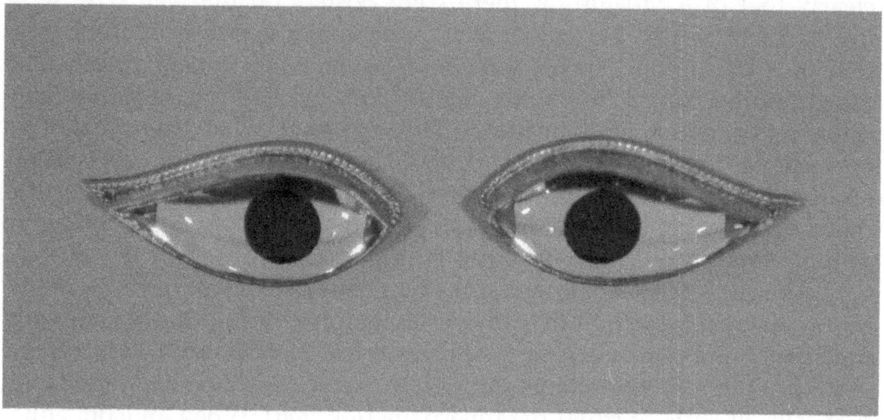

Figure 2.4. Glass *cakṣu* in collection of author. Photo © the author.

An enamel eye is also affixed to a silver base. The paint is then applied onto the enamel. Most enamel eyes have a white dot inside the black, which, according to one craftsman, helps make them look more realistic.

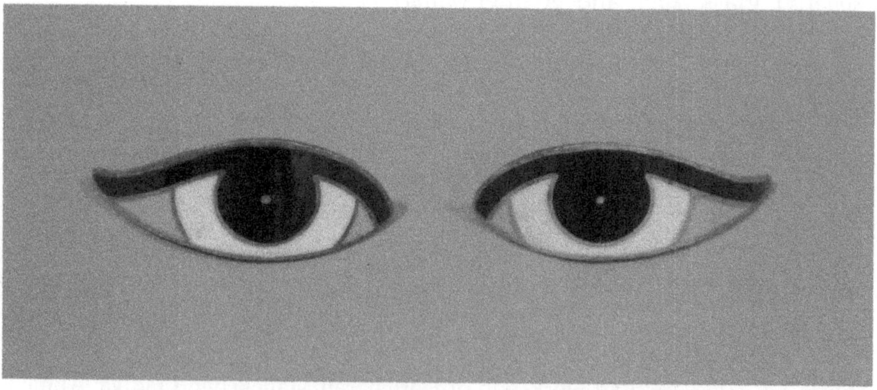

Figure 2.5. Enamel *cakṣu* in collection of author. Photo © the author.

The nature of the medium means that an enamel eye can be more fully rounded and so fits better over the carved eye of the stone icon itself. A crystal or glass eye has a small indentation in the back to center it on the carved eye of the icon, but the crystal or glass external eye as a whole is flatter than an enamel eye. Because it cannot be rounded to conform fully to the surface of the icon, a crystal or glass eye protrudes more from the icon.

As of 1995, the prices for a pair of eyes roughly two inches across were five to six thousand rupees for crystal, four hundred for glass, and three hundred for enamel.[7] One craftsman said that crystal eyes were the most popular, for they reflect the greatest amount of light. The other craftsman claimed that in recent years enamel eyes had become popular, as they were more "realistic." The largest eyes either craftsman made were eight inches across.

The craftsmen do not affix the eyes to the icons. This is done by the temple employees known as *pujārīs*. In many towns this is done by a specially trained *pujārī* who does this work for all the temples, rather than by the *pujārī* of each temple. The eye is affixed to the icon using a highly sticky resin known as *rāl* or *rāḷ*. A feature of this resin is that it will not damage the underlying stone or metal of the icon.

If an external eye on an icon becomes seriously damaged, then the temple trustees usually need to buy a complete pair. As the eyes age there is a change in their reflectivity, so having eyes of different ages on an icon would result in undesirable asymmetry in the reflections.

External Eyes in History

The metaphor of sight and the eye for divine insight into the true nature of reality is a common one in the world's religious traditions. In Jainism, *ananta-darśana* or "infinite perception" is one of the four characteristics of the *siddha*, the enlightened and liberated soul. This is also embodied in the eyes of the Jina himself. The eleventh-century monk Śāntisūri wrote in his *Ceiyavandana Mahābhāsa* (verse 328), "I bow to those eyes, clear-sighted, eyes of stainless scripture and knowledge, a gift to the mass of beings in the darkness of illusion."

Śāntisūri may have been referring to the eyes of the Jina himself, through an act of devotion in which the worshiper imagines himself to be in the presence of the now-absent Jina. Since Śāntisūri was writing a commentary on the liturgy of the rite of worshiping the Jina icon (Sanskrit *caitya*, Prakrit *ceiya*), it is likely that he was referring equally to the eyes of the icon. What is not fully clear is whether Śāntisūri was describing the eyes carved into the stone or metal icon, or external eyes that were affixed onto the icon such as we see today. Elsewhere in his text Śāntisūri described the ornamentation of the Jina icon, so the practice of applying external eyes as ornamentation might have begun by the eleventh century.

It is possible that early stone Jina icons were painted, although there is no clear archaeological evidence for this. If so, then the eyes would have been painted to enhance their effect. We do know that some early bronze icons were painted, and that the eyes of some were inlaid with silver to make the eyes stand out. That this was an ancient tradition is indicated by one of the oldest Jain bronzes yet found: the c. mid-sixth century icon of Jīvantasvāmī Mahāvīra from Akota (Shah 1951 and 1959, 26–28; Cort 2010, 155–216) contains traces of paint and has silver inlaid in the eyes.[8]

The eyes of some medieval metal icons had precious stones inlaid in them. A gilt copper icon of Pārśvanātha originally installed in a temple in Broach in 988, later in a collection in Kadi in north Gujarat as of the early 1950s, and now in the collection of the Los Angeles County Museum of Art (Pal 1988, 137–39; Pal 1994, fig. 30; Shah 1955–56, 60), formerly had inlaid eyes.

Figure 2.6. Śvetāmbara icon of Pārśvanātha, dated 988, originally from Broach, now in collection of Los Angeles County Museum of Art (M.71.26.38). Gilt copper inlaid with silver and gemstones. Gift of Mr. and Mrs. J. J. Klejman of New York.

While the precious stones in the eyes were removed at some point, the holes in the silver inlay indicate where the stones would have been, and there are still inlaid stones elsewhere on the icon. The many extant medieval icons with silver inlaid eyes are all small portable icons, which would have been found as often in private home shrines as in public temples. Temple icons tend to be larger and are usually made of stone. Most of the few bronze icons that have served as main icons in temples do not have inlaid eyes and instead feature external eyes, as do stone icons.

It is not necessarily the case, however, that the inlaid silver eyes of metal icons translated directly to the practice of affixing external eyes onto stone icons. In fact, it seems unlikely that the one led to the other. We find icons with inlaid silver eyes elsewhere in India, not just in western India. It was a widespread practice in both medieval Bengal (Mitra 1979; Pal 1988, 186–211) and medieval Kashmir (Pal 1975; Pal 1988, 61–84). In neither of these regions, however, do we find external eyes affixed to icons. There is no inherent connection between the two practices.

Another explanation for the origin of the external eyes was advanced by W. Norman Brown (1929; 1933, 16–17). Medieval western Indian Jain paintings are distinctive in the way they portray what art historians call the "farther" or "protruding" eye of a face. If the face is in three-quarter profile, the near eye is fully depicted. In a naturalistic painting only part or none of the farther eye should be visible. Medieval western Indian painters, however, depicted the entire farther eye so that it protruded awkwardly beyond the plain of the face. Brown argued that this feature "is best explained as having its origin in the copying of images with their additional glass eyes as found in Śvetāmbara temples" (1933, 17). Since this visual motif has been found on western Indian Jain paintings from as early as the middle of the eleventh century (Kramrisch 1975, 389–91), and gradually emerges out of earlier western Indian painting styles in the period between the latter part of the tenth century and the middle of the eleventh century (Shah 1976, 1–4), it might appear to help us in dating the introduction of external eyes onto Jain icons. Subsequent research, however, has shown that the same motif is found in Buddhist paintings at Ajanta as early as the sixth century (Khandalavala and Chandra 1969, 2; Kramrisch 1975, 388), as well as in paintings at the Buddhist monastery of Sumstek at Alchi in Ladakh (Guy 1994, 95), so it is unlikely that the protruding farther eye found in paintings is directly related to the external eye found on icons. This point has been argued most recently by Lalit Kumar, who wrote that the farther eye "had nothing to do with the Shvetambara tradition in which extra eyes were affixed to the Jina images, as has also been suggested, but was, in fact, a faithful rendering of the sculpted face in three-quarter profile by the early painters" (Kumar 2000, 65).

References to the offering of various ornaments to icons in the context of *pūjā* are found in texts from at least the middle of the first millennium CE. On the basis of these descriptions, as well as the evolving practice of *pūjā*, medieval authors gave standardized lists of offerings. While the best-known of these is the eightfold offering (*aṣṭa-prakārī pūjā*),[9] most Jains in their worship actually offer more items,[10] and so there are also standard lists of seventeen and twenty-one offerings (Williams 1963, 219–20). Some of these are transient items, such as fruit, flowers, incense, and the flame of a lamp, which are offered only once. Others are longer lasting items such as cloth and jewelry, which can be offered repeatedly. It may well be that many of the ornaments offered to the icon as part of the daily worship were left on it to enhance the visual impact of *darśana* of the icon. The Digambara insistence that icons should not be ornamented, however, even though Digambara *pūjā* involves offering the same substances, warns against this.

Among the items found in descriptions of the offerings to icons is a "pair of cloths" (*vastra-yugala*), in which two pieces of plain cloth are held up before the icon as an offering. The twentieth-century Śvetāmbara Tapā Gaccha monk-scholar Paṅnyās Kalyāṇvijaygaṇi (1888–1975; hereinafter Kalyāṇvijay) noted that the offering of the pair of cloths found in standard lists of the seventeenfold (*sattar-bhedī*) *pūjā* was replaced by a pair of eyes (*cakṣur-yugala*) by Ācaryā Ratnaśekharasūri in his Sanskrit *Śrāddhavidhi*, composed in 1450 (Kalyāṇvijay1957, 46; 1966, 94). Ratnaśekharasūri was head of the Tapā Gaccha, one of the dominant Śvetāmbara mendicant lineages from medieval times until the present (Dundas 2007). The printed versions of the *Śrāddhavidhi* that I have seen prescribe either the offering of a pair of eyes (*cakṣu-yugala*) or of the sanctified sandalwood powder known as *vāsakṣepa*.[11] There is no ambiguity concerning the other sixteen offerings. We can interpret this single ambiguity, therefore, to indicate that the practice of offering a pair of eyes was still fairly new as of the mid-fifteenth century. This same option is found two centuries later in the commentary on the *Dharma Saṅgraha* of Mahopādhyāya Mānavijayagaṇi that was compiled by the great Mahopādhyāya Yaśovijaya, also of the Tapā Gaccha, sometime between 1681 and 1688. In his description of the seventeenfold *pūjā*, Yaśovijaya quoted an unknown Prakrit text that said the second offering should be either a pair of eyes or *vāsakṣepa* (1984–87, II:33–4).

The ambiguity between whether the offering should be of cloth or eyes is found again in a vernacular Gujarati text of the seventeenfold *pūjā* composed by Upādhyāya Sakalacandragaṇi (hereinafter Sakalacandra), also in the late seventeenth century. In fact, Sakalacandra explicitly referred to the alternate offerings in his liturgy. This *pūjā* is still performed regularly today on the occasion of the annual anniversary of a Tapā Gaccha temple, for it is understood to cleanse the temple of all negative karmic residue caused by unintentional mistakes (*āśātnā*) in the performance of daily *pūjā* over the preceding year.[12] The third offering in Sakalacandra's text is titled by the modern publishers as "a pair of eyes" (*cakkhu yugal*), but again there is uncertainty as to whether the offering should be of eyes or cloth. The instructions for the third offering read: "On a very beautiful, sweet-smelling, priceless pair of cloths make a saffron *svastik*, hold them both before the face of the icon, and sing the text of the third *pūjā*. This is the offering of the pair of cloths." In only one of the three performance editions of the text I have consulted does an anonymous modern editor add that the offering may be "of two eyes."[13] Clearly by the late-seventeenth century there was no consensus within the Tapā Gaccha as to which should be offered. In his text Sakalacandra first described the offering as follows:

> Divinely made, divinely made,
> the two stainless garments made of light shine greatly.
> The smell of good virtues spreads all around,
> complete, unbroken, unequalled.
> Offer the pure bridegroom's gift,
> like stainless and cool moon-beams.
> This is the third *pūjā* to the blissful Jina.
> Feeling supreme bliss as they look closely,
> all the Indras honor Him.[14]

Sakalacandra then gave a different instruction:

> The faithful establish on the Jina's face
> the jewel eyes that close off darkness.
> O God, give enlightened knowledge and enlightened vision,
> they are like the two eyes.[15]

The next verse indicated that there was no consensus in the community as to whether cloth or eyes should be offered:

> Here in the third *pūjā*
> there is a textual variant (*pāṭhāntar*):
> The Jina lights up the world

like the sun.
Offer the pair of cloths
like divine raiment.
Ask that the play of the lord
grant all pleasures.[16]

Sakalacandra was not finished, however, with giving the worshiper both options, for a few verses later he mentioned them in succession:

I place the pair of eyes, like gems and jewels,
on the face of my Lord.
They are like enlightened knowledge and enlightened
  vision.
O Lord, have mercy on me.
Do the third *pūjā* of the Lord
with two cloths
that are like divine cloths.
Offer two eyes
that express the sentiment of calm.
Look, look,
drink the nectar of the Lord's face.[17]

Sakalacandra did not explicitly address the options in his autocommentary. He specified that the eyes should be inlaid with gems (*ratna-jaḍit*) or made of precious stone (*māṃṇik*), and that the cloth should be the sort worn by the gods (*dev-dūṣya*), and therefore used to adorn icons, but did not address why the two different offerings were possible.[18]

This ambiguity has continued into the modern period. The liturgies for the seventeenfold *pūjā* composed by Ācārya Vijayānandsūri (1837–1896, better known as Ātmārāmjī) in 1882, and by Ācārya Vijay Amṛtsūri in 1951, two modern leaders of the Tapā Gaccha, both mention the pair of cloths and the pair of eyes.[19]

In sum, neither the evidence of silver inlay in the eyes of bronze icons, nor of the farther eye in manuscript illustrations, is of sufficient relevance to our inquiry to help us date when Jains started applying external eyes. When we turn to the literary evidence, a study of the texts allows us only to say that by the mid-fifteenth century the practice had developed within Tapā Gaccha circles of offering external eyes to the Jina icon; that presumably these eyes were affixed to the icon, and therefore account for the now widespread practice of external eyes; and that there was some difference of opinion as to whether this offering should be of eyes or cloth.

The practice of affixing external eyes is found on icons belonging to all the different Śvetāmbara Mūrtipūjaka *gaccha*s (mendicant lineages). The above textual discussion, however, looked only at Tapā Gaccha authors. Turning to the texts of the seventeenfold *pūjā* as performed by two other influential Mūrtipūjaka *gaccha*s in western India, the Kharatara and Acala (or Añcala) Gacchas, indicates that the practice may have arisen within the Tapā Gaccha. In the Kharatara Gaccha text, composed by Sādhukīrtimuni in 1561, there is no mention of offering eyes to the Jina, only of offering a pair of cloths.[20]

Meghrājmuni, who in the late sixteenth- or early seventeenth-century wrote the Acala Gaccha text, was aware of the practice of offering eyes instead of cloths. The first verse of the third *pūjā*, labeled the offering of the pair of cloths (*vastra-yugal*), explicitly referred to the difference of opinion:

> The third *pūjā* to the Jina
> is a pair of cloths.
> Some, however, say it is a pair of eyes (*dṛṣṭi-yugal*).
> The ultimate meaning is the same.[21]

For the remainder of this *pūjā*, Meghrāj mentioned only the pair of cloths, thereby dismissing in practice the alternate offering of eyes. While his rejection of the change was not unequivocal, he indicated a clear preference for the older offering of cloths and did not really entertain the offering of eyes as a valid option.

Critique 1: Conservation

A critique of external eyes was advanced in the 1950s from within the Śvetāmbara tradition by Kalyāṇvijay. He devoted many years to studying all aspects of Jain temple and icon culture. His 1957 Gujarati *Jin Pūjā Paddhati* ("Manual for Jina Worship"), also published in 1966 in Hindi as *Jin Pūjā Vidhi Saṅgrah* ("Collection of Rites for Jina Worship"), was a carefully researched defense of the Śvetāmbara worship of icons. In 1956 he published his mammoth two-volume *Kalyāṇ Kalikā* ("The Flower Bud of Kalyāṇ"), a *śilpa śāstra* (manual on temple arts), in which he synthesized from a wide range of Śvetāmbara texts a modern manual on the making and consecrating of temples and icons. His dedicated study of the history of the Śvetāmbara textual tradition earned him the sobriquet *itihās-vettā*, "Expert in History" (Cort 2010, 262–63).

Kalyāṇvijay was not, however, an uncritical defender of all aspects of the contemporary Śvetāmbara culture of icons. He argued that the textual injunction found in Ratnaśekharasūri's 1450 *Śrāddhavidhi* to offer eyes to the Jina icon, and therefore to affix those eyes onto it, was in fact only a scribal error that had crept into the manuscript tradition (1957, 46–47; 1966, 94–95). Kalyāṇvijay asserted that whereas Ratnaśekharasūri had written that one should offer a pair of cloths (*vastra-yugala*), some copyist had mistakenly written that one should offer a pair of eyes (*cakṣur-yugala*).

This was one of a number of harmful excesses that had crept into Śvetāmbara ritual culture, according to Kalyāṇvijay. He argued that whereas icons formerly were lustrated and ornamented only on special occasions, the enthusiasm of pious Jains had led to an unnecessary growth in these practices (1957, 45–46; 1966, 93–94). To ornament the icons, temples now kept many gems, silver body-covers, and other costly items. As a result, the number of thefts in Jain temples had increased greatly. Further, affixing the eyes and other ornaments onto the icons damaged them. But, complained Kalyāṇvijay, the faithful devotees of the Jina did not seem to mind what was happening and so gave it no thought.

Critique 2: Aesthetics

Kalyāṇvijay also argued that people had lost all sense of proportion in the size of the eyes they affixed onto icons. Earlier, people had affixed enamel eyes that were in scale with the icon and so looked natural (*svābhāvik*). Now, by affixing such unnaturally large eyes people were obscuring the natural beauty of the icon.

Figure 2.7. Śvetāmbara icon of Ādeśvara (Ādinātha), Aṣṭāpad temple, Patan, North Gujarat, August 13, 1996. Photo © the author.

The objection that affixing such large eyes rendered the icons aesthetically unpleasing has been echoed by many others. I have heard this criticism from contemporary Jains, especially those who have a more intellectual and less devotional stance within the tradition, and lean more toward intellectual understanding (*jñān*) and less toward ritual orthopraxy (*kriyā*). I have also heard it from art historians, both in India and in the United States.

This criticism has a lengthy pedigree. In November 1822 the celebrated Colonel James Tod visited Mount Śatruñjay, the holy mountain of the Jains in Saurashtra that has become the most important Jain pilgrimage destination in western India. Tod commented that the main temple was "an imposing edifice" (1835, 285), but found it seriously wanting in comparison with the Jain temples of Mount Abu, which he had visited a few months earlier, on June 14, 1822. He had written of the Ādinātha temple at Abu, "Beyond controversy this is the most superb of all the temples of India, and there is not an edifice besides the Taj Mahl that can approach to it. The pen is incompetent to describe the exuberant beauties of this proud monument of the Jains" (1835, 101).

In particular, Tod objected to the external eyes affixed to the main icon of Ādinātha at Śatruñjay. "The crystal, or table-diamond eyes," he wrote, "do not improve the expression, any more than the golden collar and bracelets, with which he has been decorated by the tasteless zeal of some modern votary" (1835, 285–86). Tod went on to decry what he saw as the "incongruities of this sanctified abode," with its gilded paintings in a Dutch style, lamps from England, and a temple bell "from some Portuguese man-of-war." He attributed what he termed the "base taste" of the temple to some Jains having visited the nearby Portuguese churches at Diu. Clearly, Tod's displeasure at seeing the eyes and other ornaments on the Jina icon was shaped in part by a Protestant dislike of Catholic ornamentation and piety.

A generation later the architectural historian and colonial administrator James Burgess voiced a similar complaint. In his 1869 *The Temples of Śatruñjaya,* Burgess gave an extensive account of the temples that cover this mountain. His descriptions on the whole were much more complimentary than Tod's, but he did express some misgiving about the Śvetāmbara Jain love of extensive (and expensive) ornamentation of icons. In describing the large white marble icons in the seventeenth-century Caumukh temple atop the mountain, he wrote, "The aspect of these, and all the images, is peculiar: frequently on the brow and middle of the breast there is a brilliant, set in silver or gold, and almost always, the breasts are mounted with one of the precious metals,[22] whilst there are occasionally gold plates on the shoulders, elbow, and knee joints, and a crown on the head,—that on the principal one in the Motiśáh [temple] being a very elegant and massive gold one." It was the external eyes, however, that earned his harshest criticism, as he continued, "But the peculiar feature is the eyes, which seem to peer at you from every chapel like those of so many cats: they are made of silver overlaid with pieces of glass, very clumsily cemented on, and in every case projecting so far and from such a form as to give one the idea of their all wearing spectacles with lenticular glasses over very watery eyes in diseased sockets" (Burgess 1977, 20).[23]

This has continued to be a leitmotif in European and American response to the external eyes. In the early decades of the twentieth century, the Irish Presbyterian missionary Margaret (Mrs. Sinclair) Stevenson spent a number of years researching Jains in Saurashtra in Gujarat. In her first publication on the subject, the 1910 *Notes on Modern Jainism,* she included an account of her visit to the famous temple of Vimala Shah on Mount Abu, where she had presumably gone to escape the summer heat. This was the same temple described by Tod a century earlier. Stevenson also complained about the ornamentation, saying that the interior of the temple "was disfigured by quantities of vulgar hanging glass shades and cheap mirrors" (Stevenson 1910, 94). Her criticism of the eyes was less harsh than those of her predecessors, as she merely said, "In contrast to the simple, unadorned Digambara figures, the images throughout the Śvetāmbara temples are given staring glass eyes" (1910, 94–95), a phrase she repeated a decade later in her essay on Jain worship in the *Encyclopaedia of Religion and Ethics* (Stevenson 1921, 799). For an Irish Presbyterian missionary, however, to prefer an icon to be "simple" and "unadorned" is expected, for this is also how she would prefer a church to look in her home country, in contrast to the elaborately adorned icons of Catholic piety.

As we saw above, however, it is not only Protestant Europeans who have objected to the outsized external eyes. While Kalyāṇvijay was a widely read, learned monk, and I am confident that he had read at least Burgess's account, and possibly also those of Tod and Stevenson, I doubt that his aesthetic judgment was shaped by the European criticisms. Other complaints, however, bear evidence of a more complicated pattern of influences.

In a 1968 article on a few of the earliest (and for the historian therefore most important) inscribed icons on Śatruñjay, the lay Śvetāmbara pandit Ambalal Premchand Shah described an icon that he said was "one of the finest examples of sculptural art of Gujarat in V. S. 1064 (1006 A.D.), the date of the inscription" (A. P. Shah 1968, 163). He then criticized what more recent devotees had done to the icon: "Unfortunately, part of the beauty of this sculpture is marred by modern black paints, glass eyes, and studded metal pieces on different parts of the body." He concluded with a harsh judgment of this devotional alteration of the icon: "This is a practice which has undermined the beauty of many a Jaina sculpture, old or new" (1968, 163–64).

We cannot trace a genealogy of aesthetic judgment in the case of Kalyāṇvijay. We can, however, for Pandit A. P. Shah. This very learned layman, author of many articles and an encyclopedic three-volume guide to all the known Śvetāmbara temples of India (Shah 1953), was an employee of Āṇandjī Kalyāṇjī, the Ahmedabad-based Śvetāmbara Jain temple trust that controls Śatruñjay and a number of other important pilgrimage shrines in western India. Āṇandjī Kalyāṇjī and its trustees have also become important arbiters of Śvetāmbara temple practices throughout western India. While Āṇandjī Kalyāṇjī has emphasized a "classical" temple aesthetic since at least the early-twentieth century, one that valorizes the architecture of the eleventh- through thirteenth-century Caulukya dynasty (Kim 2007), it is particularly the role in the middle decades of the century of its powerful chairman, Kasturbhai Lalbhai (1894–1980), that is of note here.

Lalbhai was a member of the leading family of Ahmedabad Jains, a family that traced its descent to the seventeenth-century Śāntidās, a banker to the Mughals who was recognized as the *nagarśeṭh* or "mayor" of the city.[24] Kasturbhai was chair of Āṇandjī Kalyāṇjī from 1925 until his death in 1980. During these five decades he exercised enormous influence on the Śvetāmbara Mūrtipūjaka community of western India. The trust came to control directly an increasing number of pilgrimage shrines, and financed the renovation of many more. Kasturbhai Lalbhai was, arguably, the person most responsible for setting the standard for Śvetāmbara temple architecture and culture.

I have elsewhere (Cort 2000, 116–18) discussed the influence of the British architect Claude Batley on Lalbhai's aesthetic training, which I will briefly summarize here. Batley designed residences for Lalbhai and advised him on temple renovation. Batley praised traditional over modern Indian architecture. In particular, he emphasized the clean, uncluttered, and unornamented lines of classical forms. I do not know if Batley voiced an opinion concerning the external eyes of Śvetāmbara icons. I do know, however, that he taught Lalbhai to prefer the unornamented over the ornamented, and that Lalbhai was well-known in Jain circles of western India for publicly chastising local congregations for the common practice of brightly painting both the exteriors and interiors of temples. As we have seen in the case of both Kalyāṇvijay (who spent several years in the Ahmedabad area, and no doubt met Lalbhai) and A. P. Shah, as well as the European authors, the aesthetic criticism of the external eye is directly tied to a broader criticism of ornamentation in general (Cort 1996b, 2007), and a modernist preference for the underlying form itself.

Critique 3: Theology

The role of external eyes in Śvetāmbara ritual and devotional culture has also been criticized by Digambara Jains. Digambaras have rejected affixing eyes onto icons and criticize Śvetāmbaras for doing so. They say that this transforms the Jina from a lord who has renounced and transcended the material world—a *yogī*—into a king who still lives in and enjoys the material world—a *bhogī*. Not only do Digambara icons lack the external eyes, but also the eyes of the stone icons are often carved differently to accentuate the Digambara understanding of the Jina. The eyes on a Śvetāmbara icon are carved so that they look straight out, engaging the viewer in their powerful gaze (figure 2.1). The eyes on a Digambara icon are frequently carved so that they look down in meditation, gazing into the perfect soul rather than out upon the imperfect world (figure 2.2). Digambaras say that whereas Śvetāmbara icons emphasize the material, external eyes of the imperfect and transient human body that look out upon and are ensnared by the impure world of desires and karma, Digambara icons emphasize the spiritual, internal eyes of the perfect and eternal soul that look inward upon the tranquility of the infinite knowledge, perception, bliss and potential of the pure soul.

Śvetāmbaras are well aware of this criticism. Some medieval authors advanced a theology of ritual in which the worshiper is instructed on how to engage in his meditative interaction with the icon with the Jina in all the phases of his life (Cort 1996b, 2007). Just as each Jina progressed from unenlightened king to enlightened and ultimately liberated spiritual victor, so the worshiper should understand himself or herself to be on a similar path. Few Śvetāmbaras can actually enunciate this theology, however, any more than most Christians can enunciate the doctrinal details of the sacramental theology taught by their particular denominations. Instead, the Śvetāmbara defense of the external eyes on the Jina icons rests upon a valorization of the experience of *darśana* of the icon.

The External Eye in the Jain Devotional Gaze

While the texts of the seventeenfold *pūjā* do not allow us to determine with great precision when the practice of affixing external eyes developed, they do allow us to see the Śvetāmbara devotional sentiment that motivates affixing external eyes to the icon of a Jina. In *Lives of Indian Images*, Richard Davis has spoken of a "devotional eye," a "specific, influential way of looking at images and icons" (1997, 37), which is shaped by regional, historical, and sectarian location.[25] Since there are already enough eyes in this essay, I term this a "devotional gaze."[26] This is a culturally shaped set of devotional expectations that a Śvetāmbara Jain brings to his or her viewing of a Jina icon, and its large, highly reflective external eyes.

Sakalacandra sang that the two eyes are like infinite knowledge (*anant-jñān*) and infinite perception (*anant-darśan*), two of the characteristics of the enlightened and liberated soul: "O God, give enlightened knowledge and enlightened vision, which are like the two eyes."[27] The eyes enable a visual interaction between worshiper and Jina, through which the Jina's mercy (*kṛpā*) is showered upon the devoted worshiper: "I place the pair of eyes, like gems and jewels, on the face of my Lord. They are like enlightened knowledge and enlightened vision. O Lord, have mercy on me."[28]

Ātmārāmjī also sang of the importance of *darśana* of the icon. In the words of the refrain of one of his hymns in the seventeenfold *pūjā*, this ritual act "drives away delusion and washes away the stain of sin" (460). Further, he sang, in offering the pair of eyes the worshiper seeks the certainty (*nirdhārā*) of the Jina's enlightened vision. Amṛtsūri also equated the eyes with the eyes of enlightenment: "I offer up two jeweled eyes to you, the two eyes of enlightenment" (599).

These monastic authors tied the physical offering of the external eyes to the spiritual realization of insight into the true nature of the world. Śvetāmbara Jains—both mendicants and laity—with whom I discussed the external eyes, on occasion gave voice to a more direct and even magical experience of the eyes, in addition to this more doctrinal interpretation. Most simply, they said that the eyes made them feel that the Jina was actually seeing them.

The eyes certainly enable *darśana* in a powerful manner. Many Śvetāmbara temples intentionally shun the use of electric lights due to the violence (*hiṃsā*) that electricity entails. As a result, often the only illumination in the inner sanctum of a temple comes from a single-wick lamp. I have often observed that this is sufficient to create a powerful reflection in the external eyes of an icon even when viewed from thirty feet away, standing on the other side of the inner pavilion (*maṇḍap*). This is a highly desirable trait for the performance of *darśana*, for it enables the devotional gaze. While conducting fieldwork in Pune, Whitney Kelting was instructed to be sure that when photographing an ornamented Jina image, the flash reflected off the eyes, so that one experienced the full effect of *darśana* when viewing the photograph (2001, 221).

Figure 2.8. Ornamented Śvetāmbara icon of Pañcāsar Pārśvanātha, Patan, North Gujarat, August 13, 1996. Photo © the author.

In a conversation about external eyes, one layman said that the external eyes of Śaṅkheśvar Pārśvanātha, probably the most popular Jina icon in Gujarat due to its wonder-working powers (Cort 1988), change color during the course of the day. While this may not be scientifically explainable, he asserted, if one sits in the temple all day one will definitely perceive the change.

Kalyāṇvijay's criticisms of external eyes did not go unchallenged, either. In 1958, another monk in the Tapā Gaccha, Muni Abhyudaysāgar, published his *Jinpūjā Paddhati kī Samālocnā*, "Critique of the 'Manual for Jina Worship.'" In his far-ranging disputation with Kalyāṇvijay, Abhyudaysāgar touched upon the importance of the external eyes affixed onto Jina icons. He wrote, in a comment I have heard echoed by many other Jains, "The eyes are attractive. From seeing the eyes, which are full of peaceful compassion, people feel the Lord is right in front of them. Thus from the eyes of the Lord, devotion especially arises in the viewer" (Abhyudaysāgar 1958, 91). Many Śvetāmbaras with whom I have spoken have commented on the powerful religio-aesthetic impact of the large, reflective eyes of an elaborately ornamented icon. In the words of one Śvetāmbara monk, "To us, a Digambara image seems blind. With the eyes, it seems that He is seeing us."[29]

Concluding Observations

This essay focuses on a feature of Jain material culture that is almost totally absent from standard text-based accounts of the Jain tradition. Those accounts describe the central doctrinal differences between the Śvetāmbaras and Digambaras: whether or not monks should be naked or can wear simple clothes; whether or not women can attain liberation; whether or not the Jina between the time of his embodied enlightenment and his final disembodied liberation performs human functions of speech, eating and evacuation. With the exception of the issue of whether monks should be naked or clothed, however, none of these differences is as readily visible as the practice of either affixing external eyes to Jina icons or forbidding them.

Once one is alerted to the simple fact that Śvetāmbara Jains affix external eyes to most important temple icons, whereas Digambara Jains eschew this practice as a matter of principle, one sees that the presence or absence of external eyes is ubiquitous in Jain temples. There are tens of thousands of Jain temples in India (and a growing number in the countries where Jains are now settling in their global dispersion), and the sectarian identity of each one of them is marked by the eyes of the icons enshrined in it. The presence or absence of external eyes on icons is therefore a central defining characteristic of Jain sectarian identity.

Pursuing this difference takes us to core issues of what it means to be a Jain. A Jain literally is a person who is a follower of the Jina. Who the Jina is, therefore, lies at the heart of the Jain tradition. Several of the doctrinal disagreements mentioned above between Śvetāmbaras and Digambaras pertain to the definition of the Jina. There are also important disagreements between the two sects concerning elements in the biographies of several of the most important of the twenty-four Jinas. The material practice of whether or not one affixes external eyes to an icon of the Jina, therefore, is an important marker of who a Jain understands the Jina to be, and also of how one understands oneself as a Jain.

The names "Śvetāmbara" ("White Clad") and "Digambara" ("Sky Clad") literally place monastic practice at the center of Jain sectarian identity. This essay has shown, however, that if we start from Jain material culture, an alternate way to understand Jain sectarian identity is that the Śvetāmbaras are those Jains who affix external eyes to icons of the Jina, and therefore experience the Jina as visually interacting with them in the temple, whereas the Digambaras are those Jains who reject this practice, and experience the Jina as looking inward in eternal contemplation of the perfections of pure soul.

Notes

I thank Surendra Bothara, Corinne Dempsey, Lalit Kumar, Tracy Pintchman, Selva Raj, and Joanna Williams for their assistance with this chapter. It was originally written for presentation at Symposium XIII of the American Council for Southern Asian Art, held at the Asian Art Museum of San Francisco, March 2–4, 2007. A short discussion of this material appeared as an object narrative on the website of the Material & Visual Cultures of Religion (MAVCOR) project at Yale University; see Cort 2013. This essay is dedicated to the memory of Lalit Kumar.

1. A perusal of the lavishly illustrated coffee table books devoted to the many Śvetāmbara pilgrimage shrines (*tīrth*), and which allow the devoted reader/viewer to engage vicariously in the sacred viewing (*darśana*) of the icons, shows that the majority of these icons have external eyes (as well as other permanent and temporary ornamentation) affixed to them. See, for example, Jinendrasūri 1999–2000, Kuśaḷcandravijay 1990, and *Tīrth Darśan* 1980.

My discussion here pertains only to the icon-worshiping Śvetāmbara Mūrtipūjaka Jains, as the Śvetāmbara Sthānakavāsī and Terāpanthī traditions eschew the worship of icons as a matter of principle. Whenever I say "Śvetāmbara" in this essay, the reader should understand the full reference to be Śvetāmbara Mūrtipūjaka.

2. This is equally evident from a perusal of the volumes dedicated to cataloguing the Digambara pilgrimage shrines, B. Jain and L. Jain 1974–88.

3. I intentionally use the theologically charged term "God" for the Jina. In this I follow common Jain practice in English (as well as Indian languages, in which the Jina is often referred to by terms such as Bhagavān, Īśvara, Deva, and Paramātmā). This is also a methodological choice. There are significant differences between the Jain understanding(s) of the Jina as "God" and the understandings of "God" found in the three Abrahamic traditions and the many strands of Hinduism; but they are disagreements about the nature and definition of "God," not the existence of "God." See Cort 2001, 91–93.

4. I use the word "icon" to refer to three-dimensional Jina images of stone and metal, but here shift to "idol," since that word is appropriate to convey a Muslim theological sense of disapprobation.

5. Baidyanath Saraswati reported that up until about 1950 one of the most highly skilled icon sculptors in Banaras was a Muslim named Babu Miyana, "who had the reputation of being the only person who could make *sriyantra* according to the canons of *shilpashastra*" (1975, 30n1). Many of the carvers who work on structural and ornamental carvings on the Jain and Hindu temples throughout western India, such as those at Osian in Rajasthan, are also Muslim. The distinction between work and worship is fairly widespread among Muslim craftsmen who work on the material culture of the icon-worshiping traditions of South Asia.

6. A similar division of labor according to religious tradition exists among the craftsmen in Jaipur who carve stone icons for Śvetāmbara Jains, Digambara Jains, and Hindus. Most workshops carve icons for only one group, although there are a few that carve a wider repertoire of iconographies.

7. In U.S. dollars, these were roughly $150 to $175 for crystal, $12 for glass, and $9 for enamel.

8. See in particular the beautiful photographs of this icon at Shah 1988. For other illustrations of medieval icons with silver inlaid eyes, see the following: Granoff 2009, figs. S21, S22; Pal 1988, 145–47; Pal 1994, 148, catalogue 35; Shah 1955–56, 59, figs. 7 and 60, figs. 13–14; Shah 1975, 277, figs. 9 and 11–12; Shah 1978, 55–58, fig. 181; Shah 1982, 325, fig. 31; and Van Alphen 2000, 156–58, figs. 81–83.

9. See Babb 1996, 84–91 and Cort 2001, 61–99.

10. Humphrey and Laidlaw 1994.

11. For the relevant passage in the *Śrāddhavidhi*, see p. 141 of the 1980 edition, p. 91 of the 1995 edition, and p. 57 of the 2004 edition. On *vāsakṣepa* (Gujarati *vāskep*) see Cort 2001, 115.

12. On *āśātnā* (Sanskrit *āśātanā*) see Cort 2001, 71 and Williams 1963, 225–29.

13. 1986 Sivana edition, p. 514; 1984 Ahmedabad edition, p. 165; and 1986 Palitana edition, p. 316. Only the last includes the mention of eyes.

14. 1984 Ahmedabad edition, pp. 165–66.

15. P. 166.

16. P. 166.

17. P. 166.

18. Sakalacandragaṇi, *Sattar Bhedī Pūjā Sastabak*, pp. 46–47.

19. *Sattar Bhedī Pūjā* of Ācārya Vijayānandsūri, p. 459; and *Sattar Bhedī Pūjā* of Ācārya Vijay Amṛtsūri, p. 598.

20. *Sattar Bhedī Pūjā* of Sādhukīrtimuni, p. 219.

21. *Sattar Bhedī Pūjā* of Meghrājmuni, p. 838.

22. He here referred to the *śrīvats* found in the middle of the chest of most Śvetāmbara icons.

23. Such an extreme response is not limited to nineteenth-century observers. Several years ago I gave a slide-talk to faculty colleagues at Denison University. When I showed a slide of a close-up of a Śvetāmbara icon with extraordinarily large external eyes, a colleague from the history department blurted out in a shocked voice, "Who is that?!"

24. Information on the family comes from Tripathi 1981; see especially pp. 198–202 on Kasturbhai's long leadership of Āṇandjī Kalyāṇjī.

25. Davis derives this concept from Michael Baxandall's (1988) concept "the period eye."

26. "Gaze," of course, has become a central concept in contemporary art historical theory. See Olin 2003, and the sources in her bibliography. See also Morgan (2005, especially 2–6), who employs the concept of "gaze" within a specifically religious framework.

27. 1984 Ahmedabad edition, p. 166.

28. 1984 Ahmedabad edition, p. 166.

29. Digambaras, of course, do not agree with this Śvetāmbara judgment. I provide an extensive analysis of the north Indian Digambara devotional gaze in Cort 2012. For one example, let me call attention to a nineteenth-century Hindi hymn known as *Darśan Pāṭh* ("*Darśan* Recitation") by Budhjan, a lay Digambara poet who composed texts between 1778 and 1838 (see also Cort 2009). This is frequently sung by contemporary North Indian Digambara Jains as part of the ritual of taking *darśana* of a Jina icon in a temple. While Budhjan makes no explicit reference to the eyes of the icon, he does refer to the meditative, non-interactive gaze of the icon:

> The naked form of the dispassionate Lord is beautiful
> as He gazes intently on the tip of His nose.

References

Classical and Liturgical Sources

Ceiyavandana Mahābhāsā of Śāntisūri. Bombay: Jinśāsan Ārādhnā Ṭrasṭ, 1988.

Dharma Saṅgraha of Mahopādhyāya Mānavijayagaṇi, with *Svopajñavṛtti* compiled by Mahopādhyāya Yaśovijaya. Three volumes. Edited by Muni Municandravijay. Bombay: Jinśāsan Ārādhnā Ṭrasṭ, 1984–87.

Sattar Bhedī Pūjā of Meghrājmuni. In *Vividh Pūjā Saṅgrah,* 835–56. Ahmedabad: Jain Prakāśan Mandir, 1984; 12th printing.

Sattar Bhedī Pūjā of Paṇḍit Sādhukīrtimuni. In *Pūjā Saṅgrah,* edited by Tilakvijay Panjābī, 215–41. Bikaner: Bābū Dānmal Śaṅkardān Nāhṭā, 1929.

Sattar Bhedī Pūjā of Sakalacandra Upādhyāya. In *Vividh Pūjā Saṅgrah,* 158–84. Ahmedabad: Jain Prakāśan Mandir, 1984; 12th printing.

———. In *Pūjā Saṅgrah Sārth,* 309–49. Palitana: Kāntilāl Ḍī. Śāh, 1984.

———. In *Vividh Pūjā Saṅgrah,* edited by Paṁnyās Jitendravijaygaṇi, 507–56. Sivana: Tapā Gacch Jain Saṅgh, 1986.

———. With *stabak* of author. Edited by Sādhvī Dīptiprajñāśrī. *Anusandhān* 39 (2007), 39–75.

Sattar Bhedī Pūjā of Ācārya Vijay Amṛtsūri. In *Vividh Pūjāmṛt Saṅgrah,* edited by Paṁnyās Jinendravijaygaṇi, 596–613. Lakhabaval Shantipuri: Śrī Harṣpuṣpāmṛt Jain Granthmālā, 1979.

Sattar Bhedī Pūjā of Ācārya Vijayānandsūri (Ātmārāmjī). In *Vividh Pūjā Saṅgrah,* 457–74. Ahmedabad: Jain Prakāśan Mandir, 1984; 12th printing.

Śrāddha Vidhi Prakaraṇa of Ācārya Ratnaśekharasūri, with his *Śrāddha Vidhi Kaumudī*. Gujarati translation by Paṇḍit Dāmodar Govindācārya. Edited by Paṁnyās Vajrasenvijaygaṇi. Ahmedabad: Harīfārm Korporeśan, 1980. Reprint Ahmedabad: Bhadraṅkar Prakāśan, 1995.

———. Hindi translation by Paṁnyās Ratnasenvijaygaṇi. Unjha: Tattvatrayī Prakāśan, 2004.

Modern Sources

Abhyudaysāgar, Muni. 1958. *Jinpūjā Paddhati kī Samālocnā*. Beawar: Śrī Rājasthān Jain Saṁskṛti Rakṣak Saṅgh.

Babb, Lawrence A. 1996. *Absent Lord: Ascetics and Kings in a Jain Ritual Culture*. Berkeley: University of California Press.

Baxandall, Michael. 1988. *Painting and Experience in Fifteenth Century Italy*. 2nd ed. Oxford: Oxford University Press.

Brown, W. Norman. 1929. "Early Śvetāmbara Jaina Miniatures." *Indian Art and Letters* 3: 1–11.

———. 1933. *The Story of Kālaka: Texts, History, Legends, and Miniature Paintings of the Śvetāmbara Jain Hagiographical Work the Kālakācāryakathā*. Washington: Freer Gallery of Art.

Burgess, James. 1977. *The Temples of Śatruñjaya*. Gandhinagar: The Gujarat State Committee for the Celebration of 2500th Anniversary of Bhagwan Mahavira Nirvan. Originally Bombay, 1869.

Cort, John E. 1988. "Pilgrimage to Shankheshvar Pārshvanāth." *Center for the Study of World Religions Bulletin* 14, 1: 63–72.

———. 1996a. "Art, Religion, and Material Culture: Some Reflections on Method." *Journal of the American Academy of Religion* 64: 613–32.

———. 1996b. "King or Ascetic? Ornamentation of Jain Temple Images." American Committee for South Asian Art, Symposium VII, Minneapolis, May 10–12.

———. 2000. "Communities, Temples, Identities: Art Histories and Social Histories in Western India." In *Ethnography and Personhood: Essays from the Field*, edited by Michael W. Meister, 101–28. Jaipur: Rawat Publications.

———. 2001. *Jains in the World: Religious Values and Ideology in India*. New York: Oxford University Press.

———. 2007. "Dios como rey o asceta." In *La Escultura en los Templos Indios: El Arte de la Devoción*, edited by John Guy, 171–79. Barcelona: Fundación "la Caixa."

———. 2009. "Budhjan's Petition: Digambar Bhakti in Nineteenth-Century Jaipur." *Jaina Studies: Newsletter of the Centre of Jaina Studies* 4: 39–42. (Accessible at www.soas.ac.uk/jainastudies).

———. 2010. *Framing the Jina: Narratives of Icons and Idols in Jain History*. New York: Oxford University Press.

———. 2012. "Situating *Darśan*: Seeing the Digambar Jina Icon in Eighteenth- and Nineteenth-Century North India." *International Journal of Hindu Studies* 16: 1–56.

———. 2013. "External Eyes On Jain Temple Icons." Material & Visual Cultures of Religion, Yale University. http://mavcor.yale.edu/conversations/object-narratives/external-eyes-jain-temple-icons.

Davis, Richard H. 1997. *Lives of Indian Images*. Princeton: Princeton University Press.

Dundas, Paul. 2002. *The Jains*. 2nd ed. London: Routledge.

———. 2007. *History, Scripture and Controversy in Medieval Jain Sect*. London: Routledge.

Granoff, Phyllis, ed. 2009. *Victorious Ones: Jain Images of Perfection*. New York: Rubin Museum of Art; and Ahmedabad: Mapin Publishing.

Guy, John. 1994. "Jain Manuscript Painting." In *The Peaceful Liberators: Jain Art from India*, edited by Pratapaditya Pal, 89–99. Los Angeles: Los Angeles County Museum of Art.

Humphrey, Caroline, and James Laidlaw. 1994. *The Archetypal Actions of Ritual: A Theory of Ritual Illustrated by the Jain Rite of Worship*. Oxford: Clarendon Press.

Jain, Balbhadra, and Lakṣmīcandra Jain (eds.). 1974–88. *Bhārat ke Digambar Jain Tīrth*. Five volumes. Bombay: Bhāratvarṣīya Digambar Jain Tīrthkṣetra Kameṭī.

Jinendrasūri, Ācārya Vijay. 1999–2000. *Śvetāmbar Jain Tīrth Darśan*. Two volumes. Lakhavabal Shantipuri: Śrī Harṣpuṣpāmṛt Jain Granthmālā.

Kalyāṇvijaygaṇi, Paṅnyās. 1956. *Kalyāṇ Kalikā*. Two volumes. Edited by Muni Bhadraṅkarvijay. Jalor: Śrī Kalyāṇvijay Śāstra Saṅgrah Samiti. Volume one reprint 1987.

———. 1957. *Jin Pūjā Paddhati*. Jalor: Śrī Kalyāṇvijay Śāstra Saṅgrah Samiti.

———. 1966. *Jin Pūjā Vidhi Saṅgrah*. Edited by Pandit Śobhācandra Bhārill. Jalor: Śrī Kalyāṇvijay Śāstra Saṅgrah Samiti.

Kelting, M. Whitney. 2001. *Singing to the Jinas: Jain Laywomen, Maṇḍaḷ Singing, and the Negotiation of Jain Devotion*. New York: Oxford University Press.

Khandalavala, Karl J., and Moti Chandra. 1969. *New Documents of Indian Painting—A Reappraisal*. Bombay: Prince of Wales Museum of Western India.

Kim, Hawon Ku. 2007. "Re-Formation of Identity: The 19th-century Jain Pilgrimage Site of Shatrunjaya, Gujarat." PhD diss., University of Minnesota.

Kramrisch, Stella. 1975. "Jaina Painting of Western India." In *Aspects of Jaina Art and Architecture*, edited by U. P. Shah and M. A. Dhaky, 385–404. Ahmedabad: Gujarat State Committee for the Celebration of 2500th Anniversary of Bhagavān Mahāvīra Nirvāṇa.

Kumar, Lalit. 2000. "The Jain Manuscript and Miniature Tradition." In *Steps to Liberation: 2,500 Years of Jain Art and Religion*, edited by Jan Van Alphen, 57–69. Antwerp: Etnografisch Museum Antwerpen.

Kuśaḷcandravijay, Pravartak, ed. 1990. *108 Jain Tīrth Darśanāvalī*. Palitana: Śrī 108 Jain Tīrth Darśan Bhavan Ṭrasṭ.

Mitra, Sisir Kumar, ed. 1979. *East Indian Bronzes*. Calcutta: Centre of Advanced Study in Ancient Indian History and Culture, University of Calcutta.

Morgan, David. 2005. *The Sacred Gaze: Religious Visual Culture in Theory and Practice*. Berkeley: University of California Press.

Olin, Margaret. 2003. "Gaze." In *Critical Terms for Art History*, edited by Robert S. Nelson and Richard Shiff. 2nd ed., 318–29. Chicago: University of Chicago Press.

Pal, Pratapaditya. 1975. *Bronzes of Kashmir*. New York: Hacker Art Books.

———. 1988. *Indian Sculpture: A Catalogue of the Los Angeles County Museum of Art, Volume 2, 700–1800*. Los Angeles: Los Angeles County Museum of Art, in association with University of California Press.

———, ed. 1994. *The Peaceful Liberators: Jain Art from India*. Los Angeles: Los Angeles County Museum of Art.

Saraswati, Baidyanath. 1975. *Kashi: Myth and Reality of a Classical Cultural Tradition*. Simla: Indian Institute of Advanced Study.

Shah, Ambalal Premchand (Ambālāl Premcand Śāh). 1953. *Jain Tīrth Sarva Saṅgrah*. Three volumes. Ahmedabad: Śeṭh Āṇandjī Kalyāṇjī.

———. 1968. "Some Inscriptions and Images on Mount Śatruñjaya." In *Śrī Mahāvīr Jain Vidyālay Suvarṇ Mahotsav Granth*, English section, edited by A. N. Upadhye et al., 162–69. Bombay: Śrī Mahāvīr Jain Vidyālay Prakāśan.

Shah, U. P. 1951. "A Unique Jaina Image of Jīvantasvāmī." *Journal of the Oriental Institute* 1: 72–79.

———. 1955–56. "Bronze Hoard from Vasantgaḍh." *Lalit Kala* 1–2: 55–65.

———. 1959. *Akota Bronzes*. Bombay: Government of Bombay, Department of Archaeology.

———. 1975. "Jaina Bronzes—A Brief Survey." In *Aspects of Jaina Art and Architecture*, edited by U. P. Shah and M. A. Dhaky, 269–98. Ahmedabad: Gujarat State Committee for the Celebration of 2500th Anniversary of Bhagavān Mahāvīra Nirvāṇa.

———. 1976. *More Documents of Jaina Paintings and Gujarati Paintings of Sixteenth and Later Centuries*. Ahmedabad: L. D. Institute of Indology.

———, ed. 1978. *Treasures of Jaina Bhaṇḍāras*. Ahmedabad: L. D. Institute of Indology.

———. 1988. "Jain Bronzes from Western India: Akota, Vasantgadh and Valabhi." In *Indian Bronze Masterpieces: The Great Tradition*, edited by Asha Rani Mathur, 54–69. New Delhi: Brijbasi Printers.

Śīlcandrasūri, Ācārya Vijay. 2007. "Śrīvācak Sakalacandragaṇi-viracit Sattarbhedī Pūjā–Sastabak: Avalokan." *Anusandhān* 39: 24–38.

Stevenson, Margaret (Mrs. Sinclair). 1910. *Notes on Modern Jainism*. Oxford: B. H. Blackwell; and Surat: Irish Mission Press.

———. 1921. "Worship (Jain)." In *Encyclopaedia of Religion and Ethics*, vol. 12, 799–802. Edinburgh: T. & T. Clark.

Tīrth Darśan. 1980. Two volumes. Madras: Śrī Mahāvīr Jain Kalyāṇ Saṅgh.

Tod, James. 1839. *Travels in Western India*. London: Wm. H. Allen & Co. Reprint New Delhi: Munshiram Manoharlal, 1997.

Tripathi, Dwijendra. 1981. *The Dynamics of Tradition: Kasturbhai Lalbhai and His Entrepreneurship*. New Delhi: Manohar.

Van Alphen, Jan, ed. 2000. *Steps to Liberation: 2,500 Years of Jain Art and Religion*. Antwerp: Etnografisch Museum Antwerpen, India Study Centre Universiteit Antwerpen, and Antwerp Indian Association.

Williams, R. 1963. *Jaina Yoga: A Survey of the Mediaeval Śrāvakācāras*. Oxford: Oxford University Press. Reprint Delhi: Motilal Banarsidass, 1983.

3

North Indian Materialities of Jesus

MATHEW N. SCHMALZ

Introduction

In Uttar Pradesh, people associate the Catholic Church with materiality. Of course, there are the red buildings, so conspicuous in rural environments and only a little less obvious in the overgrowth of North Indian cities like Varanasi. People are also quite well aware that these red Catholic buildings are schools, hospitals, and dispensaries. Whether through the advancement promised by education, or the healing provided by medicine, the Catholic Church is deeply involved in materiality of North Indian life. North Indian Catholics themselves are also deeply enmeshed in the material aspects of everyday existence, at the least in the minds of some. The phrase referring to North Indian Catholics is "Rice Christians"—a description most often repeated in English to emphasize how these Indians have chosen a foreign religion for its manifest material benefits.

In North Indian cities, one finds communities of South Indian Catholics predominantly from Kerala and Tamilnad. The clergy generally hails from those states, as well as from Karnataka and the Jharkhand. Catholics born in Uttar Pradesh are almost exclusively Dalits ("crushed ones") from various Untouchable castes. Upon their conversion to Catholicism, Dalits usually find that the material conditions of their lives do not change as substantially as is popularly thought. Some remain sharecroppers; others are bonded laborers; some still practice their traditional occupations of tanning; and others work as catechists or village educators for rural Catholic missions. One rarely finds indigenous

North Indian Catholics in the prestigious English medium schools that the Catholic Church administers in North Indian cities. Instead, one finds indigenous North Indian Catholics in Catholic Hindi medium schools maintained by Catholic missions in the countryside. There were days when these Catholic missions were flush with funds from Catholic Relief services and had storehouses filled with milk, butter and grain. The missions would distribute clothes, build homes, and provide start-up funds for businesses. But legal restrictions have made foreign contributions both less frequent and less sizable. The Catholic Church itself has also stopped the most aggressive forms of aid, having decided that it did indeed create "Rice Christians" more interested in goods than graces.

Dalit Catholics have a different view of matters. For them, the Catholic Church used to be their patron. For generations, Dalits had been denied even the most basic forms of social interaction by their segregation in separate "colonies" and by being denied commensality and access to drinking water. There was participation in the *jajmānī* system, especially for members of the Chamar caste who would remove dead cattle, eat the meat, and tan the hide. The Catholic Church inserted itself into this material context and became the *jajmān*, a kind of benevolent landowner for a community quite understandably concerned with rice and other staples. But while they acknowledge their material dependence, Dalit Catholics also argue that the interweaving of religion with material interests is not unique to them. Dalit Catholics often point to the Catholic institutions themselves, with their brick and electricity not to mention their wheat fields and servants, as evidence that they are not alone in thinking of their material surroundings. Moreover, as Dalit Catholics observe, having requisite numbers of indigenous converts is quite a good marketing point when making appeals for funds from abroad. From this perspective, the most appropriate symbol for institutional Catholicism is not rice but meat. For North Indian Dalit Catholics, the Catholicism is not so much a rice church as it is a meat church, since meat indicates material means far beyond the mere subsistence of a rice diet.

Jesus is traditionally believed to have said, "My kingdom is not of this world." As corollary to this position, it has often been thought that true "Christianity" is somehow disengaged from materiality and its concerns. Perhaps in part to challenge such implicit Gnostic biases, we have the perspectives of observers such as Karl Marx (Marx and Engels 1964) and Antonio Gramsci (1994) who understand religious belief and practice as intimately connected to the material base that grounds all forms of cultural expression. Indeed, Catholicism has often been singled out for the ostentatious materiality of its images and symbols (for example, see Hislop 1858). Of course, these images and symbols are in some way tied to the Catholic understanding that Jesus can be experienced under the material forms of the sacraments. For their part, Indians, particularly Hindus, have also long been known for their love of image and symbol. Not only do we find early ethnographic commentators remarking rather pejoratively on the "idolatry" of the "Hindoos" (Buchanan 1986 [1934]; Crooke, 1978 [1896]; DuBois 1992), but we also find contemporary works that attempt, in a much more sensitive way, to understand and characterize the importance of material images and symbols to Hindu religious belief and practice (Davis 1997; Eck 1984).

Given the emphasis upon materiality in both Hinduism and Catholicism, it should come as no surprise that in North India Jesus has multiple materialities. In these North Indian materialities of Jesus, we can see a variety of themes that scholars have long reflected upon in their ethnographic studies of Indian material religion and devotional life. Among these themes, most crucial is interaction, for the images of Jesus that draw most attention, not to mention devotion, are those that allow an intimate and continuous engagement and exchange. Indeed, interacting with specific material representations of Jesus becomes a focal point for the reworking of identity and the creation of community—potentialities and goals often understood to be activated and achieved by material religion in its diverse forms (see McDaniel 1995). But what is finally most interesting is how engaging, or ignoring, particular material representations of Jesus becomes a way of commenting on the materiality of North Indian Catholicism itself, since materiality takes its shape and contours from the relationships in which it is situated. Accordingly, to consider the materialities of Jesus in North India, we will explore three North Indian Catholic material contexts: the mission, the ashram, and the cathedral.

The Mission

North of Varanasi lies the Shantinagar mission. It was established in the late 1940s by Capuchins from Canada, who had come on mission to what was then called the Prefecture of Allahabad-Gorakhpur. Over time, the mission grew from a simple house to a large compound with a school and a dispensary. It was during the 1960s that the Shantinagar mission became a center for local development efforts in addition to freely distributing clothes, milk, and grain. These programs continued through the 1970s, a decade that also saw the rise of the "inculturation" movement that attempted to "Indianize" Catholicism by adapting it to Hindu custom and practice (see Schmalz 2001). As part of this inculturation effort, the mission was proclaimed an ashram: meat was not prepared or eaten in the ashram's precincts, and nuns wore ochre saris to complement the ochre-colored vestments that priests wore when celebrating a form of the mass adapted to North Indian sensibilities. Jesus Christ became the "guru," of the ashram, and this status was proclaimed at the entrance to the mission's church by a large picture of Jesus sitting in a full lotus position. From its position above the threshold of the church, this other-worldly image of Jesus as guru illuminated the most "worldly" dynamic of material religion at this rural Catholic mission: that of touching and being touched.

Jesus as Guru

Mid-January often provides good weather for cleaning and refurbishing the mission. The weather is cool, and the harvest has not yet begun in earnest. Such was the case back in 1995, when a group of young Catholics volunteered to sweep out the mission's church and clean and re-hang the picture of Jesus the Guru (Figure 3.1). Usually, "service" at the mission can become a rather contentious affair, since many local Catholics understand doing manual labor for the mission as disturbingly similar to the tasks they often perform for landowners. But this wasn't an issue that day since the young men needed something to pass the time. None of them had steady work and, for the last couple of weeks, they had been mostly playing volleyball on the dirt court they had created next to a row of cannabis plants behind the mission. Over time, volleyball had become rather dull so the cannabis patch had proved invaluable. And so, the young men swept out the mission's church. The picture of Jesus was taken down, and its frame and glass were polished. With due deliberation, several of the young men positioned it once again above the entrance to the mission's church.

The perfunctory nature of this winter-cleaning might seem to merit little notice, let alone commentary. But as far as materiality is concerned, this "perfunctoriness" should be understood as the crucial point. Across the compound from the church is a shrine to the Virgin Mary where a statue of Mary is venerated with offerings of coconuts and coins. By contrast, the image of Jesus, the guru, merited no such special treatment. In fact, the image was placed in a position where it effectively looked down on worshippers: it was distant, otherworldly, and afforded no opportunity for interaction. The young Catholics did not even bother to remove their sandals when they handled the image, something they most certainly would have done if they had approached an image of Mother Mary or entered the chapel. The materiality of Jesus as Guru was an inert materiality, devoid of feeling and life.

Figure 3.1. Catholics hang a picture of Jesus as Guru at the Mission. © Mathew N. Schmalz.

Jesus as Child

In addition to Jesus as Guru, there was another material representation of Jesus, one that evoked feelings of reverential warmth instead of perfunctory coldness. To meet this other North Indian Jesus, we need to travel back again to 1995, this time to Christmas Eve, when Ghura Master asked me to take him through the bazaar of his village before traveling to the Shantinagar mission for midnight Mass. Ghura Master had been a catechist for the Shantinagar mission for a number of years. He had also been the headman, or *pradhān*, of his village—the first

Untouchable and Communist to ever hold the position. Ghura Master was forced to resign his position as headman, in addition to leaving his catechetical work, when an acid attack left him blind and disfigured (see Schmalz 1999). Even though it was past dark that Christmas Eve, Ghura Master insisted on wearing a white cloth over his face to avoid drawing reproachful gazes and questions. As Ghura Master and I walked through the bazaar in his village, we stopped at numerous stalls selling perfume. Ghura Master insisted on sampling as many scents as possible. After the shopkeeper would put a touch of perfume on his wrist, Ghura Master would smell it and then shake his head, saying, "No, that's not right." Finally, he settled upon a vial of musk perfume. We then left for the bus stand and the Shantinagar mission.

There were over five hundred Catholics gathered in the mission compound for midnight Mass. This was the primary festival for the many people present who would only attend church sporadically. A central part of the service was the veneration of the infant Jesus, represented by a doll resting in a hastily constructed crib. Since Ghura Master was blind, he could not see that the doll was almost as white as I was—a fact commented upon by some members of the congregation. As Ghura Master and I stood to make our obeisance to the child Jesus, Ghura Master asked me to give him a cotton ball infused with the perfume he had purchased several hours earlier. Ghura Master whispered, with a quick laugh, that we were like the wise men who came upon the manger of Jesus in Bethlehem. Ghura Master thought that the musk he had chosen most closely resembled the myrrh that the wise men had brought with them on that night. So I led Ghura Master to the front of the altar, and with silent reverence Ghura Master touched his forehead to the feet of the infant Jesus and then gently anointed them with the musk perfume.

Touching the feet of an elder or an image of the deity is a deep form of respect in Indian culture. South Indian Catholics, for example, often hold the feet of a statue of a saint as they pray and put forward their petitions and requests for intercession. Ghura Master was taking a traditional form of devotion, present throughout the broad expanse of Catholicism, and reinterpreting it within the terms most familiar to him: touching the feet of the infant Jesus was the natural way to express his devotion to his god. Underlying this act was an understanding of purity, for Ghura Master was acknowledging that the feet of Christ were far purer than the most elevated part of his own body.

Perfuming the infant Jesus also had its psychological resonances. Ghura Master would often say that his feet had become smooth as a baby's: since he no longer went out on his village rounds, his feet had lost their calluses. Whenever he would make this point, Ghura Master would smile sadly and say that this was a good thing since he had led such a dissolute life as headman and catechist. Perhaps the smooth plastic skin of the baby Jesus recalled this childlike innocence and its associated sense of sinlessness. But what was most crucial was that Ghura Master was touching the image and interacting with it. One of Ghura Master's strongest memories as an Untouchable was being prevented from entering temples because his very touch was considered to defile. Now, as a Catholic Christian, he could touch his god, a god that had come down from heaven, become incarnate, and placed himself in human hands. The infant Jesus, in its white and plastic material form, "materialized" a different register of power and value. The intimate nature of the interaction was underscored by the musk perfume that Ghura Master applied. As the anthropologist McKim Marriott (1990) has argued, Hindu understandings of the self-rest upon notions of its inherent changeability or "dividuality." Within this "fluid" Hindu world, human interactions are exchanges of "coded substances" that alter and transform the self. While the term "Hindu" perhaps is too bounded a category, at least for talking about a midnight Mass at a Catholic mission, it is clear that Ghura Master was taking advantage of a kind of dividuality that worked both ways, since he and the child Jesus were partaking of each other's essence. Ghura Master was instantiating a new, "touchable," identity that he believed Christianity had brought him.

The contrast between the infant Jesus and the guru Jesus could not be more striking. The image of Jesus as guru represented an identity that the mission's Catholics had rejected. Jesus as guru "taught" from on-high and permitted no interaction from his hierarchical elevation. Although the image of Jesus as guru was intended to articulate an otherworldly vision of salvation, the mission's Catholics saw its message as very worldly indeed. By proclaiming itself an ashram, the mission was attempting to adapt to North Indian religious sensibilities. But while the mission embraced the guru Jesus as an image of renunciation, it certainly had not renounced its own material possessions, such as its motorcycle, generator, television, and refrigerator. What the mission had effectively renounced was being involved in the materiality of the lives of the mission's Catholics: it did not distribute food as it once did, and it now charged Untouchable families for education at the mission's school. Therefore, the mission's Catholics effectively brought down Jesus the guru into materiality, into the dirt and pollution that they themselves experience—and are considered to embody—in their daily lives. The disdain that the Catholics showed the guru Jesus expressed their disdain for how the Catholic Church had selectively inserted itself into

North Indian rural life. Indeed, Catholicism no longer "touched" these Untouchables as it once did.

The Ashram

While Catholic missions like Shantinagar are often called "ashrams," they are so really in name only. The word "ashram" literally means "no work," and Catholic missions are certainly institutions that are designed for "work." Closer to Varanasi city, however, there is another kind of ashram, built self-consciously on a Hindu model of what an ashram should be. Matridham Ashram, literally "the abode of the Mother," was constructed several decades ago to be a center of "inculturation" and to proclaim a more authentically North Indian religious style. The ashram's primary ministry was its "Indian Christian experience" program that introduced members of Catholic religious orders to Hindu religious themes and practices. More recently, however, the ashram has also become a center for charismatic Catholicism, a movement that centers on acquiring and using "charismatic" gifts of healing and prophecy. While one might think that the contemplative emphasis of the ashram would have been in tension with the vocal and quite active ministries of charismatic healers, this did not turn out to be the case. In fact, the ashram in effect had two Jesuses to express the different aspects of its mission. These Jesuses, interestingly, were constructed on very Western patterns. But in spite of their foreign origin, these images of Jesus instantiated particular relationships of giving, receiving, and exchange that were very Indian indeed.

Jesus as Contemplative

At the center of the ashram compound is the chapel, designed and constructed with eight sides to represent the four cardinal directions and the intermediate spaces between them. These eight sides are brought together into "one pointedness" (*ekāgratā*) by a spire (*śikhar*). This cosmic symbolism continues on the inside of the chapel, with three levels representing the underworld, the earth, and the realm of the gods. The altar in the chapel is hewn from a single stone and is close to the ground so the priest can sit on the floor as he celebrates Mass. The tabernacle is in the shape of a lotus to remind us, in the words of the ashram's head priest (*ācārya*) that "we are called to live in the world without blemishes, like the lotus that rises from the mud." To cultivate such a blemishless life, retreatants gather in the chapel three times a day for a prayer service. While the prayers themselves are often Christian-inspired Sanskrit verses, the main ritual act is *ārati*—the rotation of an oil lamp to make the shape of the sacred mantra "OM" before a sepia-toned image of Jesus placed before the altar.

The religious life of the ashram used materiality for two closely associated purposes. The first purpose was to present Catholic Christianity in what was understood to be an authentically Indian idiom. The most fundamental point was obviously that what was going on in the ashram's chapel was intended to be similar to Hindu temple worship. This, in turn, was an effort to communicate that Catholic Christianity was not foreign, threatening, or somehow opposed to common Hindu devotional practices. The second purpose was to present Hindu materiality as something that could be imbued within Catholic Christian meaning. So, with regard to *ārati*, the three wicks in the oil lamp were presented as symbolic of the Trinity; the flame was associated with God's presence, such as in the burning bush; OM was equated to Christ as the eternal word; *agarbattī*, sandalwood incense, was likened to purity because as it burns all extraneous matter is consumed, leaving only ash. Materiality thus was envisioned as a way for Hinduism and Catholicism to meet in practice and to provide an opening for a shared experience of the sacred.

In spite of this great effort to express a suitably indigenous and palatable version of Catholicism, the daily cycles of prayer were only sparsely attended by residents from the surrounding villages. For many of the Catholics attending the Indian Christian experience, this was their first introduction to "Hinduism," and they often had rather conflicted thoughts about the practices: some were struck by the apparent similarities between the material aspects of Hinduism and Catholicism; others feared that adapting to Hindu religiosity would lead to a loss of Catholic distinctiveness. But what Hindus from the village and Catholic retreatants unquestionably agreed upon was the significance of the image of Jesus near the chapel's altar. On days when charismatic healings services were held, Hindus from the surrounding villages would come to place fruit and sweets before the picture after fully prostrating themselves before it.

Given that this was an ashram, one would have expected the image of Jesus in the chapel to be like the guru Jesus that stood watch over the church at the Shantinagar mission. But this image of Jesus was quite different. The picture was a straight-on view of Jesus's face: his eyes were quite prominent, and the long tresses of his hair rested gently on his shoulders and framed his face:

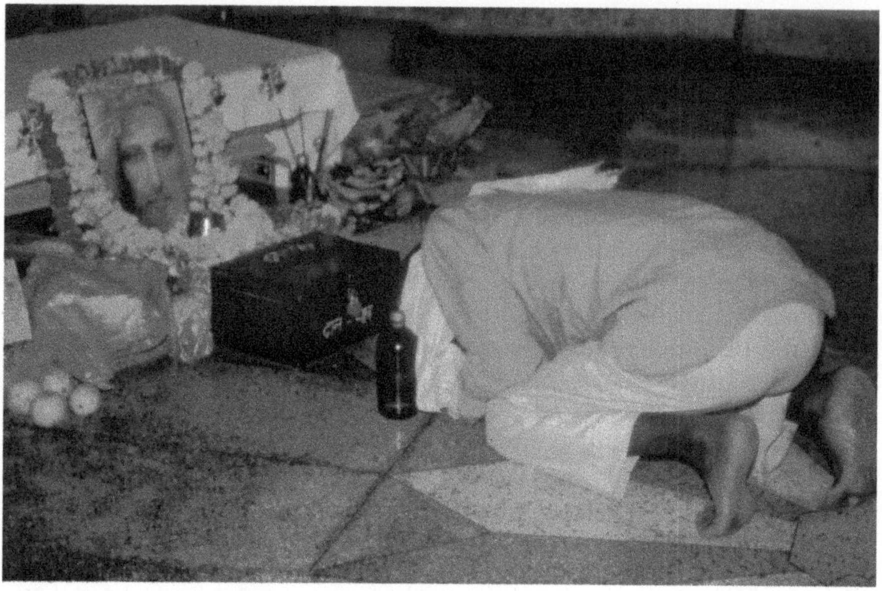

Figure 3.2. A worshipper prostrates himself before an image of Jesus in the Ashram's chapel. © Mathew N. Schmalz.

The image's understated sepia tones also made it seem as if Jesus were floating in otherworldly ether. But this image was not unique to the ashram, for it was a colorized version extrapolated from the image on the Shroud of Turin, a relic that some believe to be Jesus's burial shroud—although the Catholic Church has never officially endorsed such views. In 1898, photographic negatives of the Shroud showed an almost three-dimensional face whose features were far clearer than the faint, positive lines and impressions on the Shroud that can be seen by the naked eye. After seeing those negatives, the photographer Secundo Pia reportedly exclaimed, "It is the Lord" (see Rinaldi 1975).

Worshippers at the ashram's chapel knew nothing of the image's background or history. But they did comment on the image's eyes. At an Indian Christian Experience session immediately following a charismatic healing service, a group of sisterhood postulants from Tamil Nadu mentioned how they heard the image of Jesus "speak" through his eyes and "touch" each one of them with his gaze. Diana Eck (1984) has argued that within Hindu temple worship, the act of seeing (*darśan*) is often understood to be a way of touching and being touched by the deity. Since the image of Jesus in front of the altar was very close to the floor, its eyes could only be fully engaged from a kneeling or prostrate position. Seeing and being seen, and touching and being touched, were thus combined with postures that expressed not only hierarchy but also intimacy.

But the interaction between worshippers and the chapel's image of Jesus was not limited to seeing. Initially the offering of fruits and sweets would seem to correspond to *pūjā* (worship) that involves an exchange of substances between worshippers and the deity (on this theme see Babb 1975, 31–68). In conventional *pūjā*, whether at a temple or during a ritual at home, the deity is understood to consume part of the offerings after which worshippers take back the offerings, now infused with the essence of the deity, to consume themselves. But these offerings made to the image of Jesus were not taken back; they were simply left there, to be taken away by a priest or brother after the service.

Normally, giving implies reciprocation. But in diverging from this pattern, interactions with the image of the Jesus at the ashram seem to correspond to those Indian cultural contexts in which reciprocity is forbidden. For example, L. A. Babb (1975, 75–80) talks about the "Mahabrahman" who plays a special ritual role after a cremation by effectively taking the place of the deceased and receiving gifts that he does not reciprocally return later. By accepting these gifts during the post-cremation ritual, the Mahabrahman is consuming the remaining inauspiciousness associated with death. Gloria Goodwin Raheja (1988) has identified a similar pattern in the *jajmānī* system in which a dominant caste presents gifts to the lower castes that serve them. While the *jajmānī* system has often been taken to represent the self-contained reciprocity of village life, Raheja argues with substantial ethnographic evidence that the lower castes are in fact receptacles for inauspiciousness. A similar structure and intent seems to underlie worshippers' approaches to the ashram's image of Jesus. When asked about Jesus, worshippers most often would say, "He takes our sins." In village contexts, like Shantinagar (see Schmalz 2005), worshippers often bring sacks of wheat and rice and place them by the altar. Sin thus has a materiality that can be transferred and effectively burned away by the contemplative "austerity" (*tapasya*) of Jesus, the god-man who accepts whatever worshippers choose to give him.

Jesus as Charismatic

In popularity, monthly charismatic prayer services surpass the Indian Christian Experience as the ashram's primary form of outreach. To accommodate the large number of worshippers who attend such prayer services, a pavilion had to be constructed between the chapel and the ashram's refectory. Prayer services would follow a standard pattern: there would be sermons given by both priests and lay people, followed by the collective repetition of stock Christian phrases, such as "Jesus gives liberation," then testimonies of healing, and finally the laying on of hands (see also Schmalz 2011). Before entering the enclosure, participants would remove their sandals and discard intoxicants like betel nut and tobacco. The importance of purity was also emphasized by offering worshippers bread and water during breaks in the service, as opposed to tea, which Catholic charismatics consider to be an intoxicant that dangerously heats the body. Complementing this emphasis on purity was the theme of renunciation as participants were encouraged to place monetary offerings in a large box at the foot of the stage.

Unlike the giving that took place in the chapel, the giving that took place during the charismatic prayer service was based upon reciprocity and obligation. The central theme of the speakers from the podium was the transformative power of Jesus. This power becomes available when one creates space for it through surrender and renunciation. One speaker, a Protestant lawyer known by his professional title "Waqil Saheb" (see also Schmalz 2002), spoke of how Jesus fills the empty spaces in the human heart. In one sense, Waqil Saheb was talking about how the feeling of despair creates an opening for divine love. In another sense, Waqil Saheb was talking about how letting go allows Jesus to enter or, in other words, how emptying one's pockets allows them to be filled again. Accordingly, worshippers would make their offerings of money along with petitionary prayers. Through this exchange, Jesus was effectively obligated to reciprocate. Indeed, as many speakers from the podium emphasized, when an earnest worshipper asks something from God, God has to say "yes."

Symbolically overseeing the exchanges that took place during the charismatic prayer service was a large cardboard Jesus. This Jesus was not dressed in an ochre robe, nor was he in a full lotus position. Instead, this Jesus was dressed in a white robe with a yellow mantle, his arms outstretched (Figure 3.3). Even though his skin color was rather light, this "charismatic" Jesus bore a striking resemblance to the ashram's head priest. This similarity not only had become a running joke, but also presented numerous opportunities for inter-religious dialogue, especially when the head priest was asked to bless postcards that bore the image of Jesus's face. Worshippers were not drawn to this Jesus's eyes but to his arms and hands. The arms and hands were not articulated to traditional *mudrās*, or gestures of Hindu iconography, in which palms down represent the bestowing of boons, while palms up represent a blessing or a fear-not gesture. Instead, the palms were outstretched to

Figure 3.3. Jesus as charismatic healer at the Ashram. © Mathew N. Schmalz.

show Jesus's stigmatic wounds. While this was clearly intended to depict the resurrected Christ as victor over death, the worshippers I talked to interpreted Jesus's outstretched arms in different ways: Jesus was praying in charismatic fashion; he was accepting; he was bestowing blessings; he was embracing; or he was flying. But whatever he was doing, Jesus *was doing something*: he was active, and most certainly larger than life. To this extent, he was the material representation of what the charismatic movement attempted to create: active, inspired selves, larger than life in their supernatural power.

The Cathedral

Several miles from Matridham ashram stands the building that is now most commonly associated with Catholicism in this part of Uttar Pradesh. Built at a cost of Rs. 1.5 crore and completed in 1992, St. Mary's Cathedral was intended to constitute a new model of Indian Catholic architecture that did not rely upon European models. In his overview of the design, chief architect A. G. Menon (1993, 26) listed the characteristics of "Indian" architecture that the cathedral design embodied: an overall shape "generated" by simple geometric patterns, slopping tiled roofs, the use of *jālīs* or aluminum grilles, and the use of "corbelling" or stone bracketing to span distances in the construction. Most fundamentally, the Cathedral was designed as a Mandala, a spatial representation of the universe, which, in this case, took the form of a series of squares superimposed on each other to create a complex multi-sided space. This design also made the architectural outlines of the Cathedral resemble those of a Hindu temple, particularly in its overall mountain-like upswing with its distinct levels or porches (*mandap*). Also like a Hindu temple, the Cathedral was constructed to be circumambulated. The most conspicuous external aspect of the temple is the series of *jālīs* that portray events in the life of Jesus, often accompanied by a Hindi commentary. Under the Cathedral, however, is a different kind of display that also includes the life of Jesus: the Jeevan-Darshan ("Life Vision") exhibition, a sound-and-light presentation of elements of the Hebrew Bible and the New Testament, complete with mannequins. An examination of these different material representations of Jesus will then return us to the issue of Catholicism's own presence in the materiality of North Indian life.

Jesus as Archetype

By Varanasi standards, St. Mary's Cathedral is fairly tall: it stands approximately 100 feet high, including the thirty-foot steel cross that tops the structure. The lower level of the Cathedral has sixteen sides, created by the angular positioning of two 30 × 30 meter squares. Recessed in these sides are the *jālīs* that are intended to present a "Christ-story" or "Khrista-Katha." These twenty-one *jālīs* are meant to be read during circumambulation (*parikrama*): they begin with "A Voice Crying in the Wilderness" and "Jesus's Baptism," and extend through key points in Jesus's life such as the Temptation, the Marriage at Cana, and the Sermon on the Mount. After portrayals of The Agony in the Garden and the Crucifixion come Jesus's Descent into Hell and Ascent into Heaven, and the series concludes with images of the New Jerusalem and the Healing River. According to Jyoti Sahi (n.d.: 2–3), who designed the *jālīs*, this Khrista-Katha tells the story of "the cosmic Christ."

The "cosmic Christ" has been a favored theme of Indian theologians like Raimundo Panikkar (1993) and popularizers like Bede Griffiths (1989). The idea of a cosmic Christ is intended to emphasize how Christ represents the eternal divine principle that appears in history but is not limited by it: Jesus is the archetypical man who contains within himself the entire universe. The cosmic Christ thus is a creator and a healer who calls humans to a new kind of consciousness that embraces the interconnectedness of all existence. This "consciousness transforming" journey is internal and neither revealed in nor actuated by the course of historical events. This ahistoricism reflects how the theology of a cosmic Christ attempts to adapt to what is perceived to be the ontological devaluation of history in Hindu thought. In his writings on Indian Christian art, Jyoti Sahi (1986) argues that art is a form of "spiritual communication," as opposed to cultural critique, that in an Indian context can become a meditative way to fully inculturate Christianity. Central to this effort is the use of archetypes. Drawing upon the work of C. G. Jung and Mircea Eliade, Sahi understands archetypes as symbols or forms that are fundamental to the human mind and are present throughout the diversity of human culture. For example, Sahi argues that the "square" is an archetypical form seen not only in the Hindu temple, but also in the eschatological temple in "Ezekiel" (Ibid., 165–167). Sahi's theology of art thus relies upon a kind of morphology of the sacred in which materiality is in some way "accidental" in that it conveys but does not limit the meaning of the archetype.

A basic example of this notion of the cosmic Christ as archetype can be found in *jālī* number fourteen, "The Resurrection" (*punrūthān*). Christ is wreathed in flame and is depicted in a Bharatnatyam dance posture: left leg bent outward with the foot touching the right knee.

Figure 3.4. The resurrection of Jesus depicted in an aluminum grille at the Varanasi Cathedral. © Mathew N. Schmalz.

With his right hand, Christ gives the *dharma chitra mudrā,* formed by touching the index finger to the thumb to represent the "counting" of the laws of *dharma* on the hand. Two figures kneel before Christ, but his gaze seems to be focused on something in the distance. The Hindi couplet below the *jālī* refers to the resurrection as a continuation of "circle of light" (*jyoti paridhi*) for an already "immortal (*amartya*) soul." In his explication of the image, Sahi (n.d., 2–3) states that the flaming circle represents the cosmos (*brahmānd*), and Christ beckons his disciples to dance with him. While Jesus seems to be wearing a loincloth in this portrayal of the Resurrection, Sahi (1986, 76–77), has often stated that ideally Christ should be nude—a comment that he recalls has also brought him criticism. In the case of *jālī* number fourteen, Christ is an archetype of liberation, and his free and boundless dance creates and recreates the universe through joy.

Although Sahi has been drawing upon features of Hindu iconography since the 1960s, the extensive use of his artistic work in a Catholic ritual context is relatively new. It is perhaps because of this newness that the *jālīs* do not seem to be a focus of attention for Indian Catholic worshippers who generally only circumambulate the Cathedral during Eucharistic processions. The "Christ-story" or Khrista-katha" that does draw worshippers is found inside the Cathedral: the tried and true Stations of the Cross. As far as Hindu perceptions of the image are concerned, over a year and a half in Varanasi, it was very difficult to find "Hindus," or anyone else for that matter, lingering over the *jālīs* and exploring their meditative possibilities. Theoretically, however, *jālī* number fourteen could be perceived in a variety of ways. For example, this portrayal of Christ could be linked to destruction, since it is quite clearly patterned after the Shiva-Nataraja image in which Shiva dances to bring about the dissolution of the universe. But perhaps the main reason why the *jālīs* have not received a great deal of attention has nothing to do with their strangeness or ambiguity. Instead it could simply be because they are mounted significantly above eye level, preventing any sustained visual or physical interaction. If Jesus is indeed an archetype, then his symbolism is rather hard to see.

Jesus as Hero

Even though its exterior has not been the focus of significant devotionalism, the Cathedral has certainly become a place of interest, even of pilgrimage. In the basement of the Cathedral is the Jeevan-Darshan Bible Exhibition, the aforementioned display that comes complete with lights, sound and mannequins that depict scenes from the Hebrew Bible and the Christian New Testament. The display "In the Beginning God" starts off the exhibit with light and sound. Included among the twenty-three exhibits are Adam and Eve, the Tower of Babel, Moses and the Burning Bush, the Nativity, the Baptism of Jesus, the Prodigal Son, the Crucifixion, Sepulcher and the Resurrection. If the exterior of the Cathedral was designed for circumambulation, the Jeevan-Darshan exhibition was designed as a linear journey resembling something like a pilgrimage since visitors pass through key points in humanity's own "pilgrimage" to Christ. But what is perhaps most crucial is that the exhibits are at eye level, and the taped Hindi narration in the background seems to explicitly address visitors who move through the exhibition. Perhaps the overall effect is best characterized as "cinematic" in that viewers find themselves immersed in a kind of Catholic Christian movie that has actors and a sound track, as well as a beginning, middle, and end.

The materiality of the Jeevan-Darshan exhibition could be best described as self-consciously "incarnational" since it presents key figures from the Judeo-Christian tradition in Indian garb. Moses, for example, is presented with a black beard, in white face, and wearing an ochre robe, renunciant style. Mary and other women from the Christian gospels are depicted wearing saris, or at least brightly colored head coverings that seem reminiscent of traditional Indian village styles often seen in advertisements. The mural depicting the Last Supper is particularly interesting. Clearly, the effort is to present the disciples as "Indians" from a variety of backgrounds: some wear *kurtā-pājāmā* or *dhotīs;* some have turbans, although others do not. But because Jesus's *kurtā* is a particularly bright shade of yellow, it almost appears as though Jesus is performing at a music concert—an image, it should be added, that is certainly very much in line with the whole "cosmic Christ" motif found outside. Overall, however, the representational idiom of the Jeevan-Darshan exhibition is far more familiar and accessible than the rather abstract *jālī* on the exterior. The vivid colors all recall standard portrayals of Hindu gods and goddesses. What is perhaps most interesting is that the Jeevan-Darshan exhibition has a parallel in the depiction of the *Rāmāyaṇa* in the Tulsi Manas Mandir across town. In that white marble temple, key characters and scenes from the *Rāmcaritmānas* are portrayed in dioramas—a feature of the temple that draws much more attention than the text of the Manas itself. Perhaps because of these material similarities, residents of Varanasi call the Cathedral a "temple" (*mandir*) instead of a "church" (*girjā-ghar*).

Like Jesus as guru, the Jesus in the Jeevan-Darshan exhibition is dressed in the ochre colored robes of a renunciant.

Figure 3.5. Jesus depicted in the Jeevan-Darshan exhibit at the Varanasi Cathedral. © Mathew N. Schmalz.

Interestingly, the Beatitudes, written in Hindi and English, extend from Christ's body, not unlike the multiple arms that characterize the iconography of Hindu deities. But most unlike the image of Jesus as guru, the Jeevan-Darshan Jesus has unmistakably white skin. The whiteness of the features is framed but a quite stylish haircut that also departs from the standard Jesus as guru form. Clearly, some point is being made through this particular material representation because Jesus's face could have been darkened to portray a more Indian or Semitic appearance, depending upon whether the aesthetic is "cosmic" or "historical." The point could simply be that Christianity, a foreign religion, is now Indian. But given the whole cinematic quality of the exhibition, as well as Jesus's own "fair" complexion and coiffure, the primary association that comes to mind is Jesus as a movie star, or "film-hero." The materiality of the Jeevan-Darshan exhibit is meant to be captivating, dramatic, and bold. For all the images associated with renunciation, the Jeevan-Darshan is about not only transcending the world, but also gaining it.

Conclusion

One summer weekend at the Shantinagar mission, a group of seminarians came for a visit, led by the head priest of the seminary. The group went to the villages surrounding the mission and prayed, in charismatic fashion, over those in need of healing. After returning to the mission, the priest and the seminarians sat down for a meal. Discussion centered on the poverty in the area and how the Catholics, all from the Untouchable Chamar caste, seemed to have advanced very little, in spite of the literacy they had gained from their Catholic education. I mentioned that the Cathedral had become an object of particular resentment among the mission's Catholics, especially because of its expense. I asked the priest whether there had been any discussion in the diocese about whether the funds would have been better spent on something else, like job programs, scholarships, land purchases or the like. The priest was surprised and said to me in English, "What? It's [the Cathedral] a masterpiece! No, there was no discussion."

The notion of a "masterpiece" is a particular interpretation of the significance of materiality. A masterpiece is a material artifact that has transcended its own materiality: it's no longer the sum of the conditions of its creation, it's unique, timeless. In using the term "masterpiece," the priest was attempting to remove the Cathedral from its context, he was objectifying it.

Many scholars have identified the process of "objectification" as central issue in theorizing materiality—after all, a commonsensical view would see "the thingness of things" as a result of a process of objectification. Most recently, as Daniel Miller (2005) observes, there has been a theoretical push to problematize the subject/object distinction, leading, in Miller's words, to a distinct tendency to "recreate the 'philosophical wheel'" in which "we cannot distinguish between subjects per se or objects per se" (40). Miller finds evidence of this philosophical wheel in Karl Marx's understandings of dialectic and commodity fetishism as well as in Bruno Latour's (1996) points about the agency of objects.

While more abstract-minded scholars might attempt to philosophize out of this conundrum, anthropologists begin with it and, to a large degree, can never move beyond it except by deploying self-consciously tentative and heuristic formulations such as "culture."

For their part, North Indian Catholics find agency through the mutability of the material and within the shifting relationships between subject and object. The conventional view of Catholics in North India is that they are concerned with the crass-materiality of access to "goods" or "commodities." But what Catholics understand is how the material connections between dependence and hierarchy also have an affective or symbolic dimension. Accordingly, through their relationship with material objects, North Indian Catholics offer a kind of commentary on the shifting dynamics that they themselves confront and navigate both as Catholics and as North Indians. The Catholics at the mission saw the Cathedral, particularly with its artistically abstract renditions of Jesus, as an objectification, as they did the image of Jesus as guru: these were images that were distant, much like the institutional Catholic Church, as they understood it. Of course, the image of Jesus at the Ashram was also an otherworldly, ethereal Jesus. But this was a Jesus who was at eye level, who was accepting—one could connect with him and give him offerings. The plastic baby Jesus in the crib was also accepting—accepting of touch, and accepting of pollution. One could also engage the Jesus in the Jeevan-Darshan exhibit by walking through the narrative. While one could not directly interact with the large image of Jesus at the Ashram, one could embody its larger-than-life qualities by cultivating supernatural gifts. What was materially significant about these images of Jesus was the level of interaction and its potential intimacy. Material religion quite simply "materializes" particular relationships: it forces the issue by making explicit what is often implicit. Most obviously, the various North Indian materialities of Jesus are intended to represent and thus give form to new ways of being. When the materiality is close and tactile, it can evoke intimacy and tenderness. But when the materiality lies out of reach, it evokes distance and disdain.

References

Babb, L. A. 1975. *The Divine Hierarchy*. New York: Columbia University Press.

Buchanan, Francis. 1986 [1934]. *An Account of the District of Shahabad in 1812–13*. New Delhi: Usha Publications.

Crooke, W. 1978 [1896]. *The Popular Religion and Folklore of Northern India*, Volume One. New Delhi: Munshiram Manoharlal Publishers Pvt. Ltd.

Davis, Richard. 1997. *The Lives of Indian Images*. Princeton, NJ: Princeton University Press.

DuBois, Abbé J. A. 1992. *Hindu Manners, Customs and Ceremonies*. Translated by Henry K. Beauchamp. New Delhi: Asian Educational Services.

Eck, Diana L. *Darsan: Seeing the Divine Image in India*. Chambersberg, PA: Anima Press.

Gramschi, Antonio. 1994. *Letters from Prison*. Edited by Frank Rosengarten, translated by Ray Rosenthal.

Griffiths, Bede. 1989. *A New Vision of Reality: Western Science, Eastern Mysticism and Christian Faith*. London: Collins.

Hislop, Alexander. 1858. *The Two Babylons*. (Available: http://biblebelievers.com/babylon).

Latour, Bruno. 1996. *Aramis, or the Love of Technology*. Cambridge, MA: Harvard University Press.

Marriot, McKim. 1990. "Constructing an Indian Ethnosociology." In *India Through Hindu Categories*, edited by McKim Marriot, 1–39. Delhi: Institute for Economic Growth.

Marx, Karl and Friedrich Engels. 1964. *On Religion*. Chico, CA: Scholars Press.

Menon, A. G. Krishna. 1993. "St. Mary's Cathedral, Varanasi," in *St. Mary's Cathedral, Varanasi, India, 1993*. Varanasi: Jauhari Printers.

Miller, Daniel. 2005. "Materiality: An Introduction." In *Materiality*, edited by Daniel Miller, 1–50. London and Durham, NC: Duke University Press.

McDanell, Colleen. 1995. *Material Christianity*. New Haven, CT: Yale University Press.

Panikkar, Raimundo. 1993. *The Cosmotheandric Experience: Emerging Religious Consciousness*. Maryknoll, NY: Orbis Books.

Raheja, Gloria. 1988. *The Poison in the Gift*. Chicago: The University of Chicago Press.

Rinaldi, Peter M., S. D. B. 1976. *It Is the Lord: A Study of the Shroud of Christ*. New York: Warner Books.

Sahi, Jyoti. n.d. *Window Designs for St. Mary's Cathedral, Varanasi*.

———. 1986. *Stepping Stones*. Bangalore: Asian Trading Corporation.

Schmalz, Mathew. 1999. "Images of the Body in the Life and Death of a North Indian Catholic Catechist," *History of Religions* 39 (November): 177–201.

———. 2001. *Ad Experimentum*: Theology, Anthropology and the Paradoxes of Indian Catholic Inculturation," *Theology and the Social Sciences*, edited by Michael Barnes, 161–180. Maryknoll, NY: Orbis Books.

———. 2005. "Dalit Catholic Tactics of Marginality at a North Indian Mission," *History of Religions* 44 (February): 216–251.

———. 2011. "Boundaries and Appropriations in North Indian Charismatic Catholicism" In *Engaging South Asian Religions: Boundaries, Appropriations and Resistances*, edited by Mathew N. Schmalz and Peter Gottschalk, 85–112. Albany, NY: SUNY Press.

4

Celebrating Materiality

Garbo, a Festival Image of the Goddess in Gujarat

NEELIMA SHUKLA-BHATT

Introduction[1]

Every year, as the torrential rains of the Indian monsoon give way to a cool and clear autumn, Hindu neighborhoods in Gujarat in western India throb with preparatory activities for their favorite festival, Navarātri ("Nine Nights"), which falls in the month of Ashvin in the Indian lunar calendar. While this festival honoring the great goddess and her several manifestations is celebrated in many regions of India, in Gujarat it is well-known for *garbo* (plu. *garbā*), a popular ritual dance traditionally performed by women in open spaces around festival image(s) of the goddess and without the presence of a priest. The genre of songs to which the dance is performed is also called *garbo*. Both the dance and the song genre derive their name from the image at the center of the dance circle, known as *garbo*, which is a perforated globular clay pot with a lit lamp inside. In popular understanding, this image represents the womb of the divine mother who bears the universe inside her. The world is a part of the goddess's being, and therefore everything within it is inherently sacred.

While the concept that the universe is a part of the divine has been expounded by many Hindu theological texts since ancient times, the popular festival image *garbo* engages this concept materially, giving it a distinct immediacy and concreteness.[2] People from different strata of society who engage with the image during the Navarātri festival weave an array of other meanings into this basic understanding, relating it to their own lives. Some of these interpretations are expressed in conversations, some in songs and dance. They constitute what one may term a "popular theology" that celebrates all life and materiality and carries important religious and cultural implications. The *garbo* image offers a range of options for religious involvement through which people are able to relate the abstract theological concept of the sanctity of the universe to everyday life. The dance is performed in an open area with no priestly presence and no formal demarcation of ritual space. During the ritual, along with songs expressing devotion, folk songs expressing the dancers' social and material aspirations are freely sung around the image, concretizing and expanding the sphere of the sacred to include worldly concerns. In recent years, the *garbo* dance has also become popular as a cultural form in India and among diaspora South Asians. It is regularly performed at wedding receptions, cultural shows, and carnivals. While the *garbo* image is not present in these secular contexts, the celebration of life and materiality remains at the heart of the dance performances, expressed through song and dance movements.

In this chapter, through an examination of the *garbo* image, I suggest that a popular sacred object with which people from diverse strata of society engage, accrues layers of meaning with wider cultural implications than ritual objects handled and controlled exclusively by persons with religious authority. Drawing on field research in Gujarat and the United States as well as my participation in *garbā* for many years, in the first part I examine the processes of meaning-making around the *garbo* image that take place during its production and sale by potters, its worship in homes, and the dance around it in the ritual space. I then discuss how these multilayered meanings focusing on materiality provide a basis for transportation of songs and dance performed in the ritual arena to spaces beyond the realm of religion. I illustrate that as a popular sacred object, the *garbo* image allows articulation of messages with larger cultural significance that bridge the gap between religious and ostensibly nonreligious spheres of life.

Scholars studying religion from a variety of perspectives have argued that the production and handling of sacred objects and spaces is at the heart of religious life (Goa et al. 2005, 5; McDannell 1995, 2). A shift from an exclusive focus on texts, their messages, and beliefs to embodied expressions and material objects is recommended even in the study of religious traditions that are traditionally considered highly mystical and austere (Cort 2007, 630–631; Keane 2008, 231). Studies of sacred objects from many parts of the world have brought to our attention the complex ways in which they contribute to meaning-making within specific cultures (McDannell 1995; Liu 1998). Anthropologist Webb Keane points out the crucial role played by material things in circulation of beliefs because they can be transported from one place to another. Meanings and beliefs associated with objects circulate with them and in the process also get modified. Keane stresses that, due to their materiality, things are situated in history—multivalent and not reducible to singular stable meanings. They are necessarily open-ended in their meanings and usages (Keane 2008, 230–231). Art historian David Morgan draws attention to the role of human agency in creating meanings for objects. He stresses that meanings are activated when human agents engage material objects with their values, feelings, and even obsessions. The study of material culture looks at the ways in which people engaging with objects generate meanings that are not simply "abstract and discursive, but embodied, felt, interactive, and cumulative" (Morgan 2008, 228–229). Religion scholar David Chidester emphasizes that the democratizing impulse that informs the study of material religion, due to its consideration of the views of all who engage with specific sacred objects rather than those of the religious elite, is its most important contribution to the field (Chidester 2008, 232–233). Thus, scholars in diverse disciplines draw attention to the multivalence of sacred material objects, human agency in meanings associated with them, and the significance of their study because it can lead to an understanding of the views of the many agents who engage with them in different contexts.

The generation of meanings in different contexts is, however, not free-ranging. Umberto Eco's views about culturally constructed texts help us in considering how multiple meanings that are generated around objects remain related to one another. Critiquing Derrida's radically deconstructionist views about the stability of meanings of texts, Eco argues that while texts are in theory subject to infinite interpretations, every text operates within a particular universe of discourse. This universe provides an important point of reference for its interpretation without curtailing the possibilities of multiple meanings.[3] In other words, while contexts are important to the generation of meaning, the contribution of a text to a particular cultural discourse at the time of its composition provides an important point of departure for each subsequent meaning. Such a view is also expressed by Catherine Besley, who stresses the reciprocity between text and context in the generation of meaning (Besley 2010, 7–15). The following examination of the *garbo* image will show that the insights of Eco and Besley are also applicable to sacred objects. While multiple agents and contexts lead to the generation of a variety of meanings around the *garbo* image, the religious discourse about the sanctity of the universe in which it is embedded provides a point of departure for their emergence. This discourse forms the basis for varied cultural articulations about the inherent worthiness of all beings, things, and places.

Garbo *in the Traditional Context*

The exact origins of *garbo* as a sacred object and ritual dance remain unknown. There are no authoritative texts that comment on the image or the dance. R. V. Pathak and Govardhan Panchal trace the origins of the *garbo* dance to a dance mentioned in the ancient text *Harivamsha* (ca. first to third century CE), which contains narratives about the Hindu deity Krishna. In the Vishnu Parva section of this text, one chapter is devoted to a circular dance of cowherd women and Krishna, in which women provide rhythm by clapping. Another chapter refers to women clapping, dancing, and imitating Krishna's Hallisaka dance in Dwarika, Gujarat, where he had established his capital (Harivamsha 2.20, 2.89.7, 2.89.68). Pathak and Panchal think that the *garbo* dance could have developed from this early form in Gujarat. They also refer to a twelfth-century text, *Sangīt Ratnākar*, which credits Krishna's daughter-in-law Usha with teaching a dance of graceful movements she had learned from the goddess Parvati to the women of Gujarat (Pathak and Panchal 1954, 22–25, 33–35). These textual references indicate that a circular dance similar to *garbo* could have prevailed in Gujarat since ancient times. However, the earliest literary references to *garbo* as both a sacred object and a ritual dance specifically associated with the goddess are found in the poems of Gujarati poet Bhandas in the seventeenth century (Raval 1992, 122). Since that time at least, *garbo* has been a cherished component of the region's cultural heritage as an image and a dance.

Today, the *garbo* image and the ritual dance form a part of the cluster of objects and practices associated with Navarātri in Gujarat, some of which are pan-Indian and others are distinctively Gujarati. A large number of these objects and practices express the inseparability of the world from the goddess's being. Two pan-Indian practices of this type—recitation of the pivotal Sanskrit text glorifying the goddess, the *Devī Māhātmya* (ca. fifth century CE), and the worship of geometrical diagrams called *yantra*s, drawn on materials such as copper, silver, cloth, or wood—have ancient roots and authoritative texts associated with them.[4] The *Devī Māhātmya* contains several verses glorifying the goddess as the ultimate source of the material universe and identifying the universe as the manifestation of the goddess (1.57, 65–67, 4.6, 5.33; Coburn 1991, 37, 48, 54). Worship of *yantras*, a practice associated with Tantrism, establishes the presence of the goddess in material objects that represent the cosmos as "both the source and portal of her manifestation" (Rodrigues 2003, 39). Even though the theological content of these rituals remains abstract and is not easily accessible to lay worshippers, they form part of the cluster of practices that contribute to the discourse of sanctity of life and materiality within which the *garbo* image also operates.

Another practice that reinforces the same themes and is popular in many parts of India is the worship of a household image of the goddess installed during Navarātri. This image is formed by a clay pot filled with water and decorated with a colorful sari as well as jewelry. On its top is placed a clay platter or a basket filled with soil. A coconut is placed in its center, and five types of grain are scattered around it. The image is put on an altar made of soil where grains are scattered as well. With the water seeping through the pot, the grains sprout during the festival. The sprouts are considered a part of the image. As Hillary Rodrigues points out in his discussion of the worship of this image in Bengal, the wide body of the pot, the soil, and the altar with sprouted grains vividly communicate the motifs of pregnancy and birth (Rodrigues 2003, 262). The goddess is both the source of life and life itself. This message is explicitly conveyed in the *mantras* chanted by the priest often employed for the worship of this goddess representation. Alongside the age-old practices of recitation of the *Devī Māhātmya* and ritual offerings to *yantras*, the worship of this image contributes to the discourse about the sanctity of life on earth. Since symbolism of this worship is drawn from everyday life in an agrarian milieu, it is more accessible to people. The Gujarati practice of *garbo* participates in this discourse through the image representing the goddess's womb.

Garbo, *the Image*

Like the popular pan-Indian water pot image, the *garbo* image is also a globular clay pot with a wide round mouth. Through its shape, it shares with the water pot image an association with fertility conveyed in an accessible manner. But some aspects of its appearance and ritual handling also connote the goddess's relationship with the cosmos rather than only with life on earth. Since the *garbo* image is a perforated pot with a lit lamp inside, its visual appeal also derives from light sieving through its perforations. The pot represents the womb of the goddess, and the lit lamp represents the created universe within it. The lamp is lit when the pot is installed by a woman in her home on the first day of Navarātri and is kept lit for the duration of the festival. The image is offered simple worship inside homes during the day and is brought to the open space of the ritual dance at night. Its worshippers refer to it as an embodiment of *ādyaśakti* (primordial energy) and sing around it a Gujarati *āratī* (hymn) that addresses the goddess with this title. Unlike the worship of the water pot image, there is no priestly presence at any ritual associated with the *garbo* image.

Most Gujarati scholars agree that the term "*garbo*" is derived from the Sanskrit term "*garbha*," meaning "womb" or "fetus."[5] These connotations are reinforced by the fact that in Gujarat, the main focus of popular worship during Navarātri is the goddess's nurturing form, Ambika (mother), and not Durga, her beautiful but martial manifestation worshipped in other regions. The *garbo* image is also associated with the cosmic giver of life Surya or the Sun deity, and his consort Randal, who is in turn associated closely with fertility in Gujarat and is worshipped on auspicious occasions such as weddings and baby showers.[6] The late Khodidas Parmar, a scholar of Gujarati culture, sums up the various threads of fertility symbolism in the following:

> This vessel . . . is a symbol of a female womb, into which the light of life has entered, and this symbolizes fertility, reproduction, and motherhood. . . . The Mother, The Holder of Bhag or . . . Lamp of Life is Bhagavati Ma. . . . *Garbā* is thus a vessel that symbolizes the Womb, and the Mother Goddess is worshipped through the worship of this Vessel. (Parmar 2003, no page numbers provided)

While both the water pot image and the *garbo* image share fertility symbolism, the water pot image with sprouting grains around it is more closely linked to life on earth. The *garbo* image, on the other hand, stresses the cosmic scale of the goddess's motherhood with its association with the sun and with its light symbolizing life. Under the open sky, the light spreading out of the perforation of the *garbā* images placed at the center of the dance arena seems to establish a visual connection with the stars of clear autumn nights. At times, when the dancing women hold the images on their heads and move in the circle, they emulate the movement of the dome of the sky studded with stars. The visual appeal of the scene is profound, especially in rural areas where electric bulbs do not interfere with the light coming out of *garbā* images.

Figure 4.1. *Garbo* arena in Naranpura Village, October 2004. Photo by Neelima Shukla-Bhatt.

The poet Bhandas alludes to this custom in his famous lyric when he sings of the *garbo* held by the goddess on her head. Building on the belief that the goddess dances in the ritual arena, the poet refers to the cosmic bodies such as the sun and the moon as parts of the goddess's *garbo*. There is no reference to the goddess's own beauty or splendor in the lyric. She is praised entirely through the praise of her *garbo*.

> The dome of the sky forms the pot of that beautiful *garbo*.
> With it, the goddess dances. I sing of that fine *garbo*.
> The sun is the lamp within that beautiful *garbo*.
> The moon's light too is in it. I sing of that fine *garbo*.
> . . .
> There is a lid on that beautiful *garbo*.
> That is the endless sky. I sing of that fine *garbo*.
> Thirty-three million holes are on that beautiful *garbo*.
> Its light is beyond measure. I sing of that fine *garbo*.
> (Trivedi, Jani, and Modi 1998, 176. Translation mine.)

The understanding of the *garbo* image as representing all of creation as expressed in the above lyric is not simply a matter of poetic imagination. Ordinary worshippers also express it, linking it with their daily experiences.

During the fieldwork I conducted in 2004, almost all the men and women I interviewed clearly associated the *garbo* image with the universe (*jagat*) in the womb of its mother (*jagatjanani*), the goddess. They also expressed in different ways that everything in the world is within the mother. The image provided for them a channel to articulate their own theology about the sanctity of life and the material world, giving them a sense of connection to the divine without priestly intervention. Some members of lower caste communities indicated that, in reality, the *garbo* image draws attention to the irrelevance of such intervention. One of my informants, Baldevbhai, for example, is a potter from Vastrapur village near Ahmedabad whose family has been making *garbā* pots for generations. He suggested that even though potters are seen as low caste, they in fact have greater spiritual powers than the priests because they *create* objects that give worshippers immediate access to the goddess. When priests sanctify objects with chants, they have to invite the divine to descend from a transcendent sphere into that object. Potters, on the other hand, make images out of clay, a substance that represents Mother Earth. Due to the goddess's identification with the earth, she is already present in *garbo* images made by potters. These images do not need priests to invoke the divine in them.[7] Baldevbhai's pride in the production of *garbo* images, shared by other potters in the neighborhood, provides only one example of popular interpretations of the *garbo* image as symbolizing the worthiness of all life and materiality. Similar pride was also apparent among members of other artisan castes—carpenters, florists, and so forth—who participated in decorating the dance arena in Vastrapur village.

Among the contributors to the ritual arena whom I interviewed in 2004, one is non-Hindu. Ahmedbhai, a Muslim vendor who runs a small business of plastic and paper decorative items in the Tran Darwaja area of Ahmedabad, informed me that for a number of years he and other vendors from his community have been selling decorative items that surround the image in the *garbo* arena.[8] Hindu women flock to them to get these items, bypassing other vendors. Ahmedbhai went on to say that even though his community does not worship the goddess with *pūjā* as Hindus do, they may be seen as recipients of her benevolence because they earn a great deal of money during the festival season. In a cultural milieu that is charged with *garbo* fervor for nine days, it is not unusual for a non-Hindu vendor to ascribe culturally significant meaning to what appears to be a simple business transaction. For this vendor, it is a matter of both pride and gratitude that his products are components of the *garbo* arena.

In addition to the understandings of the *garbo* image among the members of artisan castes and other vendors, responses of women, the main participants in the ritual, bring into sharp focus the sense of religious agency people have in relation to the image. On the eve of Navarātri in 2004, I interviewed several women customers who flocked to the potter neighborhoods of Vastrapur village to purchase *garbā* images. They insisted that a *garbo* image must be carried home by a woman. It cannot be carried by a man because its shape and meaning are linked with motherhood. It must be installed for worship only by an actual or potential mother, that is, a married woman with a child or a young unmarried girl who hopes to be a mother in the future. Two women of the Naranpura area of Ahmedabad stressed that the *garbo* should be installed only in a household in which there is a newborn baby or hope for a child in the foreseeable future. If the flame of the lamp lit by a woman of the household remains unextinguished for the duration of the festival, it is an assurance that the goddess will protect the newborn or the child who will be conceived.[9] This belief among women stresses their own agency in making the ritual effective. At the same time, it also reinforces traditional norms about a woman's fertility, without which her life is viewed as meaningless. It may be seen as the kind of anthropomorphism of sacred objects discussed by Lohmann and Sered, one that reinforces gender roles and power dynamics extant within a society (Lohmann and Sered 2007, 5–7).

Interestingly however, many women also see the image as an empowering sacred object that opens two spaces for women where they can operate independently of men. One is the place in the home where the image is worshipped during the day. The second and more important space is the open arena where they dance at night dressed in festive clothing. Here they sing about themselves as friends of the goddess, rejoice in their finery, and freely express their material desires and concerns. In the traditional social milieu where women's movements are carefully managed and the norms of modesty restrain them from making references to their own bodies or material possessions, the image opens for them a door into a space where they can freely celebrate both. In this empowering context, the *garbo* image exemplifies gendered objects that form, in Janet Hoskins words, "part of a complex cultural field in which things can play important roles in people's lives," connecting "ritual power to other forms of agency and biographical significance" (Hoskins 2007, 119). It is significant that the form of agency with which the *garbo* image links ritual power includes explicit expressions of joy in and desire for material things.

As seen above, even before the *garbo* image is brought to the dance arena, agents from different sectors of society relate to it with interpretations that establish their sense of agency. Potters take pride in the image they create from sacred material; vendors express gratitude for its celebration during this time of the year; women refer to its shape in linking themselves to the goddess and see it as a passport to rejoicing in their self-worth. The conspicuous absence of priests among the agents who articulate their relationship with the *garbo* image indicates that the norm of ritual purity, which dominates Hindu priestly rituals, is irrelevant in relation to it. The democratizing impulse discussed by Chidester is clearly exemplified in the meaning-making processes surrounding the *garbo* image. Based on the popular understanding of the image as representing sanctity of life and the material universe, the agents weave into it meanings that relate to their own lives. In the process, they articulate notions of the sacred that are inclusive and more focused on the here and now than on the transcendent. In the ritual arena, these notions of the sacred validate the inclusion of songs that are not strictly religious but celebrate all aspects of life.

Garbo, *the Song*

The meanings that various agents associate with the image before it is brought to the ritual space are reinforced, extended, and given specificity in *garbā* songs, which serve as primary texts for the ritual. Devotion to the goddess, the celebration of all aspects of a woman's life in the traditional milieu, and an appreciation for the craftsmen who produce material objects offered to the goddess form the subject matter of *garbā* songs. Composed in colloquial Gujarati in women's voices (even when composed by male poets), these lyrics are suffused with material imagery. When the dancing begins in *garbo* space, the first three or five (auspicious odd numbers) songs are dedicated to the goddess. A number of these are in the form of an invitation to the goddess to join the dance. Others describe the cosmic dimensions of the goddess's dance. One of the most well-known *garbā* of this type is a lyric by Vallabh Bhatt (early eighteenth century) that refers to celestial bodies—the stars, the sun, and the moon—as created during the making of the goddess's *garbo* (Trivedi, Jani, and Modi 1998, 207). Identification of the *garbo* with the universe is also found in popular folk *garbā* songs such as the following.

Mother's *garbo* sports and swirls.
Today, mother's *garbo* sports and swirls.
In that *garbo* shine nine million stars,
making a glittering design.
Today, mother's *garbo* sports and swirls.
(*Saurabh Navrat Garbāvali* 1999, 22. Translation mine.)

In the above song, "mother's *garbo*" is understood alternatively as "*garbo* held by the goddess" or as "*garbo* that is the image of goddess." With the first meaning, the light coming out of the mother's *garbo*'s perforation is seen as stars, bringing to mind the cosmic scale of the goddess's dance. The second meaning implies that this small image contains the entire creation. Such songs with cosmic references reinforce the goddess's fundamental association with materiality and provide a frame for songs in which the goddess and women are linked through material references. A very popular song of this type is *Caukhaliālī Cundadī Mā Garbe Ramvā Āvo ne* ("Mother, come to dance in a speckled sari"), which invites the goddess to join in the dance wearing a sari designed with stars. The song's first stanza makes reference to the goddess's *garbo* swirling in the sky. But the last stanza juxtaposes the colorful saris of the women dancing in the village square with the endless scarf of the goddess.

Mother, come to dance in *garbo* wearing a speckled sari.
It is a beautiful night, Mother come to dance in *garbo*.
Sixteen types of jewelry (decorations) look lovely on you.
My heart is charmed by Mother.
Keeping beat with tinkling anklets, come to dance in *garbo*.

(Your) *garbo* swirls in the sky, with the shining stars.
Goddess Ambika and goddess Bahuchar dance together on
the full moon night.

In the village square and streets,
Mother's vermilion powder is sprinkled.
Colorful saris of dancing women have started to flutter.
Wearing the scarf of eternity,
Mother, come to dance in *garbo*.
(*Saurabh Navarat Garbāvalī* 1999, 32. Translation mine.)

Some popular *garbā* songs that mention the ritual contributions of potters, clothiers, goldsmiths, and gardeners also suggest how material objects can provide a means to establish a connection with the goddess. Conspicuously, these do not mention priests. The following is a popular song of this type.

> On the banks of river Mahisagar, the drum resounds.
> Yes, the drum resounds.
> From villages all around, potters arrive.
> They come. And what do they bring?
> They bring pots for the Mother.
>
> From villages all around, carpenters arrive.
> They come. And what do they bring?
> They bring daises for the Mother.
>
> From villages all around, clothiers arrive.
> They come. And what do they bring?
> They bring spotted saris for the Mother.
>
> From villages all around, goldsmiths arrive.
> Yes, they come. What do they bring?
> They bring tinkling anklets for the Mother.
> (*Ramzat Garbāvalī*, 172. Translation mine.)

In another popular song in this vein, the wife of each craftsman is asked to get someone (presumably her husband) to craft an offering to the *garbo* image. In this list, too, the priest's wife is absent. Songs of this type express devotional sentiment, but their focus remains on human participation in the ritual through material offerings to the image. While reinforcing the theme of material sanctity, they challenge caste and gender hierarchies of the traditional Hindu milieu, adding one more layer to the meanings associated with the image.

Yet other types of songs focus primarily on women's lives; the goddess and the ritual provide only a frame of reference. These reflect the social realities of women, sometimes in a humorous manner. In a song about the difference between the treatments given to a woman by her mother and her mother-in-law, dancing in *garbo* is used as the frame theme, almost an excuse.

> It is the full moon night of autumn;
> the mood of swaying prevails.
> Mother, let me go to dance [in *garbo*].

It is the full moon night of autumn;
the mood of swaying prevails.
Mother-in-law let me go to dance [in *garbo*].

Having danced I came back.
"Mother, give me something to eat."
Mother prepared a sweet
and put a spoonful of ghee in it.

Having danced, I came back.
"Mother-in-law, give me something to eat"
Mother-in-law prepared gruel
and put a drop of oil in it.
(Folk song. Translation mine.)

It is significant that in songs of this type, greater focus remains on the imagery of material things that serve as markers of the nature of relationships. In the above song, *garbo* dancing provides a frame; but the focus is on the woman's relationships to her loving mother and grumpy muther-in-law, highlighted through the imagery of "a spoonful of ghee" and "a drop of oil."

The imagery of material gifts as conveyors of love is prominent in folk *garbā* songs addressed to the husband or the lover. These songs express a woman's desire for jewelry, clothing, and other material things. In some songs, the desired responses of the lover are also included. A large number of such songs do not refer to the goddess but make multiple references to material things. The very popular *Sonā Vāṭakaḍī* ("Golden Bowl") provides a good example.

Woman: In a golden bowl, saffron-paste is made, my beloved.
Man: The plant is green and full of color, my beloved.

Woman: I will need a bracelet fitting my hand, my beloved;
Man: Two pairs of bangles for you, full of color, my beloved.

Woman: I will need a necklace fitting my neck, my beloved;
Man: Two pairs of chokers for you, full of color, my beloved.
(*Navarātri nī Ramzat Garbāvalī*, 42–43. Translaiton mine.)

In addition to such delightful expressions of love, descriptions of the harsher realities of women's everyday family and work life are also found in *garbā* songs. An extremely popular song in the form of a message from a newly married young woman to her grandfather tells of her tyrannical mother-in-law and the hardships she faces at her husband's house. She conveys that she is thinking of committing suicide. The grandfather consoles her by giving a specific date when an invitation from her natal home will be sent. Here, material items such as the water pot, pot-holder and rope powerfully convey the feeling of helplessness.

"Grandpa!"
"Yes Daughter!"
"Do not give your daughter in marriage into a family from Vagad!
The quarrelsome mother-in-law of the Vagad region is unbearable!
Friends, dance on! Friends, dance on!

She makes me grind during the day,
and makes me spin at night.
In wee hours of the morning,
She makes me fetch water from the well.

At my pillow is my water-pot holder.
At the edge of the bed is a water-drawing rope.
Right in the front room sits my water-pot.

My rope is too short. My pot does not reach water.
My day began and ended at the well.

O flying bird, my brother, take this message for me.
Tell my grandfather that his daughter will jump into the well.

Tell my grandfather, but don't tell my mother.
If you tell mother, her tears will not stop."

"Don't jump in the well daughter!
Don't plunge into a lake!
On the eighth of the bright fortnight,
someone will bring an invite to bring you home!"
(*Navarātri ni Ramzat Garbā*vali, 38. Translation mine.)

The in-law's house, however, is not the only place of hardship. For a working-class woman, work provides another context for exploitation.

A woman farm-worker's complaint is conveyed through the image of a sickle in the following folk *garbo*.

> My sickle is two-and-a-quarter pounds heavy and made by blacksmith Laliya.
> My dear, I will no longer go to cut grass on the farm lands.
> (My) husband cut five bundles (of grass), I cut ten-twenty.
> (My) husband makes only a quarter and I earn a full one-and-a-half rupees.
> (My) husband brought a quarter pound sorghum, I brought a ton of wheat.
> My dear, I will no longer go to cut grass on the farm lands.
> (Audio file online. Translation mine.)[10]

As many scholars have shown, folk songs reflecting the modalities of women's lives are found widely in many South Asian languages (Gold and Raheja 1994; Narayan 2003, 23–53). What makes *garbā* especially appealing for women is the way nonreligious folk songs can be interwoven with religious songs in the ritual arena. A large majority of the women I interviewed in Gujarat and Mumbai in 2004 stressed that free expression of material desires and concerns about social life is valid in the presence of the goddess, who is both their friend and mother in the *garbo* arena. Many indicated that as a ritual, the *garbo* is not formal. It is not like a fire sacrifice. Its informality makes room for the expression of mundane desires.[11] It is through the free expression of the ordinary social and material concerns that the basic understanding of the worthiness of the material universe seeps into the performative genres around the *garbo* image.

The ways in which the songs reinforce and expand on the theme of sanctity of life and materiality correspond with Keane's observation that material objects in religious systems accrue a range of responses and meanings as they enter different "people's projects" (Keane 2008, 230). When the *garbo* image enters the ritual arena, it becomes a channel through which female participants express their aspirations and concerns. Their expressions of worldly aspiration form a part of their devotional activity.

Garbo, *the Dance*

While *garbā* songs celebrate materiality through their lyrics, the dance reinforces this theme through its aspects that engage space and body. One of its distinctive aspects is demarcation of sacred space in it. The *garbo* ritual is performed at night in an open space in each neighborhood without formal sanctification by a priest. Further, even though women generally prefer to dance with their friends near their own homes, the ritual space is generally viewed as open to any female dancer who wants to join. Women enter and leave the dance circle as they like, changing the boundaries of the ritual arena continuously. The sacred space is demarcated by the feet of women dancing around the image. Such flexibility of ritual boundaries and the democratic nature of the ritual are consistent with the popular understanding of the *garbo* image as signifying sacredness of the whole world. As a ritual, this dance provides an unusual example for students of sacred spaces who focus on the "ways in which individuals and groups construct the environments and settings of their religious practices" (Kilde 2007, 277).

In addition to the treatment of space, another notable aspect of the *garbo* dance as a ritual is that it is carried out entirely through the medium of the female body. There are no priests, no chanting, and no offerings made during the ritual (offerings made by craftsmen precede the ritual). Women relate to the goddess through their voices by singing in unison and through simple but graceful dance movements that engage the whole body. The rhythm is provided by women's clapping hands. The exclusive use of the female body as a channel for the worship of the divine is significant. In the elite Hindu tradition, women, like the goddess, have been associated with *prakriti* or primary matter and viewed as "embodiments of both power and materiality" (Pintchman 1994, 201). The elite attitude toward *prakriti* is, however, ambivalent. *Prakriti* is honored as the basis of all life but often seen as subordinate to *puruṣa,* the male principle representing consciousness. In Hindu priestly rituals, women's presence is therefore carefully controlled. By contrast, in the *garbo* arena women's free movements validate the sanctity of their bodies and the materiality they represent.

The celebration of the female body is enhanced by clothing and jewelry. The dancing women make self-conscious references to their adornments in the songs. A woman participant interviewed by a local TV channel in Surat said that the ritual "provides women with an opportunity to get their colorful saris and jewelry out from cupboards and wear them with joy for nine nights. No questions asked." An early ethnographer of Gujarat, Jhaverchand Meghani, remarks that *garbo* brings into focus "the entire complex around the body"—the long skirt, the fluttering scarf, and the glittering jewelry (Meghani 1997 [1925], 23–25). This celebration of the body and adornments is easily transportable to nonreligious contexts. But in the ritual context, it has an additional layer that augments its significance. This is the understanding that the goddess dances along with women. A woman from Mumbai suggested that in the *garbo* arena, a woman feels a surge of energy in her body due to the understanding that the mother is dancing with her, adorned in the same way she is.[12] The bodies of Gujarati women begin to swing as soon as they hear the first sound of clapping in the *garbo* arena. As Kallolini Hazrat puts it, *garbo* is "a dance running in Gujarati women's blood-stream" (Hazrat 1981, 37). For them, it is an expression of their joy in femininity in all its aspects in the midst of the social constraints they face.

Hindu women's religious lives have been an important area in the study of Indic traditions in recent decades (e.g., Leslie 1987, Patton 2002, and Pintchman 2007). While the text-based studies have shown an inherent ambivalence toward women in texts written by men, some recent ethnographic studies have offered a nuanced understanding of Hindu women's religious and social selves.[13] Pintchman observes that hearing the voices of Hindu women as they speak about their own ritual practices helps us to understand how these practices allow them "to shape their worlds as agents in pursuit of their own desired ends" (Pintchman 2007, 13). Hearing Gujarati Hindu women articulate their agency as worshippers, dancers, and singers of songs around the *garbo* image confirms this observation. Women not only assert their roles as religious agents through this ritual, but also enjoy the freedom to socialize until late into the night and to comment, through song, on both positive and negative dimensions of their social situations.

As seen above, in the religious context, the meanings woven around the *garbo* image by agents from several non-elite groups in Hindu society—potters, carpenters, gardeners, and, importantly, women—involve the celebration of materiality at multiple levels through offerings, songs, and dance. With an expressed disregard for social hierarchies and ritual purity, these interpretations contribute to the creation of a ritual space for women that has flexible boundaries.[14] The openness and flexibility of the ritual space of *garbo* provide a justification for the performance of the dance in other spaces, which may or may not have religious associations. All spaces where materiality and life can be celebrated through dance are worthy of *garbā* performances. Taking advantage of this implication of the ritual, *garbā* performances have proliferated in many semi-religious and secular spaces in recent decades.

Organized Garbā *Events*

In most Gujarati cities and towns, there are a number of *garbā* events during Navarātri that are organized by community leaders or professional organizers. These events are not strictly religious; however, they incorporate several aspects of the *garbo* ritual. There is an image of the goddess—a *garbo* pot and/or a framed painting—present at the venue. As in the ritual, the dancing takes place with a few *garbā* songs dedicated to the goddess at the beginning, followed by nondevotional songs. The event ends with the singing of the *ādyaśakti āratī*. The dancers also enter and leave the dance circle as they wish. There are, however, some significant differences. The images in organized *garbā* events are not brought by the dancers, nor have they been ritually installed in homes. They are often rented props. These events also have an entrance fee, and the participants—a large majority of whom are young women—dance to *garbā* songs sung by professional singers on microphones from a stage.

The participants view dancing in such ritually ambiguous spaces in different ways. Some feel that the religious meaning is so deeply embedded in *garbo*'s form that it is inseparable from its performance, especially during Navarātri. Shachi Bhatt, whom I interviewed in Ahmedabad, articulated this view succinctly:

> Even if one does not know anything about *garbo* as a religious ritual, the songs make it clear that the goddess herself is a dancer here and that this world is her body. So, if you feel involved in the dance, as you take the first step with a clap of your hands, you feel *śakti* ("energy," one of the goddess's epithets) running through your whole body. The costumes enhance that feeling. One does not need to be formal or overt about devotion.

Such dancers bow to the image when they enter or leave the dance arena, and the *garbā* songs referring to the goddess have a religious meaning for them. These dancers tend not to associate the *garbo* image with child-protection and fertility but simply see the image as symbolizing the goddess's presence. By contrast, others view dancing in *garbo* circles at organized events only as a treasured cultural tradition. While the views about the religious intent of the performance vary among the dancers, all of them look forward to the organized *garbā* events, which provide them with opportunities to dance with their friends till late wearing colorful clothing and fine jewelry. As TV channel ANI News reported from Ahmedabad a few days before Navarātri 2010, "For the locals, Navarātri means not just folkdances and celebrations, but also flaunting their new clothes and jewelry."[15] Enjoyment of graceful movements and celebration of well-adorned bodies, which forms a part of the meaning of the dance in the ritual context, is effectively transported to the organized *garbā* events. The other layer of meaning associated with adornments in the ritual space, the goddess's presence as a dancer, remains only vaguely relevant here.

While young dancers and event organizers tend to remain focused on the nonreligious aspects of celebrations, the media—newspapers, television, and radio—consistently reinforce the link between the religious ritual and dancing in the organized *garbā* events. In all types of media, articles pertaining to the religious significance of the *garbo* ritual appear alongside articles describing how to dress for organized *garbā* and advertisements for outfits. They articulate a justification for spending money on Navarātri-related things. Socially approved material acquisition for the festival is evident in the sky-rocketing sales of clothing sold by rural women from Gujarat and Rajasthan who are experts in making embroidered cloth and inexpensive jewelry. The spirit of celebration manifests itself most visibly in the exchanges around material things associated with the festival and the kinetic experience of dancing. Even though some meanings associated with the image in the traditional ritual are not relevant in the organized events, celebration of life and materiality remains at the core of these events as well. From this world of organized *garbo* events, secular spaces are only a step away.

Garbo *in Secular Contexts*

In the past few decades, *garbo* as dance and song has traveled to many secular spaces including wedding parties, cultural shows, and carnivals. In these contexts, the intent of the dancing is clearly not religious. At weddings, it is an expression of joy and community bonding. In stage performances within Gujarat as well as in the South Asian diaspora, the *garbo* performance is often an expression of cultural identity and is not associated with the goddess. The *garbo* image is also not necessarily a part of these performance spaces. Only sometimes it is present as a prop. Yet, the core understanding of the image in popular imagination—celebration of life and materiality—is easily evoked in these spaces through dress, movement, and songs that are drawn from the ritual context. Both religious and nonreligious songs that are sung in the ritual context are freely used in these contexts, too. If nonreligious songs are not considered too mundane for the ritual arena of *garbo,* the songs referring to the goddess and the image are not considered too religious for these secular contexts. The fundamental signification of the image is so intricately integrated into the other components of the ritual that when these components are transported to nonreligious contexts, they evoke the same meaning even in the absence of the image.

During my college years in India, many of my co-participants in stage *garbā* were non-Hindu Gujarati girls for whom the goddess featured in the songs was not a divine entity. They were attracted to *garbā*'s fast graceful movements, colorful costumes, and the celebration of various aspects of women's lives in the songs. For many second-generation South Asian participants in the *garbā* competition organized annually by the Federation of Gujarati Associations in North America (FOGANA), whom I interviewed in September 2005, the case was nearly reversed. They could not fully access the meanings of the songs due to a lack of proficiency in the Gujarati language. But they had a keen awareness of the dance's association with the goddess and knew how this dance in its ritual form gave an opportunity for women to express their religious, social, and material aspirations. As they listed the aspects of the dance that attracted them, at the top was pride in a heritage that validates the celebration of women's lives in relation to the goddess.

In contrast to the above groups who have access to the cultural meanings of *garbo* through language or heritage, many participants in South Asian cultural shows outside of South Asia have no awareness of the dance's background. Their participation in the dance, however, leads them to decipher a similar meaning from the kinetic experience of dance. In a South Asian cultural show on November 7, 2008, at Wellesley College in Wellesley, Massachusetts, only three participants in the *garbo* performance were of South Asian descent. The song to which the dance was performed was addressed to the goddess and was about the joy of dancing in the *garbo* circle with friends as well as with the divine mother. When I asked for the reason for their participation, the choreographer of Gujarati descent mentioned heritage, while the non-Indian participants mentioned "graceful movements," "pretty costumes," and a feeling of being "connected to other women in circular formations."[16] While such comments about the dance movements and clothing are commonly made about folk dances performed in cultural shows, these comments reflect back on the folk dance-like qualities of *garbo* as a ritual. The movements in the *garbo* dance do not have strictly religious associations even in the ritual context; even there they express a celebration of life in all its aspects because of the meanings associated with the image. When transported to a secular context, they still carry the spirit of celebration, which becomes easily accessible to all participants.

Several Indian sacred dances traditionally performed in specific religious environments are now performed on stage as reproductions of the traditional performances. Secular *garbā* performances are not reproductions of the ritual. The support for the dance's performance in secular contexts is built into its form and meaning as a ritual. The basic understanding associated with the *garbo* image—worthiness of all existence—filters through and is expanded upon in the mix of songs, the demarcation of the sacred space, and dance movements in such a way in the ritual context that a validation for secular performances ensues from it. The absence of the *garbo* image marks dance performances in secular contexts as nonreligious but not as lacking in authenticity. It is significant that communities that practice *garbo* as a ritual have not objected to *garbā* dance performances at organized events or in secular contexts. All contexts are valid as signified by the image of the goddess in the ritual arena.

Conclusion

An examination of the meaning-making processes surrounding the *garbo* image in the ritual context and their implications beyond the religious sphere leads us to see the vitality of a popular sacred object to generate culturally significant meanings. At the heart of these processes is the popular theology associated with the image, which upholds all existence as a part of the goddess's being and recognizes the sanctity of creation. While such an association of the universe with the divine is also a part of elite theological traditions in the Hindu milieu, its expression through a popular sacred object allows people from different strata of the society to weave into it interpretations that relate to their own lives and are sustainable beyond the religious sphere. In its multiple layers of meaning, the agency of people from several sections of society and the democratic spirit in which the meanings are generated, *garbo* confirms the observations of Keane, Morgan, and Chidester regarding sacred objects. At the same time, as the above examination shows, the meanings generated by different people are neither random nor exclusively context-based. There is a "point of departure," as Eco would put. The meanings generated by different agents are linked through a core popular understanding of the image, which, in turn participates in the larger religious discourse about the sanctity of the creation as expressed in texts like the *Devī Māhātmya* and practices like *yantra* worship.

In the ritual arena of *garbo,* the image at the center establishes the sanctity of the created universe. This opens a space for celebrating all of life and materiality through offerings, songs, dance, and clothing. The core understanding of the image validates the interweaving of religious and nonreligious songs as well as dance movements without strictly religious associations. The meanings generated in the ritual arena about the worthiness of life and material things are so integrated in the songs and dance movements that they are transportable to nonreligious contexts where the image is not present. The popular understanding of the image thus plays a significant role in forging a link between the religious and secular performances. As a popular sacred object, the *garbo* expands a religious discourse about the sanctity of life and materiality into a cultural discourse about their celebration. It shows that unlike sacred objects whose religious signification is controlled by the religious elite, popular sacred objects with which people from different strata of the society engage have the vitality to generate meanings that resonate beyond the sphere of religion.

Notes

1. I am thankful to Wellesley College for offering me the Mellon Postdoctoral Fellowship that allowed me to travel to India during Fall 2004 and to the Mellon Foundation for its generous stipend.

2. The first verse of *Īśopaniṣad* identifies the world as pervaded by the Lord. In the Śrī Vaiṣṇava tradition of Tamilnadu, all that exists is considered to be a part of Lord Vishnu (Carman 1974, 127).

3. These are Eco's views (Eco 1990, 28, 36) as summarized in Layton 2001, 31–32.

4. References to the recitation of the *Devī Māhātmya* and worship of goddess's *yantras* as parts of Durgā Pūjā (Navarātri) festival in Bengal are found in many scholarly works (McDaniel 2004, 224, 96; Rodrigues 2003, 73, 317, 267–270; and Coburn 1991, 166, 170). Coburn has also described a recitation of the *Devī Māhātmya* by Gujarati scholar/priest A. N. Jani (Coburn 1991, 163–164). Even though the one described by Coburn took place in the lunar month of Sravan, such recitations are organized widely by goddess worshippers in Gujarat at their homes or in temples during Navarātri. These are accompanied by worship of various *yantras* as embodiments of the goddess.

5. A detailed discussion of the etymology of the term is provided by Kallolini Hazrat in her introductory essay on a compilation of *garbā* lyrics (Hazrat 1981, 21–24). The two notable exceptions to the majority view noted by Hazarat here are those of H. C. Bhayani and K. K. Shastri. Bhayani does not offer an alternative. Shastri holds that the term "*garbo*" is derived from the name of a South Indian dance, *kuruvai kuttu*, which re-enacts Krishna's dance with cowherd women. The majority view, however, is much more convincing. A separate dance form specifically associated with Krishna's dance with cowherd women—*rās*—has long prevailed in Gujarat. Even though this dance is often performed during Navarātri, it has no association with fertility or goddess worship.

6. The popularity of Surya worship in Gujarat in the early medieval period is indicated by a number of Surya temples built between ninth through the eleventh century. The city of Surat and its suburb Rander are believed to be named after Surya and Randal.

7. Interview with Baldevbhai, October 14, 2004.

8. For confidentiality, the name of the vendor is changed.

9. Interview with Bhikhiben Oza and her daughter-in-law, October 15, 2004.

10. http://www.esnips.com/doc/5c112bf9-44c0-42d3-8b4c-0046d957 64cd/SAva-Basher-Nu-Maru (Accessed October 19, 2010).

11. Conversations with women in Surat, Mumbai, Vastrapur, and Naranpura. October 10–16, 2004.

12. Conversation with Meena Divetia of Nagar Bhagini *Garbā* Mandal, Mumbai, October 19, 2004.

13. Examples of textual studies are provided by some essays in the landmark collection edited by Julia Leslie (1987). Bose 2010 continues that current. Examples of ethnography-based works are provided by Pearson 1996 and Pintchman 2005, 2007.

14. Such a positive view of the material universe and disregard for hierarchy are also a mark of South Asian Tantrism, a religious ideology that works "from the principle that the universe we experience is nothing other than the concrete manifestation of the godhead" (White 2000, 9). The parallels between sophisticated Tantric metaphysics and the lay theology of *garbo* participants are striking. However, *garbo* arguably takes the concept of the sanctity of the universe even further than Tantra. Many Tantric rituals are secretive and require initiation, whereas *garbo* is open and flexible in terms of both space and participation.

15. National news channel ANI had a segment title "Navratra brings new fashion trends in Gujarat" a few days before of Navarātri 2010. The segment is available at http://videos.sify.com/brings-new-fashion-trends-in-Gujarat-ANI-watch-Navratra-watch-kkejEfebjah.html (Accessed October 19, 2010).

16. Email correspondence with Kellye Steindel, Nisha Bedi, Julia Rowe, Nayna Lodhia, Nov. 9–12, 2008.

References

Appadurai, Arjun. 1986. "Introduction: Commodities and the Politics of Value." In *The Social Life of Things: Commodities in Cultural Perspective*, edited by Arjun Appadurai, 3–63. Cambridge (UK): Cambridge University Press.

Besley, Catherine. "The Poverty of 'New Historicism.'" In *Literature as History: Essays in Honour of Peter Widdowson*, edited by Simon Barker and Jo Gill, 7–15. London & New York: Continuum, 2010.

Bhandas. 1998. "Gaganmandal ni gagardi." In *Madhyayugin Urmikavyo* (Gujarati, "Medieval Lyrics"), edited by Chimanlal Trivedi, Balvant Jani, and Chinu Modi, 176–177. New Delhi: Sahitya Akademi.

Carman, John. 1974. *The Theology of Ramanuja, An Essay in Interreligious Understanding*. New Haven, CT: Yale University Press.

Chidester, David. 2008. "Engaging the Wildness of Things." *Material Religion* 4: 232–233.

Coburn, Thomas. 1991. *Encountering the Goddess: A Translation of the Devi-Mahatmya and A Study of Its Interpretation*. Albany: State University of New York Press.

Cort, John. 2007. "Art, Religion, and Material Culture: Some Reflections on Method." *Journal of the American Academy of Religion* 64: 613–632.

Eco, Umberto. 1990. *The Limits of Interpretation*. Bloomington, IN: Indiana University Press.

Gold, Anne, and Gloria Raheja. 1994. *Listen to the Heron's Words: Reimagining Gender and Kinship in North India*. Berkeley: University of California Press.

Goa, David, S. Brent Plate, David Morgan, and Crispine Paine, eds. 2005. "Editorial Statement." *Material Religion* 1: 4–9.

Hazrat, Kallolini. 1981. Introduction. *Maro Garbo Ghumyo* (Gujarati, "My *Garbo* Swirled"), edited by Kallolini Hazrat, 21–42. Mumbai: S. N. D. T. Women's University and Madhuri Shah Education Foundation.

Hoskins, Janet. 2007. "Afterword: Gendering Religious Objects: Placing them as Agents in Matrices of Power." *Material Religion* 3:110–119.

Jani, Arunodaya. 1978. "*Garbā* ni vyutpatti, utpatti, ane rahasya" (Gujarati, "*Garbo*'s Etymology, Origin, and Meaning"). *Swādhyāya* 1: 84–89.

Keane, Webb. 2008. "The Materiality of Religion." *Material Religion* 4: 230–231.

Kilde, Jeanne. 2007. "Space, Place, Religious Meaning." *Material Religion* 3: 277–278.

Layton, Robert H. 2001. "Intersubjectivity and Understanding Rock Art." In *The Archeology of Cult and Religion*, edited by Peter F. Beihl and Francois Bertemes, 25–6. Budapest: Archaeolingua.

Leslie, Julia. Ed. 1987. *Roles and Rituals for Hindu Women*. Delhi: Motilal Bararsidass.

Liu, Xinru. 1998. *Silk and Religion: An Exploration of Material Life and the Thought of People, AD 600–1200*. Delhi: Oxford University Press.

Lohmann, Roger Ivar, and Susan Start Sered. 2007. "Introduction: Objects, Gender, and Religion." *Material Religion* 3: 4–13.

McDannell, Colleen. 1995. *Material Christianity: Religion and Popular Culture in America*. New Haven, CT, and London: Yale University Press.

Meghani, Jhaverchand. 1997 [1925]. *Radhiyali Rat* (Gujarati, "Beautiful Night"). Bhavnagar, India: Prasar.

Mehta, Narmadashankar D. 1973 [1933]. *Shakta Sampradaya, tena siddhanto, Gujarat ma teno prachar ane Gujarati sahitya par teni asar* (Gujarati, "Shakta Tradition, its principles, its spread in Gujarat and its influence on Gujarati Literature"). Mumbai: Farbas.

Morgan, David. 2008. "The Materiality of Cultural Construction." *Material Religion* 4: 228–229.

Narayan, Kirin. 2003. "Singing from Separation: Women's Voices in and about Kangra Folk Songs." In *Songs, Stories, Lives: Gendered Dialogs and Cultural Critique*, edited by Gloria Goodwin Raheja, 23–53. New Delhi: Kali for Women.

Parmar, Khodidas. 2003. "The Ancient Traditions of *Garbā* and Raas: Folk Dances of Gujarat." In *Gujarat, a Celebration of Life*. Content Editor: Jehangir Hussein, no page numbers. Gandhinagar: Government of Gujarat.

Pathak, Ramanarayan, and Govardhan Panchal. 1954. *Ras ane Garbā, Ena Swarup ane vikas ni Ruprkeha* (Guajrati, "Ras and *Garbā,* An Outline of the Form and Development"). Delhi: Indian National Theater.

Patton, Laurie, ed. 2002. *Jewels of Authority: Women and Textual Tradition in Hindu India*. New York: Oxford University Press.

Pintchman, Tracy. 1994. The *Rise of the Goddess in the Hindu Tradition*. Albany: State University of New York Press.

———. *Guests at God's Wedding: Celebrating Kartik among the Women of Benares.* Albany: State University of New York Press.

———. Ed. 2007. *Women's Lives, Women's Rituals in the Hindu Tradition*. New York: Oxford University Press.

Raval, Anantrai. 1992 [1954]. *Gujarati Sahitya, Madhyakalin* (Gujarati, "Gujarati Literature, Medieval"). Ahmedabad: Gurjar.

Rodrigues, Hillary Peter. 2003. *Ritual Worship of the Great Goddess: The Liturgy of Durgā Pūjā with Interpretations*. Albany: State University of New York Press.

White, David. 2000. Introduction. *Tantra in Practice,* edited by David White, 3–38. Princeton, NJ: Princeton University Press.

Garbā *Anthologies*

Navarātrinī Ramzat Garbāvali. N. D. ed. Harishbhai Varan. Ahmedabad: Sastu Pustak Bhandar.

Ramzat Garbāvali. N. D. ed. Varsha Shah. Ahmedabad: Gayatri Publication.

Saurabh Navrāt Garbāvali. 1999. ed. Hasu Yagnik. Ahmedabad: Sahitya Saurabh.

5

The Goddess's Shaligrams

TRACY PINTCHMAN

The Parashakthi Temple in Pontiac, Michigan, also known in English as the "Eternal Mother Temple," sits down a side street just off a drab stretch of highway, past the Dixieland Flea Market and down the street from a rather run-down strip mall. Here the temple was built in 1999 on sixteen acres of undeveloped wooded land—or, rather, the first shell of the temple was built in that year, as the existing temple has been greatly expanded from its original form. The Divine Mother worshiped in this temple is the Tamil goddess Karumariamman, "Black Mariamman," who, the temple website asserts, has manifested herself both in the village of Thiruverkadu, on the outskirts of Chennai in Tamil Nadu, and at the Parashakthi Temple in Pontiac, Michigan.[1] An elaborately decorated icon of Divine Mother occupies center stage at the temple and easily captures the attention of devotees and other visitors. Yet since the temple's founding in 1999, many additional deities have been installed, resulting in the need to add an addition just a few years after the initial construction.

On March 21, 2009, I was present at the temple, as I had been many times before, for a ritual occasion. In this case, I had come to Pontiac to attend a day of ritual fire sacrifice, or *homam*, and ritual bathing, or *abhiṣekam*, of several deities. The culminating event at 6:30 that evening was an *abhiṣekam* of two special stones that had been brought to the temple from India. These were *śālagrāma* stones (hereafter "shaligram"[2]) that the spiritual director of the temple, Dr. G. Krishna Kumar, had brought back to Pontiac with him on two of the several trips he had made to India during the prior year. These large, round, black stones, covered with distinctive markings, had already played a role in several temple functions beginning in June 2008, although this particular evening of ritual was dedicated specifically to their worship. Shaligram stones are understood broadly in the Hindu tradition as natural manifestations of the deity Viṣṇu that form only in the Gandaki River in Nepal. In this regard, they function as an abstract or aniconic symbol of Viṣṇu, similar to the way a *liṅga* functions as an abstract image of Śiva. Dozens of devotees had gathered that night to see the shaligram stones, attend the *abhiṣekam*, and hear Kumar give a short lecture on the "Significance of Shaligram worship at the Parashakthi Temple." According to Kumar, these particular shaligram stones are extraordinary, mystical, powerful objects whose arrival at the temple was orchestrated by Divine Mother herself for a specific purpose.

How did shaligram stones, normally associated with Viṣṇu, come to play a prominent role in rituals performed at a temple nominally dedicated to Divine Mother in her form as a regional South Indian goddess? How did they get to the temple, and how did they come to be recognized and honored as mystical and powerful religious objects? What significance is normally attached to shaligram stones, and how is this meaning reconstituted in the context of the Parashakthi temple in Michigan? And by exploring these issues, what might we learn about the religious significance of materiality and material objects at this particular Hindu goddess temple? In order to answer these questions, I will first explore the nature of the Parashakthi Temple and its implicit theology of matter, for the predominant religious understanding of the shaligram stones promulgated at the temple cannot, I would argue, be separated from the larger narrative about the origins and mission of the temple or its discourse about the role that sacred material objects play at the temple as instruments of the Divine.

The Parashakthi Temple: A Brief History of its Founding

The story of the founding of the Parashakthi Temple is, among other things, a story about human reception of divine communication. It is also a story about sacred power, its manifestation in the American landscape, and its embodiment in particular places and objects. In this story, matter matters.

Like the Rājarājeśwarī Pīṭham in upstate New York that Corinne Dempsey has researched, the Parashakthi Temple, too, diverges in significant ways from patterns that tend to characterize Hindu temples in the American diaspora.[3] Like many other American Hindu temples, it has a governing temple committee; however, it is the only such temple of which I am aware where more than half of the members of the governing body are not of Indian descent but are instead Caucasian American.[4] Although the temple is nominally sectarian, focusing on Karumariamman as Divine Mother, numerous other deities have also been installed; however, their presence in the temple is not a result of committee discussion (Narayanan 1992, 175) but the direct demand of the Goddess; furthermore, deity icons are described in temple discourse as the material manifestations of the Divine Mother's vibrations (*spanda*). Finally, unlike in many American Hindu temples, the religious life of the Parashakthi Temple is shaped directly by a charismatic leader, Dr. G. Krishna Kumar, who also serves as the temple committee's president. Kumar is also a Tamil American gastroenterologist on staff at William Beaumont Hospital. While Kumar is the temple's acknowledged spiritual director and is recognized by many temple devotees as a mystic and religious visionary—a recently established website (www.drkrishnakumar.us) that includes videos of his talks as well as textual instruction describes him as a "renowned seer, modern mystic"—he refuses the moniker "guru," insisting instead that he is simply a "mailman" whose role is to deliver instructions and truths that he has received directly from Divine Mother. Kumar was also a principal founder of the temple. Many other individuals were heavily involved in establishing the temple, and many in the initial group of founders continue to support the temple financially and remain actively engaged in temple activities. However, none play the kind of central role that Kumar does in guiding the temple's ongoing religious life.

Kumar reports that he came from India to the United States from Tamilnadu (South India) in the mid 1960s to do his medical internship.[5] He advanced in his career very quickly and began teaching at Wayne State University. During his first decade in the United States, he recounts that he was not particularly religious but was instead absorbed primarily in developing his career. Sometime in the early 1970s, he began to feel restless, as if something important were missing. A friend of his offered to take him to an expert in Bhrigu *nāḍi*, a form of predictive astrology, in South India, and Kumar agreed. This *nāḍi* reader, A. N. K. Swamy, reported to Kumar that he had been a medical doctor in many previous lifetimes, which is why everything was coming to him so easily in this lifetime. A. N. K. (as Kumar calls him) revealed further that Kumar would eventually be called upon to build a temple for the Goddess. But Kumar did not know at the time what that would entail. After the *nāḍi* reading, Kumar became increasingly interested in what he refers to as mysticism and the occult, taking up a practice of meditation and doing research on a wide range of religious topics. He returned to India frequently during the 1970s and 80s, often meeting with A. N. K. and having readings done on his own behalf and on the behalf of others. But he did not yet act on the call to build a temple for the Goddess.

It was during this period that Kumar also began to develop an important spiritual relationship with a Caucasian female colleague of his, whom I shall call Jane. Kumar reports that one day, when passing him in the hall, Jane greeted him, teasing that he rarely stopped to say hello to her in the material world. But, she told him that he was coming to her in her dreams and offering her religious teachings. Kumar was surprised to hear this and didn't believe her. But when he next returned to India, he brought Jane's biodata with him and had a *nāḍi* reading done for her. This was sometime around 1988. A. N. K. confirmed that Kumar had indeed been going to Jane and offering her spiritual instruction in her sleep. Subsequently, the two reportedly developed a friendship and close spiritual relationship. Jane and her husband, who also has played a major role in creating and sustaining the temple, had a number of Caucasian friends who were spiritual seekers, engaging in Native American vision quests together, and Kumar became friendly with them as well.

The formative moment for Kumar and the temple came in 1994, when, Kumar reports, the Divine Mother first appeared directly to him in a vision while he was engaged in deep meditation. Here is how Kumar described it to me in an interview I conducted with him in 2009:

> KUMAR: From '72 to the eighties I was studying these mystical things, the occult, but I really did not communicate (with Divine Mother) . . . in '94, when Mother appeared . . . at first I didn't know who she was. . . . I was just meditating and this form came (and said,) "Build a house for me, because the world is going to go through major turmoil beginning 2000. So install me, build the house for me, and I'll protect the earth."
>
> TRACY: Had you had visions like that before?
>
> KUMAR: I had visions, but not so specific like that. I had it 27 times, same thing. . . . Then I knew it was something genuine.

The number 27 is meaningful here, and, as we will see, is especially significant with respect to the shaligram stones—a point to which I will return.

Kumar then conferred with A. N. K., who confirmed that Divine Mother was calling upon Kumar in her form as Karumariamman. A. N. K. sent Dr. Kumar a picture of Karumariamman's icon. Kumar maintains he was not at all familiar with this form of the Goddess until she appeared to him in the vision. Around this time, too, Jane called Kumar and told him that some goddess had been appearing to her repeatedly and asking that she and Kumar build a house for her. When Jane came to Kumar's office one day, Kumar showed her the photo of the icon of Karumariamman that A. N. K. Swamy had sent from India, and Jane confirmed that it was the same goddess. So, Kumar reports, they both knew the temple would have to be built.[6]

Kumar writes in the first temple newsletter, put out in 2001, that A. N. K. Swamy had described to him the land on which the temple would come to be built when he performed Kumar's first *nāḍi* reading in 1972.[7] After Kumar's vision in 1994, he began to search for this land. An Indian American acquaintance who was a real estate broker called Kumar one day and told him he had come across a plot of sixteen acres of undeveloped land in the middle of Pontiac that was for sale. It was topographically similar to the site of the Mīnākṣī Temple in Madurai, and Kumar knew that this was the land the Divine Mother wanted. When I interviewed him in Chennai in January of 2009, A. N. K. Swamy made particular note of the similarity between the name "Pontiac," the town in Michigan, and the name "Pandya," the empire that was responsible for building the Mīnākṣī Temple, claiming that Pontiac is the New World recreation of the Pandyan Empire, a South Indian Tamil dynasty that ruled parts of South India until the fifteenth century. Significant in this regard, too, is the reported role played by Dr. V. V. Svarnavenkateśa Dīkṣitar, one of the main priests of the Śaiva Chidambaram Temple, also in Tamil Nadu.[8] Kumar reports that Divine Mother told him in the 1994 *nāḍi* reading that he should seek help from the Brahmin Dīkṣitar, whom Kumar had never met. Kumar narrates that A. N. K. took him to meet Dīkṣitar, who at first rejected Kumar and was angry that A. N. K. had bothered him. However, Kumar reports that Divine Mother had given him secret information about a *yantra* in Dīkṣitar's possession, which he revealed to Dīkṣitar. The Brahmin then told his guests to leave and return the next day. When they returned, Kumar reports, Dīkṣitar accepted the meeting with them and explained that Gaṇeśa himself had told Dīkṣitar that Kumar was worthy of his attention. Kumar reports also that Dīkṣitar was a powerful tantrika and master *yantra* maker who came to Michigan to oversee the installation of the first *yantra*s and icons in the Parashakthi Temple, beginning with the *yantra* and icon of Divine Mother herself. A photo of Dīkṣitar hangs in the temple, and Kumar continues to refer to Dīkṣitar as his guru.

In the *nāḍi* reading, it was predicted that the land on which the temple that Kumar would eventually build would have been occupied previously by priests of another religion. Kumar and others intimately involved in establishing the Parashakthi Temple maintain that the temple grounds had previously been considered sacred by Native Americans in the area and had been a site of powerful shamanic activity. Kumar reports that the presence of Native American shamanic spirits was revealed to him one day when he was deep in meditation, well after he had purchased the land. One Caucasian devotee told me that she and a friend were walking on the land one day before the temple had been built, and the friend went into the woods. This friend came out a few minutes later visibly frightened because she had heard the sound of drumming in a particular pattern, as well as voices singing in a language she had never heard before, sounds that this devotee understood to be the music and voices of Native American spirits still inhabiting the area (personal interview, 2008). Kumar recounts that the Divine Mother herself had been present in the land for millennia and set up the shamanic spirits that are still present in the land around the temple. He also reports that he and others have seen on the temple grounds huge deer with large antlers, which are invisible to most humans but are the spirits of the deceased shamans. The land's connection to its reported Native American past has become well established as part of public discourse about the temple.[9]

It is not insignificant that the land chosen for the Divine Mother's house in the West, situated in a largely African-American city, is experienced by devotees as infused with the religious power of the spirits of deceased Native American shamans and is also imitative of South Indian Hindu landscape, specifically that of the Mīnākṣī temple in Madurai. The Parashakthi Temple functions as both a Tamil, Hindu Goddess temple and a divine power-spot that crosses boundaries, transcending its Tamil, Indian, and Hindu trappings. In fact, several individuals closely involved in the establishment of the temple have told me that the original plan was to make this temple a monument to the Divine Feminine in all religions, with shrines to Mary and goddesses from other traditions, but the Divine Mother appeared to Kumar in a dream after the initial structure had been built and consecrated and told him that she did not want that initial plan fulfilled. I have heard temple spokespersons describe the temple to large audiences in public temple events as a "vortex" and a place where communication with the Divine Mother functions via a "faster cable" than at other places. The ritual practices performed at the temple remain for the most part conventionally Hindu, and mostly South Indian Hindu, but the theology of the temple moves decidedly into the realm of tantra, yoga, and even New Age discourse.

It is this context that gives rise to what I will call a mystical tantric theology of matter.

Matter/Materiality at the Parashakthi Temple

While the Parashakthi Temple is recognizably Hindu and specifically South Indian in many ways, it does not situate itself squarely within any particular lineage of Hindu thought or devotion. Theological instruction—that is, the discussion of the nature and actions of the Divine—promulgated at and through the temple, shares many features with Upaniṣadic, Purāṇic, and Tantric thought, but it continues to unfold in a process of ongoing revelations that Kumar experiences as direct communications from Divine Mother, revelations that he then transmits to the temple community. While Karumariamman is perceived in other contexts to be a South Indian village or regional deity, Kumar argues that in fact she is at the ultimate level "Parashakthi," or "highest female power." He promulgates an understanding of Karumariamman as "Divine Pure Eternal Consciousness" who is the source of all other gods and goddesses (http://www.parashakthitemple.org/temple.aspx, accessed June 2012). In the video recording of a talk that was recently posted on his website, Kumar explains the evolution of material creation in terms that he attributes to direct revelation: Divine Mother has, he recounts, narrated to him directly and clearly who she is and how the created universe came about. He explains Divine Mother's ultimate, transcendent nature as Parā-Brahman, which exists as energy without attributes but gives rise to Nirguṇa Brahman, which is Divine Mother's nature with attributes but no form. From Nirguṇa Brahman evolves Saguṇa Brahman, the Divine with form, from which arises Mahāmayī. As Mahāmayī, Divine Mother both conceals her higher dimensions and projects the material universe. Because she wishes to experience herself, Mahāmayī then becomes Bindhu, the "point" of potential creation, which begins to oscillate and, through this oscillating or vibrating energy, generates extreme heat. The heat becomes material, and that is the start of the physical universe. Śiva and Śakti evolve from Bindhu as *puruṣa*, consciousness, and *prakṛti*, matter. Hence the universe consists of both matter and consciousness, and both evolve directly from the transcendent aspects of Divine Mother.[10] Many aspects of this account of creation overlap with accounts of cosmogenesis found in a variety of South Asian environments, but Kumar insists that Divine Mother has revealed this account directly to him, so he does not attribute it to any textual authority.

Because the material realm has evolved directly from the Divine, it contains within it divine energy. But not all matter is the same, for some material forms may be or may become more "charged" and active—that is, more imbued with consciousness or oscillating heat-energy—than other forms. Hence, for example, the land on which the temple itself was built is described in temple literature as not only chosen and prepared by Divine Mother herself, but also imbued in a unique way with her concentrated energy. In the temple's first newsletter, Pamela Costa writes, "Modern day visionaries have also been attracted to the land's power and sacred past. **It is apparent to many that a vortex of energy exists at the site.** We, at the Eternal Mother Temple, believe **the Holy Land is aligned with the various planetary and star systems** in such a way so as to heighten the energies at the present day site" (2001, 4). Similarly, the deities, or *devatās*, established at the Parashakthi Temple are described as vibratory cosmic forces whose power comes to be embodied at the temple when their icons are ritually installed.

Divine Mother sometimes uses particular material objects to communicate her wishes to human devotees. In 2008, for example, Kumar told the following story to me during an interview. After Divine Mother called him to build the temple in 1994 and A. N. K. Swamy revealed to him that this was the goddess in her form as Karumariamman, Kumar went to the Karumariamman temple in Thiruverkadu. Kumar reports that one of the temple priests, who was called Ramdas, saw him and called out to him. According to one of the main priests at the temple, Gaṇeśa Gurukkal, who had served at the temple for twenty-eight years when I interviewed him in South India in January of 2009, this Ramdas was the person most responsible for helping popularize the Karumariamman temple in Thiruverkadu. Kumar reports he was walking in the temple when Ramdas, whom he had never before met, approached him and said that Divine Mother wanted Kumar to pay for her chariot. As Kumar tells the story, Karumariamman had revealed to Ramdas in a vision that she wanted a chariot to be built to process her icon outside of the temple on festival days. But even though many devotees offered to pay for it, the Goddess would not allow anyone to have it built for her until Kumar came to Thiruverkadu, at which point she revealed to Ramdas that Kumar was the person she had chosen to sponsor the chariot. Kumar agreed to fund it. Kumar reports further that when he returned to the United States and was back in his home meditating, Divine Mother came to him again to reveal that the chariot had larger significance, as it represented her desire to be brought out of the Thiruverkadu temple all the way to Michigan and installed in a temple there.

Even more frequently, however, Divine Mother uses materiality and material objects at the temple to channel and transmit divine power, especially protective power. In this regard, it is important to note that the stated main concern of the Parashakthi Temple—the central mission of the temple—is explicitly described in temple literature as sharing Divine Mother's grace with those who are able to receive it. This mission was modified a few years ago to include also "experiencing and exploring the Divine." But the major impetus for building the temple in Pontiac at the precise time it was built was the protection of the Western world, during the first part of the twenty-first century, from grave danger. Kumar has noted on several public occasions that Divine Mother orchestrated the construction of the temple because the world would go through a catastrophic period during the first two decades of the twenty-first century, and the temple would function to protect humans and the earth from potential disaster. Kumar writes on a page on his website:

> We are so fortunate and blessed to be able to be part of Divine Mother's plan to have her cosmic aspects installed on earth, so that the earth can be protected from major Asura (Demonic) activities. All of us are aware how she has protected us in the past nine years. As the Mother foretold, many tragedies have happened in the world beginning with the attack on the World Trade Center Tower, and the Tsunami that followed. In the past few years, major financial crisis, which the world has not faced in the past sixty years or so have unfolded, and we are still trying to survive this major shock to the global financial infrastructure. And then we had the Swine Flu occurrence. With the Divine Mother's grace and protection, the world has come through these with minimal damage. Other tragic events that are foretold and are supposed to happen in the next decade will also be mitigated a great deal by the Divine Mother and her various manifestations, due to proper installations of various cosmic aspects of "Her" at our Temple, with her Kindness, Blessings and Grace. (http://drkrishnakumar.us/2012/asuric.html, accessed June 2012)

Kumar speaks often of *asuras* as active, malevolent forces that can be balanced and overcome with positive divine energy. In this regard, the Divine Mother of the Parashakthi Temple assumes the traditional protective function often associated with the demon- and ignorance-destroying Goddess of the Devī-Māhātmya and other Hindu Śākta and

Tantric traditions. This protective function in particular comes to be embodied in specific objects, including many of the deity icons installed in the temple. It is also embodied in the shaligram stones, the first of which Kumar brought with him from India in February of 2008.

What is a Shaligram?

Shaligram stones are forms of fossilized ammonite that develop in the Gandaki River in contemporary Nepal. They are generally black and round or oblong in shape, and they come in a variety of sizes. In his comprehensive study of shaligrams, Allen Aaron Shapiro notes that Indian Hindus tend to classify shaligrams as either perforated or nonperforated (Shapiro 1987, 5–6), with perforated shaligrams containing visible ammonite markings. Both types of shaligrams are worthy of worship, but those with perforations that resemble *cakras* are generally considered most meritorious. Many Hindus consider these *cakra*-like perforations to be the mark of Viṣṇu. Kirin Narayanan notes that in Kangra, where she has done field research, most upper caste households keep a shaligram stone in the home shrine, but married women are not supposed to touch it (Narayanan 1997, 32). More widespread, however, is the belief that Viṣṇu makes himself available to all devotees in his shaligram form, and the Skanda Purāṇa states that anyone initiated into shaligram worship, including women and Śudras, should worship shaligram stones (Shapiro 1987, 33). There is a long history in Hindu traditions of shaligrams being recognized as objects of reverence, going back to the Vedic or even pre-Vedic period (Shapiro, 44–52). In several of the Purāṇas, they are proclaimed to be natural, aniconic forms of the deity Viṣṇu in particular.

How Viṣṇu came to take the form of a shaligram stone is recounted in a well-known narrative told in a variety of versions, both textual and oral. The Devī-Bhāgavata Purāṇa (9.17–25) recounts one such version. Tulsī, a goddess who also takes form as the basil plant, marries a demon named Śankhacuda (named Jalandhara in other versions of the story). Tulsī—or in other versions, Vṛndā, another name for Tulsī—here is described as a form of Lakṣmī, and Śankhacuda is the incarnation of Kṛṣṇa's dear childhood friend, Sudama. Both Tulsī and Sudama are said to have been compelled to take human births because of a curse visited upon them by Rādhā, Krishna's consort.

Śankhacuda soon gains more and more power. His ascendency culimates in a battle between divine and demonic forces. Because Tulsī is a devoted wife (*pativratā*), she is able to generate power that protects

Śankhacuda, whom the gods are unable to defeat. Viṣṇu intervenes by going to Tulsī in the form of Śankhacuda and tricking her into having sex with him. Tulsī has now broken her wifely vow by having sex with a man other than her husband, thereby depriving Śankhacuda of the protective powers that resulted from Tulsī's spousal devotion and chastity. Śankhacuda is killed, whereupon he is reborn in Kṛṣṇa's heaven as the loyal Sudama, with his bones becoming conch shells. Conch shells are broadly used in Vaiṣṇava worship. Tulsī curses Viṣṇu to become a stone, which results in his manifestation as the shaligram. Viṣṇu invites Tulsī to become his wife, proclaiming that her body will become the Gandaki River, the only river in which shaligram stones are said to naturally manifest.

In contemporary lived Hinduism, shaligrams are associated with both Śiva and Viṣṇu. But they are most consistently accepted as natural forms of Viṣṇu (Shapiro 1987, 12–14) and are kept in many Vaiṣṇava temples. In contemporary Hinduism, shaligrams sometimes also have Tantric associations and may be seen as having special power that humans can access. Shapiro tells the following story about his encounter over shaligrams with the *pujāri*, a temple priest, of a South Indian Śiva temple, who was said to be a "learned practitioner of the 'salagrama cult'":

> This priest, whose name was Sivan, was very unimpressed with the salagrama stone given to me by the priest of the Muktinatha shrine, because it did not have any perforation, but decided to test it anyway. He placed it upon a small disk of copper and put another small piece of copper as a lid on top of the stone. We waited to see if the lid would be turned by the power residing in the stone: my stone failed miserably. However, he was more intrigued by another stone I have. . . . I cannot say what the actual reason for Sivan's interest in the latter stone was, for it, too, was unperforated. It was, however, adorned with a pair of small eyes made of conch shell, applied with wax in the manner typical of the Vrindaban area. He tried the same copper plate test on the Govardhana stone, but it also proved powerless to move the copper lid. (Shapiro 1987, 7–8)

Hence the idea that shaligram stones are powerful religious objects is part of contemporary Hindu thinking. It is their association with supernatural power, much more than their association with Viṣṇu or Shiva, that characterized the two shaligrams that came to be consecrated with an *abhiṣekam* in Michigan in March of 2009.

The Shaligrams of the Parashakthi Temple

When Kumar went to India in early 2008, he did not set out to bring shaligram stones back to Michigan. Rather, he was making one of many trips he usually makes to India annually, often at the behest of Divine Mother, to do her bidding for the temple and to visit his remaining family in Chennai. In 2008, he journeyed back to India four times, with the first trip occurring in February of that year. During this particular trip, like most others, Kumar called on A. N. K. Swamy in Chennai. Kumar reported to me in a conversation we had in February of 2009 that during that particular visit, A. N. K. wanted Kumar to meet someone residing about forty or fifty miles outside of Chennai. Kumar describes this individual as a *siddha,* an accomplished yogi who has attained supernormal powers through religious practice. Kumar usually translates "siddha" simply as "mystic" in temple lectures and discussions. Kumar reports that this *siddha* had been designated a *rājā-yogī,* "king of yogis," by other yogis at an annual festival in the Himalayas, although Kumar was not sure what yogic lineage this man belonged to or at what particular festival gathering he had been deemed to be a *rājā-yogī.* Kumar recounts that when they met, the *rājā-yogī* showed Kumar a very special shaligram stone and announced that he was going to give it to Kumar:

> KUMAR: When I saw that, it had what is called—you know, Sudarśana is called Viṣṇu's *cakra,* Visnu's emblem. And actually it looks like a spiral galaxy. And there were thirteen of them [*cakra* markings].
>
> TRACY: Okay.
>
> KUMAR: I've seen one or two. I've never seen thirteen.
>
> TRACY: So there were thirteen *cakra*s—
>
> KUMAR: Sudarśana *cakra*s.
>
> TRACY: —on this shaligram?
>
> KUMAR. On the shaligram. . . . And then he showed me—I shook it, and there was water in it, entrapped matter. . . . And this is a real valuable fossil, 140 million years old. The continent shifted, and that's when the Himalaya formed. . . . That was not enough. Mother had told him, "You have to charge it

before you give it. I want my place to be completely energized for the devotees."

"Sudarśana *cakra*" is the name given to the disk-like weapon that Viṣṇu uses to protect the world and destroy evil or obstructing forces, both external and spiritual. The language of "energizing" or "charging" objects with sacred power is well-established language at the Parashakthi Temple. While sacred objects and important temples can be found all over India, Kumar insists that most of them are lifeless. Sacred objects and temples become powerful only when they have been properly infused with divine power, which can only be done by someone who has been "thinned out," that is, someone who has become aware of the divine on an intuitive level and is able to communicate with divinity and receive divine energy. According to Kumar, most Hindu temple priests are not thinned out and hence are unable to become in any real way vehicles of divine power. Kumar himself, as well as the *rājā-yogī*, on the other hand, were immediately sensitive to the dynamics of divine energy surrounding the special shaligram stone. Kumar reports:

> He said, "I have this for you. But I want to energize it for you so you can—see, what he does is—when you have a shaligram, you have to do certain [things]. We call it feeding the cosmic forces. You've got to do that. . . . So he instilled that energy through Karttikeya.

Kumar reports that he had to return to the *rājā-yogī*'s home two or three days later to participate in a big *homam* that he and the *rājā-yogī* conducted together before an audience of about forty or fifty invited participants. He was accompanied by A. N. K. and A. N. K.'s daughter Mina, but Kumar and the *rājā-yogī* had to work together to infuse the shaligram with the appropriate energy. Kumar describes this *homam* as "the longest *homam* I've ever been to there [in India]":

> It took about four or five hours of intense, intense energy. And the herbs—we use some at the temple, maybe five, six seven—but, yeah, [there were] 153 [herbs used]. Highest I've ever seen. He must have spent years accumulating those herbs. . . . 153 of them he used, and each one used is one *devatā*. I was sitting next to it. The energy was so intense that Swami [A. N. K.] didn't even stay. He couldn't stand it; he walked away. Even the *siddha* [the *rājā-yogī*] walked away. And they're watching from outside about fifty feet away, and

> many people thought I was burnt because they said the flame engulfed me. . . . I felt like I was burnt. I felt like I was dying, but I didn't know it—I was not burnt. For them it looked like I was also part of the *homam*.

According to Kumar, everyone else at the *homam* experienced the introduction into the fire of each herb—with every herb corresponding to one *devatā*—as suffocating energy, so they were unable to remain near the *homam* fire. Divine Mother wanted only Kumar to remain with the divine energies infusing the shaligram, so she made the air impossible for everyone else to breathe. Even Kumar felt almost overwhelmed:

> I felt that suffering. I felt that intense death-like thing, but I was not burnt. But they felt I was consumed by [the flames]. Some people were trying to get up and come and open the windows. The door was closed; through the window, they were watching me.

Kumar returned to Michigan with the newly charged shaligram. It was brought to the Parashakthi Temple, and on August 9, 2008, a special *abhiṣekam* of the shaligram was performed publicly.

Kumar reports that he returned to India in November of 2008 and met again with the same mystic, who gave him a second powerful shaligram at the behest of Divine Mother. The second shaligram had fourteen perforations on it. Kumar reports:

> When I saw that, he said, "She also wants you to have it." And I said, "You know, there must be a reason." I said, "If Mother says, I'll take it." That night, when I meditated, Mother said, "I want my devotees on earth to get all the energies from twenty-seven constellations. Each [*cakra* perforation] represents one constellation. So I want twenty-seven." See, I didn't know that. When I got [the second shaligram], I didn't make the connection. . . . So twenty-seven we will have. Ours will be the most energetic [shaligram]."

The constellations to which Kumar refers are the twenty-seven fixed *nakṣatra*s, minor constellations—also called "asterisms" or "lunar mansions"—recognized in Hindu astrology. The *nakṣatras* are assigned fixed positions in the sky so that together they complete the entire 360 degrees of the zodiac. As the earth rotates, over time the moon seems to move to a different part of the sky, and hence it appears to move through the different *nakṣatras* over the course of the year. When a person is born, they are associated with the *nakṣatra* that appears in conjunction with the moon at the time of their birth. Each *nakṣatra* is also associated with a particular deity.

Kumar's understanding of what Divine Mother has revealed to him is that each *cakra* on the two shaligrams he was given corresponds to a *nakṣatra* as well as the presiding deity of that *nakṣatra*; their divine energy is being captured and channeled through the shaligrams' *cakra* perforations in such a way that every devotee coming to the temple—since everyone is associated with one or another of the twenty-seven *nakṣatras*—will receive the protection and divine grace being channeled through the shaligram stones. During the March 2009 function, Kumar again made a direct connection between the twenty-seven *cakra* perforations on the two shaligram stones, the twenty-seven *nakṣatras*, and Divine Mother's protective energy, noting that because every person has a *nakṣatra*, the shaligrams together protect everyone since they have now been infused properly with Divine Mother's energy. As I was following Kumar around the temple with my tape recorder before the shaligram *abhiṣekam*, he also stopped to shake the stones gently to allow me to hear the sound of the fluid trapped in the stone. Kumar was insistent that spiritually sensitive individuals at the temple could hear music emanating from the shaligrams; he could hear it, as could two of the priests at the Parashakthi Temple. Both Kumar and Swami Māmā, the temple priest most widely recognized as spiritually developed—thinned out, in Kumar's terms—insisted too that they distinctly heard the sound of the mantra "Om" coming from the shaligrams when they were shaken.

Figure 5.1. Shaligram stones at the Parashakthi Temple. Photo by Tracy Pintchman.

Constructing Theologies of Matter

Writing about material religion, David Morgan notes, "As an object moves from one person to the next, from one social setting or one culture to the next, it acquires different values and associations. . . . [I]t is more productive to study the response to objects as they are displayed, exchanged, destroyed, and circulated in order to determine what they mean to people" (Morgan 2008, 228). Certainly, the significance of the shaligrams that journeyed from India to America in 2009 and came to be consecrated ritually at the Parashakthi Temple in Michigan cannot be separated from the temple context or its larger narrative and sense of mission. Nor should any exploration of these shaligrams be solely about meaning, for their distinctiveness resides for temple devotees more in what they can do than in what they might mean. And the range of what these stones can do, it seems, depends on context. Webb Keane notes, in this regard, that "by virtue of their very materiality, forms can never be reduced in any stable way to particular intentions or meanings. One reason is . . . the contingent coexistence of an indefinite number of qualities in any object" (Keane 2008, 230). Hence shaligrams, normally the province of Viṣṇu, need not always be so.

In *Diaspora of the Gods*, Joanne Waghorne looks in particular at Tamil *ammans*, "mothers," and in particular at Mariamman—of whom Karumariamman may be seen as a form—as a "gentrifying" local Tamil goddess (Waghorne 2004, especially 131–142). In India, Mariamman is associated increasingly with the Hindu middle class and a form of religiosity that attempts to transcend class and caste barriers in a context of globalization and rapid economic change (139). Outside of India, Waghorne argues that temples to Murugan and Tamil *ammans* are the primary sites of what she calls the "globalization of more localized temple traditions" (172). She describes this "globalized localism" as a tendency to reproduce in diaspora regional or local Indian temples, deities, and practices. This "contemporary return to the local," as Waghorne puts it, reflects a yearning for what the "local" in India can uniquely provide; "the sense that the concrete world becomes the site for divine powers to interact with human devotees, for curing pain in the body and agony in the mind, for financial success, for general mangalam (auspiciousness)" (179). The Goddess, along with Murugan, intrudes directly into people's lives and provides a sense of divinity as a "living presence": hence in diaspora contexts where these deities come to be revered, they tend to function not as impersonal, abstract divinities but act instead as "living energy, the vibration of the universe and the pulse of each devotee" (227).

Kumar uses similar terms to describe the Divine Mother of the Parashakthi Temple, whom he describes frequently as a kind of vibratory energy who becomes personal for the benefit of her devotees. Divine Mother's protective power is made available to those who revere her at least in part through sacred objects like the shaligrams. In the case of the Parashakthi Temple, I wonder if it would be more accurate to view "the local" or "locality," especially with respect to material objects that embody the power of "the local," less as something to which those most involved with the temple return, to use Waghorne's formulation, and more as something they, in conversation with Divine Mother, creatively construct. As noted, the main reason Divine Mother has purportedly called upon human agents to build the temple is to protect the West during a dangerous period in history; to this end, the Goddess's power has had to take up residence in the American landscape, as is repeatedly emphasized in temple literature and talks that Kumar gives, through the temple that her human devotees have built at her behest. Particular sacred objects, such as the shaligrams that Divine Mother reportedly arranged to have Kumar bring to Michigan, become vehicles of her power, that is, the media through which she transcends distances and boundaries—between India and the United States, for example, or the sphere beyond form and the material world—and comes to act in the human and natural realms. But these objects are not inherently powerful; rather, the divine requires human agents—Kumar in particular, but in this case also the *rājā-yogī* and A. N. K. Swamy, among others—whose ritual interventions are needed to infuse the shaligrams with divine energy. These rituals, such as the *homam* that Kumar and the *rājā-yogī* performed for the first shaligram, and the accompanying perceptions of divine power are not simply reproduced from an "original" local context but are created according to Divine Mother's instructions based on the needs of her devotees living in the Western world and carried out by the individuals she has entrusted to do her work. Similarly, perceptions of what the shaligrams are able to do at the Parashakthi Temple is particular to that religious environment, constructed in conversation with the temple's larger mission. In the temple context, the stones' power is no longer "local" but becomes vast, conferring a degree of cosmic protection that is unleashed at the crossroads of influences that give the Parashakthi Temple its unique power and identity.

Now, at the Parashakthi Temple, the foundation for a large Rājāgopuram, or royal monumental tower, has been prepared. The tower has been in the planning stages for several years, ever since Divine Mother revealed to Kumar that she wanted him to have it built. This Rājāgopuram has been designed according to Divine Mother's wishes, as revealed directly to Kumar, and will be forty-four feet tall with a Śrī Cakra on the front and will be adorned with 520 icons (*vigraha*) of *devatās*, deities, understood at the temple to be Divine Mother's vibratory energies. These are *devatās* of the Goddess's choosing; Kumar insists they are already active at the Parashakthi Temple, but people are not yet aware of them. Hence the Rājāgopuram will bring their energies to people's awareness and thereby make it available to devotees. Kumar insists that the Rājāgopuram had to be built because of cosmic changes that occurred in December of 2012, unleashing destructive forces on the earth. Once again, Divine Mother is channeling her protective powers through a religious object—or, more specifically in this case, a structure—to keep her devotees safe from harm.

Notes

1. http://www.parashakthitemple.org/shakthi_worship.aspx (accessed June 2012).

2. I use here the Anglicized spelling common at the Parashakthi Temple and in popular usage.

3. See Dempsey 2006. For an overview analysis of Hindu temples in the United States, see Kurien 2007, 86–116.

4. For a list of the members of the Temple Committee, see http://www.parashakthitemple.org/committee.aspx.

5. The account summarized here of Kumar's life leading up to the founding of the temple is based on interviews I conducted with him in 2008–2009.

6. Prema A. Kurien notes that the initial impetus for the building of a Hindu temple both in India and abroad is often an injunction sent through a dream or religious medium by a deity demanding a home (Kurien 2007, 88). In this case, the injunction came independently to two different actors who perceived the Mother's direct appearance to them in a form with which neither of them was familiar as a clear sign that they now had no choice but to do the Mother's bidding.

7. The way that the land was obtained is also described in the Temple's first newsletter, *Om Shakthi*, as a miracle (Kumar 2001, 4).

8. For more on this temple, see Younger 1995.

9. For example, a column that temple devotee Pamela Costa wrote for the first newsletter on the temple's "Mystical Origins" notes, "Local Native American Indians were drawn to the power of the land and selected it for their sacred worship site. Several devotees have commented on feeling the presence of these ancient spirits" (Costa 2001, 12).

10. http://www.drkrishnakumar.us/teaching/divinegrace.html (accessed June 2012).

References

Websites

http://www.drkrishnakumar.us
http://www.drkrishnakumar.us/teaching/divinegrace.html
http://drkrishnakumar.us/2012/asuric.html
http://www.parashakthitemple.org/committee.aspx
http://www.parashakthitemple.org/shakthi_worship.aspx
http://www.parashakthitemple.org/temple.aspx

Print Sources

Costa, Pamela. 2001. "Mystical Origins." *Om Shakthi*, vol. 1, issue 1, (Jan.–March): 12.

Dempsey, Corinne. 2006. *The Goddess Lives in Upstate New York: Breaking Convention and Making Home at a North American Hindu Temple*. NY: Oxford University Press.

Keane, Webb. "On the Materiality of Religion." *Material Religion: The Journal of Objects, Art and Belief*, vol. 4, no. 2. (July): 230–231.

Kurien, Prema A. 2007. *A Place at the Multicultural Table: The Development of an American Hinduism*. New Brunswick, NJ: Rutgers University Press.

Kumar, Dr. G. Krishna. 2001. "Personal Note from Dr. G. Krishna Kumar." *Om Shakthi*, vol. 1, issue 1, (Jan.–March): 4.

Morgan, David. 2008. "The Materiality of Cultural Construction." *Material Religion: The Journal of Objects, Art and Belief*, vol. 4, no. 2. (July): 228–229.

Narayan, Kirin. 1997. "Sprouting and Uprooting of Saili: The Story of the Sacred Tulsi in Kangra." *Manushi*, no. 102: 30–38.

Narayanan, Vasudha. 1992. "Creating South Indian Hindu Experience in the United Stages." In *A Sacred Thread: Modern Transmission of Hindu Traditions in India and Abroad*, edited by R. B. Williams, 147–196. Chambersburg, PA: Anima Publications.

Shapiro, Allen. 1987. "Śālagrāmaśilā: A Study of Śālagrāma Stones with Text and Translation of Śālagrāmaparīkṣā." PhD diss., New York: Columbia University.

Waghorne, Joanne. 2004. *Diaspora of the Gods: Modern Hindu Temples in an Urban Middle-Class World*. New York: Oxford University Press.

Younger, Paul. 1995. *The Home of Dancing Śivaṉ: The Traditions of the Hindu Temple in Citamparam*. New York: Oxford University Press.

6

The Camphor Flame in an Age of Mechanical Reproduction

James McHugh[1]

Camphor, a white, pungently fragrant, crystalline substance has long been a highly valued material in South Asian culture. It is used in traditional Indian medical systems such as Āyurveda and is also an important ingredient in traditional perfumes and incenses. Sanskrit literature abounds in references to camphor. But for many people, the context most strongly associated with the use of camphor in South Asia is religion. To be more precise, one of the most conspicuous uses of camphor in India (as well as in Hindu religious contexts outside India) is in *pūjā* rituals of worship. There, at the end of a series of rites and offerings, a bright camphor flame is burned in front of a sacred image. Not only is the Hindu ritual burning of camphor probably the most well-known use of this substance in South Asia today, but, conversely, the camphor flame has become somewhat emblematic of Hindu worship.

In this chapter I will explore the somewhat Marxian thesis that the changing mode of production of camphor is closely tied to its changing religious significance—hence the allusion in the title to Walter Benjamin's essay on the implications of moving to an industrial mode of production. The relation between production and use, however, is dialectical. Hence the social meanings and uses of camphor have been powerful forces in changing the mode of production of camphor from a system of forest production and trade to an industrial chemical process. The story of camphor's significance in South Asia is extremely complicated, and in order to describe how people changed camphor—and how camphor changed people—I will also draw inspiration from the work of Bruno Latour, an important scholar of science and technology studies.[2] In particular I adapt Latour's ideas in the way I suggest that camphor—a substance—is also an *institution*: what camphor is at any place and time is conditioned by a *network* of social, technological, institutional, discursive, economic, and, in this case, even theological factors. Ultimately, we see that modern pressures on camphor from far outside the realm of Hindu worship have changed this material so radically that the precious and ancient camphor flame is in many cases quite threatened.

In an important 1992 study of temple Hinduism—a book entitled *The Camphor Flame*—Christopher Fuller suggested that, in relation to Hindu *pūjā*, "showing the camphor flame is the climax of worship and . . . it synecdochically represents the entire ritual." He also asserts, "When a camphor flame is shown at the climax of *pūjā*, therefore, the divine and human participants are most fully identified in their common vision of the flame and hence in their mutual vision of each other—the perfect *darshana*. God has become man and a person, transformed, has become god" (Fuller 1992, 73). As to the significance of camphor in this context, Fuller notes that the camphor flame in particular symbolizes "the deity's transcendence of its embodied form, for the burning camphor, which leaves no sooty residue, provides an intangible display of incandescent light and fragrance" (Fuller 1992, 73). Unlike wood, for instance, when camphor burns it (theoretically) leaves no residue, and exploiting this in a symbolic manner reflects South Asian proverbial wisdom (Sternbach 1974, 450). As we will see below, this popular interpretation of the significance of camphor is by no means all that one can say about the matter, nor is camphor always quite so pure in burning as supposed.

In recent years camphor, apparently so central to Hindu worship, has become the subject of a minor controversy. In August 2004, the newspaper *The Hindu* reported the following:

> The Tamil Nadu Camphor Tablets Manufacturers' Association has urged the State Government to advise the temple authorities to use camphor for 'deeparadhana' . . . The temple authorities decided against lighting camphor citing that the smoke emanated from the camphor spoiled the clean atmosphere of the sanctum sanctorum but the association came in defence of use of camphor saying that its smoke was a good disinfectant and could add to the divinity of the temple. Further, lighting any product in huge numbers would result in more smoke. Hence, judicious use of camphor would be beneficial for everyone, the association said. They also charged the temple authorities with displaying boards with words prohibiting

> use of camphor inside the temple and sought their removal. Lighting camphor in temples was a traditional practice and stopping them had disappointed many devotees. Hence, the State Government should step in and consider the demands, the association said.[3]

Apparently some temples in Tamil Nadu had abandoned the use of this traditional material, and this was a cause for concern to the camphor manufacturers for whom these camphor-burning temples evidently constitute an important market. The camphor manufacturers therefore asked the state government to intervene and persuade the temples to return to burning camphor, representing their economic concerns in religious terms. The temples seemed to be rejecting camphor in the interests of temple cleanliness. The manufacturers, on the other hand, hoped to obtain the support of the state in retaining this tradition, which was important to their business and presumably also to the manufacturing economy of the state. In this chapter, in exploring the way changes in the production and use of camphor have had implications for the material culture of religions, it is also necessary to address the following broader questions. Why do people burn camphor in Hindu temples in the first place? How did the burning of camphor become so excessive as to leave pollution and dirt? And what wider historical processes led this formerly precious and prestigious material to become so easily available and demoted from its formerly central place in ritual?

Precious, Exotic, White, and Cool: The Career of a Raw Material

How ought we to go about talking about a raw material like camphor? Igor Kopytoff (1986) famously suggested that we talk of *things* as having biographies, part of a wider move to extend categories of the social and the human to the apparently inanimate and passive world of objects and materials: now we can say that things have biographies, social lives, and actual or represented agency.[4] Or, we might take another route and think of camphor not as a stable substance moving through time and space, but rather as an *institution*. As Latour notes when stating that he would prefer to designate substances as institutions, "The word 'substance' does not designate what 'remains beneath,' impervious to history, but what gathers together a multiplicity of agents into a stable and coherent whole . . . substance is a name that designates the *stability* of an assemblage" (Latour 1999, 151). In fact, both models are useful here.

The "biography" model allows us to follow camphor over time, and the "institution" model allows us to consider the huge changes in the manner camphor is used, produced, and understood over time.

To return to the present case, what, then, is camphor and how did it ever come to be burned in lamps in Hindu temples? The sources, availability, nature, and therefore the price and uses of camphor, must have changed considerably over time, and these factors must also have varied across South Asia, not to mention in Southeast Asia. By looking at certain textual genres, such as pharmacological texts that are less set in Sanskritic stone with regard to material culture,[5] and also by examining scholarship on the history of camphor in other parts of the world, we can begin to historicize this material and explore how its use and value in religious traditions reflect a complex and changing assemblage that is social, economic, technological, political, and geographical.

The English word "camphor" is used in a nontechnical way to refer to a number of materials with different chemical formulae and origins. If we exclude synthetic camphor, the materials referred to by the English word "camphor" and the most common Sanskrit word for camphor, *karpūra*, are probably closely related materials. This makes sense if we consider that camphor, whether in Europe or India, was for a long time derived from the same geographical sources, namely Southeast Asia and parts of China.[6] Setting synthetic camphor aside for now, there are two principal types of camphor. One variety is produced from trees of the species *Dryobalanops* that grow on the island of Borneo as well as in parts of Sumatra and the Malaysian peninsula. Production of this sort of camphor is most closely associated with Borneo and this camphor is often called "borneol" or "borneol camphor." Borneol camphor is produced by felling the trees, and the camphor is then found in the form of crystals inside fissures in the wood. It seems that this variety of camphor was the first to be produced and traded, and it was, in several times and places, the most prestigious type of camphor. The second principal type of camphor is produced from the tree *Cinnamomum camphora*. This tree is found further east, growing in parts of China, Taiwan, and Japan. The camphor from this tree is not generally found "native" in the wood, but instead is produced by steam distillation of the tree. This latter camphor seems to have become available to the world later than the Borneo camphor and was less valued. In later periods, this tree and this manner of production were the most abundant source of the material.

The first camphor to arrive in India would have been the precious camphor that most likely came from parts of Indonesia (especially Barus in Sumatra), Borneo, and possibly the Malaysian peninsula, appearing around the early- to mid-first millennium CE.[7] This new material, bright white, with a cold feel to the touch, and pungently fragrant must have seemed quite remarkable at the time. We are generally so used to highly purified chemicals and strong solvent smells today—consider, for example, menthol or acetone—that it is easy to forget how striking the physical properties of camphor must have seemed many centuries ago. The overseas, exotic origins of this camphor were both noted and celebrated, with one narrative text referring to a "camphor island."[8] From this very short survey of some materials it seems that, broadly speaking, the more precious camphor from Borneo that appeared in India sometime around the early- to mid-first millennium CE was joined at a later date by the cheaper and more plentiful China camphor. Certainly by the fourteenth century this cheaper China camphor was quite familiar.

The possibility of cultivating camphor in India was explored during the colonial period, but attempts at cultivation in India were not a great success, and natural camphor was never produced on a large scale there. Instead, prior to the introduction of the manufacture of synthetic camphor, India relied on imports of camphor from East Asia (and also at a later date on imports of synthetic camphor).[9] Writing in 1958, Chopra noted that it would be worth looking into manufacturing camphor in India.[10] Chopra was also acutely aware of the consequences of the synthesis of camphor on the traditional manner of production, when he observed that "the fate of camphor industry (sic) may approach that of indigo which was formerly a very thriving industry but has been blotted out of existence by production of aniline dyes and synthetic indigo" (Chopra 1958, 124). Indigo had been a major economic product of India and changes in the supply of natural indigo, the revolution in production of this dye afforded by cheap synthesis, and the impact of the First World War on supplies of synthetic indigo all played an important role in nineteenth- and twentieth-century Indian history.[11] Unlike in the case of indigo production, the fight for control over the production of camphor at the turn of the twentieth century appears to have left India relatively unaffected, except for the impact the camphor trade war had on the supply and price of camphor. Whatever camphor might mean in India, it could never have been a powerful symbol for resistance in colonial India in the way that textiles and dyes could.

The Uses of Camphor in Premodern South Asia

Camphor was used for a variety of purposes in premodern South Asia.[12] It appears to have been particularly important in early periods for flavoring betel (*pān*),[13] another introduction from Southeast Asia. Camphor was also used as a medicine and in perfumes and incenses. These latter two uses, in medicine and perfumery, were common in most of the premodern world.[14] In South Asia, camphor was also burned in lamps—a point to which I will return in more detail below.

What did people think of camphor, or at least what did they write about camphor in premodern South Asia? Briefly stated, camphor was admired because it was white, cool, and fragrant.[15] Anyone familiar with Sanskrit poetry will note that these three qualities are generally considered very desirable. Jasmine, smiles, and, of course, the moon are all admired for their whiteness, as is camphor. Like the moon, terms for camphor were very common in figurative speech expressing whiteness. It is important to remember that, where we tend to think of perfumes as invisible and ethereal, the visual properties of such aromatics as camphor (white) and musk (black) were highly admired in medieval India (McHugh 2011b). Just as envy is green for most English speakers, so are fame and laughter white in the conventions of Sanskrit poetry. As a consequence of camphor's exemplary whiteness, in many poems the radiant fame of the king is compared to camphor (Sternbach 1974, 433). Coolness is also frequently admired in Sanskrit literary culture. Precious sandalwood is admired for its cooling tactile qualities, and another notable source of coolness is the moon, which also happens to be white. Thus, it is not surprising that one very common synonym for cool white camphor in Sanskrit is "moon" (*candra*), together with the many synonyms for "moon." Thus camphor, a precious, exotic, bright-white perfume, a veritable *terrestrial moon*, was a perfect medium for articulating many of the literary, sensory, and even political values of elite culture in premodern South Asia.[16]

I should mention that the whiteness of camphor is still admired, and one particular mass of white camphor is quite famous as a visual icon in Hinduism. This is the white forehead-mark (*nāmam*) on the image of Venkaṭeśvara at the temple in Tirumala in South India. The very distinctive and noticeable white forehead mark on this image actually consists of a considerable quantity of (borneol) camphor[17] molded onto the face of the image and divided in the center by a striking, bamboo-leaf-shaped streak of dark musk (which is mixed/diluted with sandalwood paste).[18]

For those familiar with contemporary Hindu rituals, perhaps the first thing that comes to mind when they think of camphor is the camphor flame. Burning camphor is, however, a rather strange thing to do if one considers the many uses to which this material has been put historically in other places. Camphor is indeed very inflammable and was added to incense in many parts of the world, but to fuel a lamp entirely with this valued aromatic would have been, in an early South Asian context, a profligate display of conspicuous consumption—almost literally burning money. This appears all the more excessive as camphor is totally destroyed, and rapidly so, in burning. It would appear that no other culture regularly burned quantities of camphor as a lamp fuel; thus what seems like a routine use of camphor in a Hindu context today stands out as a strange and extravagant innovation within a global historical context.[19]

These extravagant camphor lamps were evidently highly esteemed, as we see in the following passage taken from a seventeenth-century Sanskrit compendium of materials relating to *pūjā* rites: *The Elucidation of Pūjā* (*Pūjāprakāśa*) of Mitramiśra, part of an enormous digest on Hindu law (*dharmaśāstra*) and ritual called the *Vīramitrodaya* (Mitramiśra 1987).[20] The text here describes the nature and merits of the rite, known today as *āratī*, that involves waving a camphor flame before a sacred image:

> And one who performs *ārātrika*, flaming, with many wicks over Keśava [Viṣṇu or Kṛṣṇa] may dwell in heaven for ten million *kalpas*.[21]
> And the one who sees *nīrājanam* of the god of gods who has the discus may become a Brahmin for seven births and at the end [attain] the supreme state.
> And the one who with devotion performs *ārātrika* at the head of Keśava with camphor, oh best of sages, may attain imperishable Viṣṇu. (Mitramiśra 1987, 87)

Here *ārātrika* and *nīrājanam* are used as synonyms for this flame-waving rite. The latter term, *nīrājanam* is found in early (first millennium CE) texts and appears to refer to a rite of protection (often related to horses and weapons) associated with assuring victory. This rite sometimes involved fire and light and also protected against the evil eye (Losch 1951). The above passage also seems to imply that using camphor for this rite is just one option that ensures particular results, but that its use is not necessarily intrinsic to the rite. Presumably the camphor-lamp version of *āratī* was quite prestigious given the cost and rarity of camphor. Texts such as this that provide several options for rites permit greater flexibility in ritual and thus greater flexibility for religious institutions in accepting donations, great and small. On a similar note Gérard Colas suggests that the conceptual division of Vaikhānasa worship might in fact reflect and permit a more distributed funding of worship (Colas 1996, 318). Such complex opportunities for patronage could well have been desirable for donor and temple alike: by breaking down a larger rite into several parts, institutions created a situation where there were numerous possibilities for patronage, as well as a variety of patronage to suit every pocket: from a costly daily camphor lamp to a more affordable occasional ghee lamp.

Another text, not this time on *āratī* but on the lamps to be used in *pūjā* worship, presents a hierarchy of lamp fuels:

> And the one who with devotion performs *ārātrika* at the head of Keśava with camphor, oh best of sages! may attain imperishable Viṣṇu.
> And one who performs *ārātrika,* flaming, with many wicks over Keśava may dwell in heaven for ten million *kalpas*.
> One who gives a lamp with clarified butter to Śaṅkara [Śiva] or to Viṣṇu, being liberated from all evils, may attain the result of bathing in the Ganges.
> And a man, having given a lamp filled with sesame oil to Viṣṇu or Śaṅkara, attains all his desires, that best of men. (Mitramiśra 1987, 75)

As is clear there is some textual borrowing going on here, since the first two lines of this passage are also found in the previous text we considered. Here the lines we saw in the first passage are combined with two verses, giving an even greater number of choices for types of lamp, something typical of many of the other passages on lamps in this compilation. Again we see that camphor is one type of lamp among many, and apparently a rather prestigious one, for here we are told that offering this type of lamp permits the person offering it to attain/enter Viṣṇu himself.

A hierarchy of lamp fuels is not unique to this text, and in the *Mahābhārata* we are given more advice about which lamps to offer the gods. The passage in question is from a pre-camphor era and thus, unlike in the passages above, the superior material here is clarified butter (ghee). The lines are taken from a longer passage that also deals with flowers, incense, and food offerings. Although this passage on lamps does not deal explicitly with *pūjā* or *āratī* as we understand it in later Indian religious traditions (in fact, these practices are treated here as a type of ritual giving, *dāna*), nevertheless it gives us an idea of a very early hierarchy of fuels used in lamps:

> It [the lamp] is suitable with the oblation [clarified butter], and the second [best], with the liquids of herbs. It should not be made with the exudates of [animal] fat, marrow, or bone by one who desires prosperity. (*Mahābhārata* 13.101.51)

Clearly the most prestigious type of lamp uses clarified butter, which is referred to here by using a word implying its use in Vedic sacrifices. Not only is the offering of lamps in worship aligned with the orthodox practice of gift giving, but the very materials of worship reflect the material culture of Vedic religion, something that I have argued also applies to the flowers and incense as presented in this passage (McHugh 2008, 345–87). We are also told which fuels are inadvisable to use: fats from animals. Although this passage is older than the previous ones I have cited, we should not forget that this material remained in circulation in later times, possibly contributing to a complex of available theories concerning the material culture of lamps and lamp fuels in India.[22]

Several types of lamp fuels were thus available for offering to the gods in premodern South Asia, and these were in many cases evaluated hierarchically in texts that discuss the qualities of lamps. Camphor lamps are not mentioned in the earlier source we examined above, but they are mentioned in many later ones, as seen in *The Elucidation of Pūjā*. This hierarchy of lamps no doubt reflected an economic hierarchy of materials, from the more expensive camphor to the more commonplace ghee and plant oils. And of course, such an economic hierarchy of materials also had social consequences since the wealthy were better able to offer these religiously more meritorious types of lamps.

This is how lamps were represented in texts discussing rituals and donations, but what of inscriptional evidence? It is not possible in this chapter to examine the vast corpus of inscriptions available to us, so I will here focus only on some of the inscriptions collected from the temple at Tirupati (where the image of Veṅkateśvara has the famous camphor forehead-mark). This material is important to us here as it provides a dated actual use of camphor, allowing us to see how it was ideally used and also how valued it was.

An inscription dated probably 1013 CE, the first year of the reign of King Rājendra Choḷa I, is specifically about lamps. This inscription concerns an enquiry that revealed how a previous provision to provide lamps was being neglected, and that "as per the old document registered on stone, the *Sabhaiyār* of Tirumuṇḍiyam, a grant to this God, received money and undertook to light 24 lamps, including one light of camphor, but that the villagers of Tirumuṇḍiyam discontinued to burn all of them excepting the two lights which they still burn" (Sastry 1998a, 30). The king's officer who was conducting this enquiry ordered that the capital to provide these lamps be transferred to the temple treasury instead, where the priests would burn the lights, including one lit with camphor, "as long as the moon and the sun last" (Sastry 1998a, 31). We see here that the funding of lamps was serious business, no doubt involving significant expense, and that abuses required an investigation by the royal officer and a new stone inscription to record his verdict.[23] We see also that the camphor lamp was singled out as special and that there was only one such lamp, presumably as it was more costly to maintain. There is no mention here of *āratī*.

A later inscription, from 1468 CE, records the donation of the income from a certain village to supply a number of materials to the temple, including sandalwood paste, musk, rose water (a relatively new, rather Persianate, perfume product in South Asia), saffron, and two types of camphor: refined (*paccai*) and crude, the latter being for "*ālatti*" before the image in the temple (Sastry 1998b, 50–55). We might note here the reference to two types of camphor, the former being no doubt the more prestigious borneol camphor that is still used today to form the famous forehead-mark. The camphor that is burned in a rite, here specified as *āratī*, is no doubt a lower quality camphor, quite possibly one of the various other (Chinese? Distilled?) types that must have been available at that time.

Japanese Colonies, Celluloid, and Chemistry

In the early years of the twentieth century there was a revolution in the way camphor was produced. In 1845, the first synthetic plastic, cellulose nitrate, was discovered by a German Swiss chemist, and this was further developed by the English inventor Alexander Parkes who produced the new material *Parkesine*. In 1865 Parkes discovered that the addition of a quantity of camphor to this new material improved its plastic properties. Parkes's material was not a success, but his invention was taken up in America by the Hyatt brothers who also had difficulties with this material, primarily because it was unstable and inflammable: famously, early billiard balls made from this type of plastic would sometimes explode.[24] In 1870 John Wesley Hyatt refined the process of adding camphor to this material, and he trademarked this very successful product "Celluloid." Thus, in the final decades of the nineteenth century camphor found a new role in a rapidly expanding and lucrative plastics industry, which played a role in the history of film and photography.[25] Given the importance of camphor to the expanding plastics industry, huge quantities of this aromatic were now needed. So dramatically did the plastics industry transform camphor that Walter Durham, writing in 1932, reported estimates of world camphor consumption to be "80% in the manufacture of celluloid and film; 10% in medicine; 6% in Indian incense and religious ceremonies; 2% in gunpowder and smokeless fireworks; 2% in perfumes" (Durham 1932, 797).

At the very time that this new demand for camphor was rising (above and beyond the use of camphor in the pharmaceutical industry), the principal supplier of camphor was Japan and, most particularly, Taiwan, a Japanese colony at that time (Durham 1932). This lucrative Japanese monopoly on natural camphor, together with the massive demand for the material, led to a relatively short "life and death struggle" against a developing synthetic camphor industry in the first decade or so of the twentieth century.[26] The Japanese were extremely aggressive in maintaining their monopoly on Formosan camphor, so much so as to interfere with the French turpentine market in order to drive the manufacturers of synthetic camphor out of business. Nevertheless, synthetic camphor still had a future and, by the 1930s, synthetic camphor manufacturing had picked up again in America, led by the DuPont Company, which set up a plant in Deepwater, New Jersey.[27] Since then, synthetic camphor has been readily available, and it appears that the first Indian synthetic camphor manufacturing plant—Camphor and Allied Products Ltd.—was established around 1961, using technology from DuPont.[28]

But ultimately, why did this somewhat forgotten "camphor war" take place in the first place? In such a highly industrialized context as described above, the price of raw materials such as camphor is a major factor in the rate of profit. Marx explained that "as long as other circumstances are equal, the rate of profit falls or rises in the opposite direction to the price of the raw material. This shows, among other things, how important low raw material prices are for industrialized countries" (Marx 1981, 201). Thus for the manufacturers of these early plastics such as celluloid, the less they paid for camphor, the greater their profits.

This is not, however, what happened in Indian Hinduism in the twentieth century in the case of camphor. This can be attributed to the diversity of values at play in contemporary India. As Dipesh Chakrabarty has noted, we live in a plural "now," in "entangled times" (Chakrabarty 2008, 243). On one hand, synthetic camphor produced on an industrial scale was initially meant to supply the needs of a booming plastics and chemicals industry, and in the West, indeed, the cheaper the camphor, the better. Camphor was not perceived in the final product at all. The Hindu camphor market was quite different. Here the early significance of camphor had much to do with its rarity and preciousness. No doubt relatively small quantities were originally burned as an impressively extravagant and highly distinguished offering. The relatively high price of camphor maintained its prestige and also limited the quantity that could be burned. Superabundant and extremely cheap camphor, so vital to the profits of plastics manufacturers, had the disadvantage in the Hindu context of being both commonplace and polluting in excess. The

Hindu religious use-value for this material—originally closely related to its exclusivity and preciousness—was intimately connected to the early mode of camphor production (involving long-distance, global trade) in a premodern, preindustrial context. It is difficult therefore, but not impossible, to accommodate an industrial inflection of this material into more traditional practices and structures of significance. Now that camphor-as-institution has changed so radically, industrialists must either rely on other connotations of that material—properties that are not related to its vanished rarity and preciousness. In this case the Tamil camphor producers have even gone so far as to use an argument based on regionalism to make their case. In this complete turnaround, formerly exotic camphor is now articulated as a Tamil economic and industrial interest.

The title of this chapter alludes to Walter Benjamin's famous and eternally popular paper, "The Work of Art in the Age of Mechanical Reproduction" (Benjamin 2007). And here the reason I chose to invoke Benjamin's paper becomes fully apparent. The highly exploited "Formosan camphor" and contested synthetic camphor were indispensable in manufacturing the very celluloid that played such a vital role in the technologies of photography and film that Benjamin closely associates with the mass reproduction of art and theater. Without camphor there is no celluloid and no mass reproduction of images. Camphor, the exotic chemical oddity, aids and abets in the capitalist stripping of the auras and gets dragged along in the process, first in the Japanese colonies and then, once finally synthesized, in the factories of Europe and North America. But can a raw material lose an "aura"? I would argue that there is no aura to lose in such cases, but rather in being synthesized and manufactured on a mass scale, camphor does lose its associations with a certain manner of production and trade, as well as its (nowadays desirable) associations with "nature." From the point of view of medieval discourses, camphor loses its associations with remote lands/islands and voyages of trade.

Reduced in price, and freed from many of the previous economic constraints on access to this material, the possession and display of camphor lost its social prestige. Yet these same circumstances have no doubt increased the association of camphor with worship in South Asia compared to, say, the mid- to late-first millennium CE when, as we saw, this was an important but still minor material of worship. Now, camphor has become a ubiquitous and supposedly traditional smell of religion in South Asia, at least in Hindu contexts. These heightened religious associations of camphor might also have been strengthened by the changes in the sorts of perfumes used in India and among diaspora communities. To cite one example, Dempsey reports that in North America, as in India, camphor lamps have for the most part been replaced with oil and ghee lamps, yet one temple guru in upstate New York refuses to stop using this material "because its familiar blaze and smell evoke devotional emotions" (Dempsey 2006, 38–39). "Camphor" has not lost its aura; it has just changed. Formerly an exotic rarity and a quite special offering to the gods, camphor is now a commonplace olfactory icon of Hinduism.

Conclusion: From Borneo to Tamil Nadu, via New Jersey

For the Chola king who donated lamps to a temple, camphor was a very precious, exotic religious gift, a sign of status and no doubt a producer of merit that needed to be policed by the king's officers and documented in stone. At that time camphor was indeed rare and precious as well as white, perfumed, and burning with no trace. For the modern Hindu, camphor is one of the "smells of religion" and is traditional, if not terribly prestigious. As we saw at the very start of the chapter, Hindus are aware that camphor nowadays is not quite what it was; furthermore, in many temples it is banned for polluting and dirtying the temple, replaced instead with equally traditional ghee and oils. However, Tamil camphor manufacturers have a vested interest in presenting camphor as a Hindu tradition, and not only that but an important part of the local economy, such that for these industrialists it would not only be pious but also regionally loyal for the temples to worship using this latest, Indian manufactured, democratic avatar of the precious, perfumed, white crystals from Sumatra and Borneo.

Notes

1. A version of this article appeared in the journal *Material Religion* 10.1 (2014).

2. I refer here especially to Latour 1999, but I should note that in this book Latour is, as he admits, indebted to the process philosophy found in the work of Alfred North Whitehead, which he combines with a pragmatic, nonfoundationalist epistemology derived ultimately from William James.

3. "Camphor Manufacturers' Plea to Govt," *The Hindu*, August 13, 2004, http://www.thehindu.com/2004/08/13/stories/2004081317360300.htm.

4. See also Appadurai 1986, Latour 2005, and Gell 1998.

5. That is to say, pharmacological literature in Sanskrit tends to reflect the material culture of the period more accurately than the idealized world of poetics and liturgy. For example, the perfumery material civet crops up in Sanskrit pharmacological texts in the second millennium CE, but this perfume never enters the olfactory worlds described in Sanskrit poetry.

6. I base the following brief account of camphor on that given in Donkin 1999, Ch. 2.

7. On the dating of camphor in India see Donkin 1999, Ch. 3 and also Sternbach 1974, 436–39. On the earliest camphor in Barus and other parts of Southeast Asia see Guillot 2003, Ch. 2; Nouha 1998; and Ptak 1998.

8. On the fascination with and prestige of exotic materials in medieval India see McHugh 2011a. Donkin has summarized many such references in Donkin 1999, 94. Also see Sternbach 1974, 462–64.

9. Chopra provides a very detailed account of camphor production and imports in India in the early- to mid-twentieth century. Chopra 1958, 120–24.

10. Ibid. 124.

11. For a detailed treatment of the history of indigo in colonial India see Pouchepadass 1999.

12. Fortunately for us, the scholar Sternbach wrote a very thorough, almost exhaustive, article in which he collected all manner of references to camphor in Indic, mainly Sanskrit, texts (Sternbach 1974).

13. Menthol appears to have somewhat taken the place of camphor in modern betel flavoring.

14. Donkin 1999 discusses the many historical uses of camphor.

15. For example, the seventh-century CE poet Bāṇa describes a gift of camphor, part of a larger tribute to king Harṣa, as "bright-white and chilly like a splinter of a slab of frost" (. . . *tuṣāraśilāśakalaśiśirasvacchasitasya ca karpūrasya,"* (Bāṇa 1909, 291–93)).

16. Other synonyms for camphor are "cloud" (*ghanasāra*) and similar terms, in addition to "frost" (*hima*) and similar terms. See Sternbach 1974, 427–35.

17. "*paccakarpūra*."

18. I am extremely grateful to Dr. A. V. Ramana Dikshitulu, Pradhana Archaka and Agama Advisor, T. T. Devasthanams, Tirumala for explaining to me the composition and weekly preparation of the *namam* of Lord Venkateśvara in a personal interview, June 12, 2010.

19. Donkin notes that camphor has been used as a fumigant and incense, and in fireworks. One text notes that it burns when floating on water but here this is presented as a marvelous novelty, not a regular sort of lamp. See Donkin 1999, 141, 161, 31.

20. For a detailed discussion of the *Vīramitrodaya* see Kane 1975, 941–53.

21. A *kalpa* is one thousand *yugas* or 432 million human years.

22. This is not the place to discuss all sources dealing with lamps, which would also include compendiums on gift giving, and encyclopedic texts.

23. The editor notes that the earlier inscriptions in the temple often focus on religious gifts in the form of lamp lighting (Sastry 1998a, 89).

24. I am grateful to Professor Robert Travers of Cornell University for discussing the history of billiards with me.

25. I base my account here on the excellent discussions of this subject in Williamson 1994, and Mossman 1994. Another good account of the history of celluloid that also provides many details concerning the introduction of camphor technology is Kaufman 1963.

26. As reported in an excellent (and seemingly anonymous) article on this matter, "Camphor, Natural and Synthetic," *The Journal of the American Medical Association* 65.18 (1915): 1555–56.

27. Gubelmann and Elley provide a very detailed account of the economics of camphor, natural and synthetic, up to 1933. Of course shortly after this time American relations with Japan were to change (Gubelmann and Elley 1934).

28. Unfortunately I have not been able to conduct archival research in India on synthetic camphor but have had to reply instead on the website of a prominent camphor manufacturer. "Welcome to Camphor & Allied Products Ltd," http://www.camphor-allied.com/home.html (accessed March 31, 2011).

References

Appadurai, Arjun, ed. 2003. *The Social Life of Things: Commodities in Cultural Perspective*. Cambridge: Cambridge University Press.

Peter C. Ashlee. "The Bogus Butterfly Collector, Camphor and the Early Plastics Industry." *Plastiquarian* 7 (1991): 14–15.

Bāṇa. 1909. *Bāṇabhaṭṭa's Biography of King Harshavardhana of Sthāṇvīśvara with Śaṅkara's Commentary, Saṅketa*, edited by A. A. Führer. *Bombay Sanskrit and Prakrit Series*, no. 66. Bombay: Government Central Press.

Benjamin, Walter. 2007 (1955). "The Work of Art in the Age of Mechanical Reproduction." In *Illuminations, Essays and Reflections*, 217–51. New York: Schocken Books.

"Camphor Manufacturers' Plea to Govt." *The Hindu*. August 13, 2004. http://www.thehindu.com/2004/08/13/stories/2004081317360300.htm.

"Camphor, Natural and Synthetic." *The Journal of the American Medical Association* 65.18 (1915): 1555–56.

Chakrabarty, Dipesh. 2008 (2000). *Provincializing Europe: Postcolonial Thought and Historical Difference*. Reissue, with a new preface by the author. Princeton, NJ: Princeton University Press.

Chopra, R. N. 1958. *Indigenous Drugs of India*. Calcutta: Dhur.

Colas, Gérard. 1996. *Viṣṇu, ses images et ses feux*. Paris: Presses de l'École Française d'Extrême-Orient.

Dempsey, Corinne. 2006. *The Goddess Lives in Upstate New York: Breaking Convention and Making Home at a North American Hindu Temple*. Oxford, New York: Oxford University Press.

Donkin, R. A., 1999. *Dragon's Brain Perfume: An Historical Geography of Camphor*. Leiden: Brill.

Durham, Walter A. 1932. "The Japanese Camphor Monopoly: Its History and Relation to the Future of Japan," *Pacific Affairs* 5.9: 797–801.

Fuller, Christopher, J. 1992. *The Camphor Flame: Popular Hinduism and Society in India*. Princeton, NJ: Princeton University Press.

Gell, Alfred. 1998. *Art and Agency: An Anthropological Theory*. Oxford: Clarendon Press.

Gubelmann, I., and H. W. Elley. 1934. "American Production of Synthetic Camphor from Turpentine." *Industrial and Engineering Chemistry* 26.6: 589–94.

Guillot, Claude, ed. 2003. *Histoire de Barus, Sumatra: le site de Lobu Tua; II: Étude archéologique et documents*. Paris: Cahier d'Archipel 30.

Hara, Minoru. 2010. "A Note on Sanskrit Gandha." In *Studia Orientalia* 108, *Anantaṃ Śāstram: Indological and Linguistic Studies in Honour of Bertil Tikkanen*, edited by Klaus Karttunen, 65–86. Helsinki: Finnish Oriental Society.

Kane, P. V. 1975. *History of Dharmaśāstra (Ancient and Mediaeval Religious and Civil Law in India)* vol. 1, part II, 2nd ed. Poona: Bhandarkar Oriental Research Institute.

Kaufman, M. 1963. *The First Century of Plastics: Celluloid and Its Sequel*. London: The Plastics Institute.

Kopytoff, Igor. 1986. "The Cultural Biography of Things: Commoditization as Process." In *The Social Life of Things: Commodities in Cultural Perspective*, edited by Arjun Appadurai, 64–91. Cambridge: Cambridge University Press.

Latour, Bruno. 1999. *Pandora's Hope: Essays on the Reality of Science Studies*. Cambridge, MA: Harvard University Press.

———. 2005. *Reassambling the Social: An Introduction to Actor Network Theory*. Oxford: Oxford University Press.

Losch, Hans. 1951. "Nīrājanā," in *Beiträge zur indischen Philologie und Altertumskunde 7, Walther Schubring zum 70. Geburtstag dargebracht von der deutschen Indologie*, 51–58. Hamburg: Cram. de Gruyter & Co.

Marx, Karl. 1981 (1894) *Capital, A Critique of Political Economy, Volume Three*, trans. David Fernbach. New York: Vintage Books.

The Mahābhārata for the first time critically edited by Vishnu S. Sukthankar [and others] illustrated from ancient models by Shrimant Balasaheb Pant Pratinidhi. Poona: Bhandarkar Oriental Research Institute, 1933.

McHugh, James. 2008. *Sandalwood and Carrion: Smell in South Asian Culture and Religion*. PhD diss. Harvard University.

McHugh, James. 2011a. "The Incense Trees of the Land of Emeralds: the Exotic Material Culture of *Kāmaśāstra*," *The Journal of Indian Philosophy* 39.1: 63–100.

McHugh, James. 2011b. "Seeing Scents: Methodological Reflections on the Intersensory Perception of Aromatics in South Asian Religions." *History of Religions* 51.2: 156–157.

Mitramiśra. 1987 (1913). *Vīramitrodaya*, vol. 4: *Pūjāprakāśaḥ*. *Chowkhamba Sanskrit Series* 30. Benares: Chowkhamba Sanskrit Book Depot.

———. 1994. "Parkesine and Celluloid." In *The Development of Plastics*, edited by S. T. I. Mossman and P. J. T. Morris, 10–25. Cambridge, UK: Royal Society of Chemistry.

Naraharipaṇḍita. 1927. *Rājanighaṇṭusahito Dhanvantarīyanighaṇṭuḥ*, Ānandāśrama saṃskṛtagranthāvaliḥ, 33. 2nd ed. Pune: Anandasrama Press.

"Natural versus Synthetic Camphor." *The Journal of the American Medical Association* 78.11 (1922), 830–31.

Nouha, Stephan. 1998. "Le camphre dans les sources arabes et persanes: production et usages." In *Histoire de Barus, Sumatra: le site de Lobu Tua; I: etudes et documents*, edited by Claude Guillot, 225–41. Paris: Cahier d'Archipel 30.

Pouchepadass, Jacques. 1999. *Champaran and Gandhi: Planters, Peasants and Gandhian Politics,* translated by James Walker. New Delhi: Oxford University Press.

Ptak, Roderich. 1998. "Possible Chinese References to the Barus Area (Tang to Ming)." In *Histoire de Barus, Sumatra: le site de Lobu Tua; I: etudes et documents,* edited by Claude Guillot, 119–47. Paris: Cahier d'Archipel 30.

Raja, Bhoja. 1974. *Cārucaryā, A Medieval Work on Personal Hygiene.* Hyderabad: Indian Institute of the History of Medicine.

Sastry, Sadhu Subrahanya. 1998a. *Tirumala Tirupati Devasthanams Inscriptions Vol. 1: Early Inscriptions Translated and Edited with Introductions.* Tirupati: Tirumala Tirupati Devasthanams.

Sastry, Sadhu Subrahmanya. trans. 1988b. and V. Vijaya Raghavacharya. *Tirumala Tirupati Devasthanams Inscriptions Vol. 2: Inscriptions of Saluva Narasimha's Time from 1445 A.D. to 1504 A.D.* Tirupati: Tirumala Tirupati Devasthanams.

Sternbach, Ludwik. 1974. "Camphor in India." In *Vishveshvaranand Indological Journal* vol. 54, *Acharya Dr. Vishva Bandhu Commemoration Volume,* edited by B. R. Sharma, 425–67. Hoshiarpur: Vishveshvaranand Vishva Bandhu Institute of Sanskrit and Indological Studies.

Williamson, C. J. 1994. "Victorian Plastics—Foundations of an Industry." In *The Development of Plastics,* edited by S. T. I. Mossman and P. J. T. Morris, 1–9. Cambridge, UK: Royal Society of Chemistry.

7

Metal Hands, Cotton Threads, and Color Flags

Materializing Islamic Devotion in South India

AFSAR MOHAMMAD

Introduction

IMAM: What is the purpose of using a metal object for the *pīr*? How do you see this object?

SATTAR SAHEB: We need certain objects to keep our memory fresh. For us, worship begins with a material symbol and then extends into deeper aspects of Islam. For me, even a mosque is a symbol, and everything in a mosque is symbolic. In a mosque we have *qibla*, we have the book, and do you know how many people actually can read it? Similarly we have incense sticks, we have the rosary. Similarly, we have Muharram images, and we give different names to them that keep their memory alive—naming gives them a life, a great life!

IMAM: Do you think these symbols make your prayer or devotion perfect?

SATTAR SAHEB: It depends. But, having a symbol before you helps you to focus on the goal of devotion. You know, in devotion, one should become '*fana*' which means you should feel united with your God or saint. If not, it is no devotion at all.

This excerpt is from a conversation that took place between a sixty-year-old Muslim man, Sattar Saheb, and Jaffer Sharif, a local *imam* in Gūgūḍu, a pilgrimage center in the South Indian state of Andhra Pradesh. In 2007, I was in Gūgūḍu to document various public ritual performances of Muharram, the Muslim New Year event that commemorates the martyrdom of the grandsons of the Prophet Muhammad at Karbala. Since Sattar Saheb was also a regular mosque-going Muslim, the local *imam* questioned him about the use of these material objects in Muslim worship that, to the *imam,* are un-Islamic. Responding to the *imam* in Urdu, Sattar Saheb tried to explain his perception of religious objects: "No these are not mere objects; these are the *mark*s of the memories that take us back to the historic battle of Karbala, reminding us of the value of our community. Yes, some devotees worship these symbols; you see, very few 'real' Muslims just come here to perform the recital of the first verse of the Quran. Whatever way it is done, *ibādat* is *ibādat* (worship is worship), and this entire tradition is a crucial part of our life."

In his emphatic use of the term "mark" to indicate various objects used in local-specific Muslim public events, Sattar Saheb was not exceptional. Several communities that include both Muslims and non-Muslims clearly recognize these "marks" as objects of piety that transmit the "real presence" of the divine. When devotees use this religious vocabulary, they are actually evoking a broad set of historical and religious associations with specific practices that encompass a variety of local devotional agencies and networks—in this case, a blending of Hindu and Muslim sainthood traditions.

In 2006, during my stay in Gūgūḍu, the local *imam* Jaffer Sherif frequently tried to explain to me that official or normative Islam strictly prohibits all use of material objects in devotion. Most of the time he supported this assertion by reading various verses from the Quran and numerous "official" interpretations of Islam that condemn the practice of object-worship. However, the use of material objects in Islamic devotion is pervasive throughout South Asia, where numerous well-known public rituals feature the use of material objects like battle standards, flags, rags, cradles, and sacred threads. This chapter explores the multiple uses and meanings of ritual objects in four contexts: within the ritual settings of Muharram and *'urs,* and in the ritual practices of *faqīri* and offerings of rags, flags, and cradles. Muharram and *'urs* are scheduled ritual events, while *faqīri* and offerings of flags, rags, and cradles are more diffuse material practices.

Muharram occurs during the first ten days of the month of Muharram, when Shi'a Muslims commemorate the sixth-century battle of Karbala through fasting and mourning rituals. The public performance of Muharram features metal objects that represent battle standards of Muslim martyrs and members of the Prophet's family, most importantly his grandsons Hasan and Husain, who were killed on the battlefield of Karbala. These battle standards are called *'alams* in Urdu and *pīrs* in Telugu. The battle of Karbala is pivotal in the historical memory of Shi'i Islam, marking its rise as a distinctive Islamic sect that took the side of 'Ali in the dispute over the legacy of the Prophet.[1] Each year in the month of Muharram, the Shi'a remember the martyrs of Karbala and observe various mourning rituals for ten days as signs of religious identity and sectarian devotion. Muharram has become a public event memorializing each aspect of the battle of Karbala with theatrical imagery and in a ritual setting.[2]

Faqīri is primarily a ritual practice involving the wearing of red or red and yellow silky cotton-woven threads around the shoulder or wrist during the first few days of Muharram. Devotees don these threads on the first day of Muharram after performing a prayer ritual at the *pīr*-house, the shrine that marks the final resting place of a Sufi saint or, as locally known, a *pīr*. *Faqīri* is considered to be a temporary ascetic practice that devotees observe to refashion their life following the example of a local Sufi saint or a member of the family of the Prophet (Mohammad 2010, 145). When a devotee wears a *faqīri* thread, he is supposed to follow strictly the devotional path that is exemplified by the saint upon whom he is modeling his behavior.

Many Sufi shrines have been built on martyr-saints' relics, worldly items such as staffs, swords, and bowls used by those who lived and died on the battlefield fighting for their local community. The practices performed at these Sufi shrines also include the display and offering of devotional objects such as green and red flags, rags, and cradles (Flueckiger 2006, 223–32; Saheb 1998, 55–76). When devotees or pilgrims visit these shrines for the first time, they often tie a rag to a branch of the tree, which is always present at a Sufi shrine, as part of a votive request to the saint. On their second visit they offer a green flag or a model cradle as a sign that the request was fulfilled. They continue to perform flag offerings and make gifts of model cradles at set times throughout their life. Performing these ritual offerings becomes a significant part of devotees' lives, reminding them of their commitment to the devotional path shown by the *pīr*.

Practices of wearing sacred threads and making votive offerings also occur during *'urs*. *'Urs* refers to the annual death commemoration ceremonies of Sufi saints, when relics are displayed. Like the practice of offering rags, flags, and cradles described above, *'urs* also involves votive rites that devotees observe in return for a saint's fulfillment of their wishes.

For example, each year tens of thousands of devotees visit the shrines of two saints, Saida (at Jan Pahad) and Baba Fakhruddin (at Penukonda). At the end of their pilgrimage to these shrines, devotees offer green and red flags and cradles in return for their wish fulfillment. Though not all flag festivals are part of *'urs*, it is not uncommon to use flags during *'urs* as a marker of the memory of a saint. I will explore these examples below.

The deployment of religious objects in these devotional contexts, I argue, functions to help generate new narratives and ritual practices that then proliferate among South Indian Muslim communities and continue to evolve over time. The use of these objects in Islamic ritual also helps produce and sustain varied and fluid understandings of *ibādat* (worship), *īmān* (faith), and *niyyat* (pure intention), three important religious categories recognized by local Muslims and non-Muslims alike. Ultimately, I would argue that material objects play a critical role in the making of local Islamic devotion and facilitate the construction of a locally produced religious knowledge.

Severed Heads Speak Out: Displaying Metal Hands and Heads in a Public Ritual

During the first ten days of the month of Muharram, both Muslim and non-Muslim performers in South India retell and reenact the entire story of the martyrdom of the Prophet's grandsons.[3] Historically, this event marks a split between Sunni and Shi'i Muslims while clearly representing the distinctive identity of Shi'i Islam. Throughout Muharram, metal hands and heads, symbolic representations of the family members of the Prophet, play a central role in prompting performers to imagine the "real" presence of the entire family of the Prophet (Mohammad 2011, 173–96). These material symbols—or, as some devotees call them "metal gods"—become the objects of active piety and actually function as relics. They are richly decorated following the traditions of Shi'i Islam and are taken out in procession during Muharram.

Many Shi'i Muslims narrate the story of these metal battle standards in a traditional mode, stressing the historical details of the battle of Karbala. However, many stories popular among both Muslims and non-Muslims in South Asia offer locally produced narratives that emphasize the value of honoring the battle standards in ritual as a sign of one's devotion to the family of the Prophet. These objects thus become agents, inspiring the production of a new story of the battle of Karbala that, in turn, generates a new repertoire of devotional practices that actively promote image worship.

Figure 7.1. The Metal Battle Standards of the Martyrs. Photo by Afsar Mohammad.

A local story that I collected in the village of Vīrla Palle in the state of Andhra Pradesh traces the ritual of making metal objects into symbols of martyrdom back to Fatima, mother of the martyrs Hasan and Husain. According to the normative Shi'i story of Karbala, both Fatima and Hasan were already dead at the time of the battle (Momen, 1985). However, the local story describes how Fatima took on a central role in the battle while Hasan and Husain, who fought together against their enemy Yazeed, were martyred. After the death of her sons, Fatima collected their severed heads and body parts to display in public and as a means of gathering together the local community in an act of collective mourning. This local story reimagines the entire history of Karbala and attributes special ritual authority to Fatima. Many individuals familiar with this narrative also claim that the metal hands or heads used annually during Muharram commemorations were designed and modeled after the body parts that Fatima gathered on the battlefield. This claim makes these metal battle standards fall under the category of relics which is also acceptable to many groups of "*asli Islam*." While normative Muslim stories about the battle at Karbala highlight the martyrdom of Husain, numerous local variants center on the suffering of Fatima. This theme is evident in an excerpt from a song I collected in Vīrla Palle:

Mother Fatima brought out the severed heads
And made them public for the first time.
She dressed them up in new clothes
She put Husain's head on one dome
She put Hasan's head on another dome
And started telling the story of their martyrdom.

The severed heads of the martyrs are represented during Muharram by battle standards, which are prepared in precious metals and installed for rituals at memorial sites, called *pīr*-houses, which are built exclusively for their installation. These battle standards are taken out in procession on the seventh and tenth days of Muharram. The above excerpt refers to three ritual acts prominent in Muharram performances: bringing out the replicas of the severed heads, dressing them in new clothes, and garlanding them with flowers. Since these three ritual acts are central to Muharram performances, large segments of local communities participate actively in them.

Muharram narratives that I collected from the village of Gūgūḍu interpret these metal battle standards in an entirely different way. In Gūgūḍu, the battle standards are said to represent a local saint called Kuḷḷāyappa as well as the martyrs of Karbala. One narrative from Gūgūḍu recounts how, eight centuries ago, two goldsmith brothers yearned for fame, so they decided to make an incredible artifact blending all kinds of precious metals. However, they could not figure out what to make. Finally, an appropriate object appeared to them in their dreams. The *pīr* Kuḷḷāyappa appeared to them as well, asking them to install this artifact at the center of the village. In local Muslim stories, dreams are often moments of intercession by God or a *pīr*. Interpretations of these dreams typically provide resolutions to long-standing searches for material or spiritual needs. In this story, resolution comes through the creation of a beautiful metal battle standard. At first, the goldsmith brothers fail to value the sacred nature of this object, and they throw it into an old well in their village to avoid its magical powers. The village subsequently burns down, according to local legend, "due to an impure handling of the object" (Mohammad 2010, 157–88). According to the place legend of this village, these goldsmith brothers and other villagers do not realize the true importance of these objects until Kuḷḷāyappa appears to them and asks them to take care of these objects.

In Gūgūḍu, the making of these battle standards is connected to a specific caste of goldsmiths, the caste to which the goldsmith brothers in the local place legend belonged. This story reveals the importance of sacred objects and the necessity of handling them with what this caste group describes as a "pure mind and heart." This caste group is said to have vied with other artisan groups during the premodern period in Andhra Pradesh to produce the best devotional image representing Kuḷḷāyappa. The making of these standards amounts to what Kenneth George calls a "visual *dhikr*," representing "a mindfulness of god while creating an aesthetic object of god" (George 2008, 172–93). During the entire process of preparing these objects, the artisans are expected to utter the name of God or, in this case, the local saint, Kuḷḷāyappa. Tirupatayya, heir to generations of metalworkers associated with Kullayappa in Gūgūdu, including the errant metal workers of legend just mentioned, spoke of the religious import of his work. For him, the errant goldsmith brothers stand as a lesson to the rest that they must perform their craft with reverence. If not, they risk incurring the wrath of Kullayappa that once brought the village down. Recalling lessons learned from the past, Tirupatayya put it like this: "If you stop reciting, you're a failure. Also, it's not just reciting, you recite with the *niyyatu*, the pure devotion to the *pīr*. You can't hold the divine force of this object; that's what happened with my ancestors. Since they didn't know what *niyyatu* is or how to hold this divine object, they threw it away into an old well."

The active role of these metal standards comes to the fore when storytellers actually "see" and "feel" the presence of various *pīrs* during their performance of the story of Hasan's death on the battlefield of Karbala. Every evening, metal battle standards are taken out of the *pīr*-house for an evening procession. During Muharram, there can be no storytelling or ritual without a fire, so both Muslim and Hindu devotees gather huge logs from surrounding neighborhoods and prepare a fire in a fire-pit, known as *ālāvā* in Urdu, or *ālāvā gunḍam* and *nippu gunḍam* in Telugu. After the fire has been lit, a group of performers join their hands forming a circle around it.

As the battle standards are taken out and processed, the group recounts the story of Hasan's martyrdom, a story that will soon engulf them in a flood of sorrow, pathos, and tears.

Both performers and devotees believe that the various *pīrs* visit them during this ritual narration and procession (Figure 7.2). Many villages and towns in Andhra Pradesh engage in some fashion in this ritual performance, known popularly in Telugu and Deccani Urdu as *aśsey dūlā* (the bridegroom from Husain's family).

Red and Yellow Sacred Threads: The Transmission of Islamic Knowledge and Ritual Practices

During the death anniversaries (*'urs*) of Muslim saints and the commemorative events that take place on the seventh and tenth day of

Figure 7.2. Metal battle standards in a procession. Photo by Afsar Mohammad.

Muharram, the most visible ritual objects are red and yellow silk threads with a silver strand running through them.[4] Most Muslim shrines, called *dargāhs* or *pīr*-houses, are busy on Thursdays and Fridays, as these are popular days for pilgrims and devotees to visit and perform rituals such as *ziyārā* (the visitation), when devotees visit the shrines or graves of the local saints. The ritual practice of *faqīri*, the tying of red and yellow sacred threads, is reserved exclusively for annual days of commemoration for the Muslim saints or martyrs honored at these shrines during the month of Muharram. On the seventh day of Muharram, devotees who visit the shrine tie this thread either on their wrists or across their shoulders and then start observing a ritual fast.

Concerning the dynamics between the public event of Muharram and the practice of *faqīri*, Khaja Hussein, a Muslim pilgrim, said:

> For me the red and yellow thread is just a symbol of Karbala martyrdom. It reminds me of all those tragic events and

> moments and their sufferings. When you remember their martyrdom, you cannot eat food or even drink water. As a Muslim, I never forget those tragic moments in the Prophet's family. They are all etched onto my memory forever. For a Muslim, *zikr* (remembering the name of God) is itself a reminder. Though I never use a rosary, I would never forget *zikr*. For us Muslims, *zikr* is an integral part of everyday life. When you observe *tahārā*, when you go to mosque, and when you recite *fāteha*, every time you do *zikr*. But Muharram is different. It's the memory of the martyrdom. I wear the red sacred thread to remember the martyrs and to feel their presence in my body.

Khaja Hussein emphasizes values such as *zikr*, the remembering of exemplary Muslims, and the idea of purity in the everyday life of Muslims; according to him, all these aspects blend together in the practice of the *faqīri*.

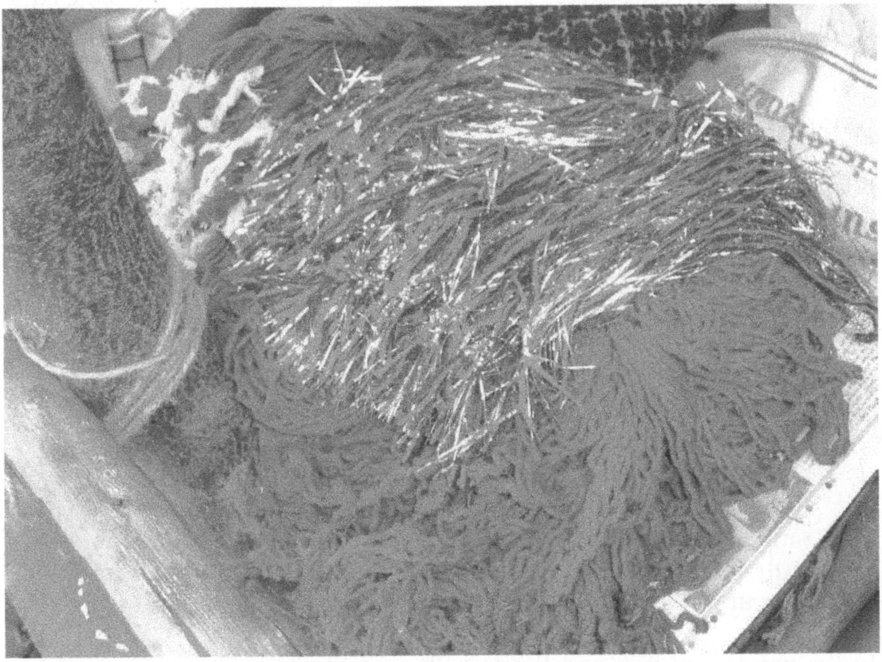

Figure 7.3. Red sacred threads for sale. Photo by Afsar Mohammad.

In another local narrative that I documented during my field research, these threads symbolize the innards of the martyrs of Karbala. As described by Mallayya, a lower-caste non-Muslim who performs storytelling sessions of the martyrs during the month of Muharram,

> Somehow we are now missing one aspect in my story. Actually the story I heard from my grandfather also tells that Fatima, the mother of the martyrs, brought the innards from the battlefield. As each body part of the martyrs began to turn into a symbol such as we see today in any metal battle standards, the innards turned into red threads. They are red because they were full of blood. When we wear this red thread, we make a pledge that we are always with them and will never allow them to be murdered by the enemies. These threads drenched in the blood of the martyrs teach us their love for the community and the ethics by which they lived.

Mallayya's words resonate with many pilgrims and devotees who visit *pīr*-houses during the month of Muharram. Most importantly, they explain the intricate process of how the body of the martyr translates into a material object and then a marker for individual and communal values.

Wearing a red sacred thread is a common practice among Muslims and Hindu pilgrims alike. However, Muslims wear these red threads reciting the *fāteha*, the first verse in the Quran, while Hindus visit a local *pīr*-house or *dargah* and make the local Muslim ritualist (*muzāvar*) recite the *fāteha* for them. All other practices around this ritual vow are the same for Muslims and Hindus.

In Hinduism, the ritual of tying a sacred thread is of central importance to Brahmin males for whom the rite signifies the coming of age. The sacred thread, as Raymond Williams describes it,

> remains a symbol of the transmission of religious tradition through the stream of generations. Possession of a sacred thread admits the young person to the storehouse of ancient wisdom through the study of sacred texts, participation in rituals of home and temple, and acquaintance with learned saints and teachers. Thus, it is thought, a boy becomes a man with a solid identity, a clear focus on a definite tradition, and a secure place in a community. (Williams 1996, 3)

In the practice of wearing the *faqīri* thread likewise, some Hindu devotees ascribe the same importance to the red thread, also perceived as a marker of their entry into adulthood, a phase defined locally as a life-changing moment when a person is expected to follow devotional acts with maturity. Many Hindu caste groups moreover consider the ritual vow of *faqīri* to be a sign of temporary asceticism. For lower caste groups that converted to Vaishnavism during the *bhakti* movement in Andhra Pradesh, this practice is especially significant. Narrating his family history connected with the wearing of the red sacred thread, Venkata Chalapati Rayalu, a local priest in a Vishnu temple, explained to me, "Though we are called Vaiṣṇavas, we are never allowed to wear the Brahminical sacred thread. Now wearing this red sacred thread gives us that authority to participate in the pure realm of asceticism."

From the time they visit the *pīr*-house to the moment they don the thread, devotees take care to keep themselves clean and pure as described in any Islamic *tahārā* practice. "If you're not clean and pure, your thread will not work," said Narsimhulu, a fifty-year-old Dalit devotee who has been performing the *faqīri* vow since his thirteenth year. Narsimhulu's annual *faqīri* ritual begins on the first day of Muharram. He prepares his own thread by interweaving red, green, and silver threads with it, whereas many other devotees purchase ready-made threads available in the market during this month. As Narsimhulu described it to me,

> This is a vow. It's not just about wearing some red thread. For me, it's a tradition that I want to continue through several generations in our family. So I want every family member in our family to prepare their own thread. The time and work that you put into this preparation is also a crucial part of the *faqīri*, which would remain incomplete if you're not making your own thread.

Due to heavy commercialization today, for many families who live by their handloom works, the production and sales of these threads has become a source of income. As Narsimhulu told me, "when something involves money, it won't remain a pure thing, and if it's not pure, it's not *faqīri*."

Rags, Flags, and Cradles: Bringing a Wish to Fulfillment

Each year 700,000 devotees visit the shrine of Jan Pahad Saida in the district of Nalgonda. A local story narrates that about four centuries ago, a Sufi saint called Saida and his disciples were martyred at this site. Each January to commemorate the *'urs* death anniversary, tens of thousands of devotees carrying green flags and model cradles throng the shrine and pay respects to the martyr-saints. When I asked a devotee about these different objects, she told me, "A rag is just a wish. A flag is a sign of wish fulfillment, and a model cradle is particularly for those whose wish to have a baby granted by the saint." For this devotee, a visit to the shrine was a journey that brought a wish to fulfillment.

Each January, to commemorate the *'urs* death anniversary, tens of thousands of devotees carrying green flags and model cradles throng the shrine and pay respects to Saida and his disciples. The key concepts of the *'urs* are expressed mainly through these objects, particularly the green flags. Along these lines, some devotees' narratives describe how Saida visits them in the form of a material object such as a blooming flower, a red and green cloth, or a well-decorated little cradle. During a night vigil at the Jan Pahad *dargāh*, when devotees spend three nights at the shrine to secure the saint's attention, I heard several dream stories from female devotees who were visiting Jan Pahad to make practical and personal requests. They told me that the *pīr* reappeared in their dreams to remind them to bring standard offerings like an embroidered blanket, a green flag, or a well-decorated model cradle. During the three-day *'urs*, the trees around this shrine looked vibrant with color thanks to the many model cradles hung on their branches.

Whereas shrines such as the Jan Pahad *dargāh* articulate a version of popular Islam, the Sufi shrine at Penukonda honoring a twelfth-century Sufi saint named Baba Fakhruddin blends aspects of both classical and popular Sufism. The material relics such as the holy staff of Baba Fakhruddin attract devotees and pilgrims both from within India and from far off places, including the United States, Sri Lanka, Malaysia, and Singapore. Thousands of Muslims and Hindus who participate in common rituals, particularly on Thursdays or Fridays and in the annual commemorative ceremony of the saint in May or June, try to emulate the teachings of Baba Fakhruddin by remembering his stories and practices. Nevertheless, we also find devotees and pilgrims who perform typical *dargāh*-related rituals such as tying rags and gifting green flags. In addition to these rituals, devotees also bring with them locks that they secure to the doors of the shrine, petitioning the *pīr* to relieve them of their psychological ailments. As explained by one devotee, petitioners believe that these locks "help in locking up the evil powers so they won't possess their bodies and mind, and this ritual offers relief as a blessing from the *pīr*."

One of the devotees I encountered at this site was forty-year-old Rasheeda, the mother of a teenage daughter, Fatima, who was suffering from an unknown psychological disorder. Rasheeda consulted several doctors and visited many places searching for a cure as she was planning to get her daughter married. Nothing worked, and finally she visited Penukonda. Like other female devotees, she brought a lock with her and secured it to one of the metal frames surrounding the tomb of the saint. Rasheeda said, "I started my *ziyārā* in 2005 and soon I could see it is working. By the end of that year we got Fatima married. From then onwards, our family made an obligatory annual pilgrimage to every *'urs*." Many devotees tell similar stories while narrating their experiences of pilgrimage to the shrine of Penukonda.

The hagiography of Baba Fakhruddin describes many material objects that manifest Baba's miraculous powers (*karāmat*), culminating in an episode when Baba plants a twig of a *neem* tree.[5] This twig subsequently is said to grow into a huge tree that is now a popular ritual site at the shrine of Penukonda. Devotees gather and submit their petitions to the saint by tying a rag to the tree or sharing sacred food, in this case sugar. It was said that, until recently, one of these trees used to rain sugar as a material sign of the pure blessing bestowed by Baba at this site. Devotees also venerate a holy, twelve-foot-long staff that Baba allegedly used to resurrect a cow as a sign of his miraculous abilities. Devotees who visit the shrine with a vow request often cleanse this staff ritually with water. If any devotee has their wish fulfilled after performing this ritual, he or she is considered to have been blessed directly by Baba.

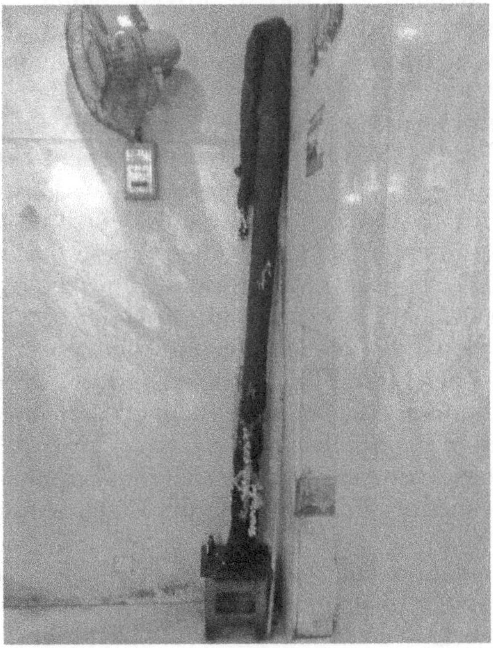

Figure 7.4. Holy staff displayed inside the *dargah* of the Baba Fakhruddin. Photo courtesy of Ashfaq Ahmad.

As we can conclude from the above examples, South Indian Sufi saints like Jan Pahad Saida and Baba Fakhruddin are absorbed into local place histories through stories that link these places to specific relics, such as the body parts of the saints or objects they used during their life. Despite the fact that sacred relics and the stories that go with them are surrounded by larger belief systems that blend global and local Islams, their historicity is most often secured through materials such as flags, rags, cradles, and sacred threads. When I inquired about the historicity of these traditions, most of my informants simply asserted, "This is our history. This history comes from our stories, our family and caste stories that we heard from our elders. And see all these things that tell the story!" When these devotees say "things," they refer proudly to the memorials, ritual objects, and relics that surround Sufi shrines.

Debating Materiality in Living Islam and Sufism

The recent "materialist" turn in contemporary scholarship informs us of the importance of material religion in helping us, as Vasquez puts it, "disentangle some of the epistemological knots that have characterized the discipline of religion as a way to provide fallible yet effective tools to explore the rich and diverse everyday activities of situated actors who have come to identify what they do as religious" (Vasquez 2011, 9). In this regard, the ritual deployment of the above-described objects is closely connected to processes of embodiment and emplacement in the making of local South Asian Islams. The engagement of religious objects in ritual practice involves the usage of several key Islamic themes, such as death, martyrdom, and Sufi mysticism, as well as the construction of Islamic community (*ummāh*) and ethics. These objects are not static entities with fixed, context-neutral meanings; rather they are dynamic entities that "mean" only in relationship to larger devotional networks, including those that have a predominantly local base. In spite of the importance of understanding the public display of sacred objects within larger religious systems, they remain unmapped in the case of Islamic practices, particularly in South Asia (Abrahams 1981, 303–21). The question of what material sources show and tell thus requires much attention as they reveal deeper implications of living Islam, particularly in public ritual contexts.

Recent debates on material culture, materiality of religions, and sensory characteristics of religious practices help us to see the implications of using objects in a ritual context. As Birgit Meyer et al. observed, "Materializing the study of religion means asking how religion happens materially, which is not to be confused with asking the much less helpful question of how religion is expressed in material form. A materialized study of religion begins with the assumption that things, their use, their valuation, and their appeal are not something added to a religion, but rather inextricable from it" (Meyer et al. 2010, 207–11). Reflecting these concerns, I used the term "materializing" in the title of this chapter yet the question of materializing Islamic devotion is as problematic as it is understudied. It is problematic since normative Islam contests any form of materialization associated with God, condemning it as *shirk,* associated with practices of "idolatry" or "polytheism" that are opposed to the foundational idea of the singular god (*tauhīd*) in Islam (Mohammad 2010, 141–69). However, in the practices of lived Islam like those discussed here, devotees depend minimally at best on textual sources or mosque-centered activities. Objects assume crucial ritual roles in such religious practices, which resist conceptual distinctions between materiality and spirituality.

The agency of religious objects is evident in the creation of a local religious identity formed through ritual. We find an example of this in the book *On Wings of Diesel: Trucks, Identity and Culture in Pakistan,* where Jamal Elias observes that

> [t]he truck is, therefore, not a static artifact of so-called 'popular' or 'folk' art traditions, or even necessarily of vernacular expression, but a manifestation of the processes of societal change that get reflected, projected, re-absorbed, and reflected again through the decorative and epigraphic program of the vehicle. (Elias 2011, 207)

Elias's observations help us to see how truck designs eventually become religious objects with the ability to promote a specific identity. Although this example is not specifically about public religious events such as Muharram and *'urs,* the question of agency remains intriguing. In this context, as Frank Korom explains it, "material culture embodies potentialities that are not necessarily in the control of creative human agency. They rather work reciprocally, for man-made objects can assume their own sense of volition once created" (Korom 2012, 1–19).

Most religious objects in South Indian Islam acquire agency by manifesting the powers widely associated with saints. For example, although the battle standards used ritually during Muharram are made by human beings, the stories that surround them imbue them with divine life and give them an aura of the miraculous (*karāmat*). Narratives about the metal battle standards and local interpretations attribute to them divine or a saintly intercessory agency. Similarly, relics of Sufi saints or local holy figures are widely accepted in South Indian Islam as nothing less than the living presence of the saint and hence are seen as embodying saintly power. In a recent essay on relic practices, Kevin Trainor observed:

> The relics of the saints, as mediated through the embedded symbolism of their material containers, serve as privileged interfaces between a celestial realm in which the saints enjoy a special intimacy with God's presence (as well as intercessory access), and the faithful who, through their interactions with these extraordinary objects, come to embody *reverentia*, a particular mode of bodily deportment that can be seen as an appropriate engagement with the saint's transformative power. (Trainor 2010, 272)

In the public ritual settings I have explored here, Muslims clearly divide into two separate groups. One group supports the usage of all kinds of material objects in worship, arguing that they are part of genuine Islamic devotion and help guide devotees to follow the path of Muslim saints. The second group such as "*asli Islam*," however, upholds an idea of "true" or "pure" Islam that rejects many the above-described practices involving worship of material objects. Some reformist Muslims have criticized the very act of using objects or "marks" of memory and piety in a devotional context as un-Islamic, considering them to arise from Hindu influences that pollute the message of Islam. Other Muslims such as those who prioritize local Muslim practices found in the second group, however, accept the value of relics as marks of local Muslim saints and members of the family of the Prophet while rejecting the Islamic use of non-reliquary objects. The ways these groups argue against each other's perspectives reflect tensions concerning what is believed to be the proper or legitimate use of different kinds of objects in Islamic ritual practice.

Efforts to remove objects from public Muslim spaces have been persistent. As the local *imam* Jaffer Sherrif put it, "actually all this stuff is just polluting the pure worship that Islam teaches us." Many devotees, however, both Muslim and non-Muslim, offer a contrary viewpoint. As one devotee named Shafi explained it to me,

> I come from a lower class Muslim family and my knowledge of Islam is confined to my frequent visits to a local mosque. But I learn more from these public commemorations, whether

> Muharram or *'urs,* where I see numerous metal battle standards, green flags, and colorful swings. Then I start talk to my parents, grandparents and older people here at this site. I learn more when I come here. We share more stories when we see things. Above all, I really like the beauty of these objects and their colorful festive costumes.

The experience reflected in these words resonates with tens of thousands of devotees who visit Sufi and Islamic shrines. Muslims who visit these shrines inevitably blend and, in ways that work to support devotional expressions and understandings, strike a balance between material and non-material Islam.

Notes

This paper is an outcome of a long personal and academic journey since 2006. All interviews and conversations used in this paper were from my field research in Andhra Pradesh in 2006 and 2007. I am greatly indebted to the people of Gugudu, Veerla Palle, and Penukonda, the three major sites of this research. I am grateful to the storytellers and local devotees who were always there to respond to my questions and share their stories. This fieldwork was made possible by a generous funding from the American Institute of Indian Studies. During the workshop of the AIIS fellows in Delhi in 2007, and later at a workshop and conference on Ethnography and Theology at the Emory University in 2009, Joyce Flueckiger and Luke Whitmore made me rethink the aspects of materiality such as red sacred threads and, particularly, Luke made me read extensively, raising numerous questions from time to time.

Earlier versions of this paper were presented at the Conference of Material Objects and Religious Narratives at Duke University in 2008, and the Ethnography and Theology Conference sponsored by the *Journal of the Practical Matters* at the Emory in 2009. I still remember those fascinating and thought-provoking discussions led by Ann Gold, Leela Prasad, Kirin Narayan, and Karen Ruffle. I am very thankful to Tracy Pintchman and Corinne Dempsey for their careful reading and patience throughout this writing process.

1. Karbala, which is within the geographical boundaries of present day Iraq, symbolically refers to the entire history of Shi'i history and the gradual enactments of Muharram events. An intensely powerful and definitive Karbala represents, as David Pinault put it, "an overriding paradigm of persecution, exclusion and suffering." For more on this aspect, see Pinault 2001.

2. For more on this dramatic aspect of Muharram performances in Iran, Trinidad and South India, see Chelkowski 1979, Korom 2003, and Sharif 1975 (1921).

3. The paradigm of Karbala functions in various ways in religious and literary realms. For an understanding of its religious and literary implications, see Hyder 2006.

4. For an idea of other paraphernalia or material objects used during *'urs* events, see Werbner, Pnina, and Basu 2003.

5. For more on the idea of *Karamat* in a South Indian *dargah* context, see Narayanan 2007.

References

Abrahams Roger D. 1981. "Shouting Match at the Border: The Folklore of Display Events." In *"And Other Neighborly Names": Social Process and Cultural Image in Texas Folklore,* edited by Richard Bauman and Roger D. Abrahams, 303–21. Austin: University of Texas Press.

Bashir, Shahzad. 2011. *Sufi Bodies: Religion and Society in Medieval Islam.* New York: Columbia University Press.

Bellamy, Carla. 2011. *The Powerful Ephemeral: Everyday Healing in an Ambiguously Islamic Place.* Berkeley: University of California Press.

Chelkowski, Peter J., ed. 1979. *Tazi'yeh—Ritual and Drama in Iran.* New York: New York University Press.

Elias, Jamal. 2011. *On Wings of Diesel: Trucks, Identity and Culture in Pakistan.* Oxford: Oneworld.

Flueckiger, Joyce Burkhalter. 2006. *In Amma's Healing Room: Gender and Vernacular Islam in South India.* Bloomington: Indiana University Press.

George, Kenneth. 2008. "Ethical Pleasure, Visual *Dhikr* and Artistic Subjectivity in Contemporary Indonesia." *Material Religion* 4, 2: 172–92.

Hyder, Syed Akbar. 2006. *Reliving Karbala: Martyrdom in South Asian Memory,* New York: Oxford University Press.

Korom, Frank J. 2003. *Hosay Trinidad: Muharram Performances in an Indo-Caribbean Diaspora.* Philadelphia: University of Pennsylvania Press.

———. 2012. "The Presence of Absence: Using Stuff in a South Asian Sufi Movement." *AAS Working Papers in Social Anthropology,* 23: 1–19.

Meyer, Birgit, David Morgan, Crispin Paine, and S. Brent Plate. 2010. "The Origin and Mission of Material Religion." *Material Religion* 40: 207–11.

Mohammad, Afsar. 2010. "Telling Stories: Hindu-Muslim Worship in South India." *The Journal of Hindu Studies,* 2: 157–88.

———. 2010. "Following the Pir: Temporary Asceticism and Village Religion in South India." In *Transfer and Spaces,* edited by Gita Dharampal-Frick and Robert Langer, 141–69. Wiesbaden: Harrassowitz Verlag.

———. 2011. "Sita is Fatima and Fatima is Sita: Performing Sita and Fatima in a Muslim Public Ritual." *Journal of Vaishnava Studies,* 20: 173–96.

Narayanan, Vasudha. 2007. "Religious Vows at the Shrine of Shahul Hamid." In *Dealing with Deities: The Ritual Vow in South Asia,* edited by Selva J. Raj and William P. Hartman, 65–85. Albany: State University of New York Press.

Pinault, David. 2001. *Horse of Karbala*. New York: St. Martin's Press.
Orsi, Robert. 1985. *The Madonna of 115th Street: Faith and Community in Italian Harlem, 1880–1950*. New Haven, CT: Yale University Press.
Sharif, Ja'far. 1975 (1921). *Islam in India or the Qanun-i-Islam,* translated by G. A. Herklots. London: Curzon Press.
Suvorova, Anna. 2004. *Muslim Saints of South Asia*. London and New York: RoutledgeCurzon.
Vasquez, Manuel A. 2011. *More Than a Belief: A Materialist Theory of Religion,* New York: Oxford University Press.
Trainor, Kevin. 2010. "Relics in Comparative Perspective." *Numen: International Review for the History of Religions,* 57, no. 3–4: 267–83.
Werbner, Pnina, and Basu, 1998. *Embodying Charisma: Modernity, Locality and Performance of Emotion in Sufi Cults*. London and New York: Routledge.
Williams, Raymond Brady, ed. 1996. *A Sacred Thread: Modern Transmission of Hindu Traditions in India and Abroad*. New York: Columbia University Press.

8

Monastic Matters

Bowls, Robes, and the Middle Way in South Asian Theravāda Buddhism

Bradley Clough

Just as a bird takes wings with it wherever it flies, so the monk takes his robes and his begging bowl with him wherever he goes. He is content with robes for his body and a begging bowl for his stomach.

—Dīgha Nikāya [hereafter DN] I.71; Majjhima Nikāya [hereafter MN] III.35; and Anguttara Nikāya [hereafter AN] II.209

As the words above indicate, the bowl and robes of a Buddhist *bhikkhu*[1] or monk[2] are material objects that are central to his life. Throughout the history of Theravāda Buddhism in South Asia, monks were not allowed to give ordination to candidates who came forth without these possessions (Vinaya I.90). The robes and bowl are such markers of monastic identity that the monastic code (Vinaya) warns against those imposters who wear the robes and carry the bowl, and thus are assumed to be monks, until it is found out that they are not ordained. Such persons are considered to have taken the very signs of a monk by theft (Vinaya, Mahāvagga I.63). Furthermore, one of the central questions asked during an ordination ceremony is, "Do you have your robe and bowl in order?" (Vinaya, Mahāvagga I.63). And when Mahāpajāpatī and some of her fellow Sākyan women wished the Buddha to institute a nuns' order, they put on the robes and took up the bowl to show their readiness for the vocation. A bowl and robes also constitute half of the "eight monastic 'requisites'" (*ata-pirikara*): alms-bowl, three robes, girdle, razor, water-strainer, and sewing needle.

In this chapter, we will look at the role that these material objects have had in the religious lives of Theravāda Buddhists in South Asia. Looking primarily at the monastic code of Theravāda Buddhism, the Vinaya Piṭaka of the Pāli Canon, we will examine the greater meanings that these items have had in this tradition, meanings that go well beyond ideas concerning the well-being of monastics' bodies and stomachs.[3] Among the Vinaya's minutiae regarding the use of the robes and bowl, we find rules applied to their usage that address many of Buddhism's central values. I will argue that Theravāda Buddhism has employed regulations concerning the use of the robes and bowl as parts of a social process that has involved interaction with and conversion of lay people, in order to inculcate in monks many central principles of the religion's "middle way," such as equanimity, mindfulness, detachment, and generosity.

This chapter will also consider ritual exchanges of these material objects. Ritual is often a place where cultural dynamics and the meanings of material objects involved come alive, and arguably the two most important Theravāda rituals are concerned with monastic-lay exchanges of these material objects and the use of begging bowl and robes. These are the daily almsgiving rounds and the annual ceremony of donating to the monastic *saṅgha*. In these rituals, how the material objects are used—handed over, received, held, stored, and consumed—also teaches lessons about Buddhism's central principles. These rituals allow for the making of karmic merit (*puñña*), which is of great interest to those participating in them.

Lastly, I will show that although Theravāda Buddhism has always encouraged detachment from material objects, the particular objects discussed here serve important practical purposes nevertheless.

Robes and the Middle Way

Robes: Introduction

Monks' robes[4] are one of the most important symbols of the religious life. Many Vinaya passages describe a well-defined way of dressing in Buddhist monasticism. Rules on the subject were much more numerous than rules about other "requisites," as Buddhism calls them, that monks are allowed to possess. In the Vinaya, nineteen offenses calling for forfeiture and confession, and seven offences calling for confession only, deal with clothing. And three full chapters are devoted to specific details about cloth. In conveying the teaching of renunciation to his monks, the Buddha originally had his itinerant *bhikkhus* make robes from cast-off bits of cloth found in burying grounds and dump areas, cloths that they would then wash and don. Thus the monastic robe was known as *paṁsukūla* or "rag-robe." In order to instill detachment, the monk was urged to be content with this humblest of clothing. This clothing signified the same spirit of renunciation that forbade monks from wearing ornaments, using combs, mirrors, and ointments, and required shaving of the head. Still, the Buddhist monastic mode of dress did not conform to notions of detachment held by renouncers of other early Indian *samaṇa* traditions, some of whom took to wearing tree bark, animal skins, or nothing at all.[5] At the same time, Buddha forbade any personal decoration or coloring of clothes, thus negating vanity and assuring that a uniform mode of dress put all members of his *saṅgha* on equal footing (Wijayaratna 1990, 40). We see here the Buddha pointing to a middle way, between the ways of stark asceticism and self-indulgent vanity.

In the Vinaya, the Buddha seems to be concerned that his *saṅgha* not be confused with other groups of renouncers (*samaṇa*). There is no specific rule specifying certain colors, but the texts show that robes were to be saffron or yellow, apparently for the sake of distinction, simplicity, and uniformity. The Buddha and his *saṅgha* were very concerned with conversion, especially in the early phases of the religion, and so they did not want any poor behavior exhibited by other *samaṇas* to be mistaken for Buddhist monks' ways. Furthermore, it was said that wearing different colors was the habit of householders who still enjoy the pleasures of the senses, and thus doing so was forbidden (Dhīrasekere 1984, 184). So, to wear robes was to instill and convey a sense of contentment with yet also detachment from the barest of material necessities, leading to a middle way where a monk would be neither overly attached to nor too dismissive about possession of certain material objects.

This practice went on for the first twenty years of the *saṅgha* (Wijayaratna, 33). Then, at a defining stage of evolution of the community (the twenty-year point) (Vinaya Aṭṭhakathā [hereafter VA], 1119), the Buddha permitted monks to wear robes given to them by laypersons (*gahapativīcara*). Robes given by the laity could be made of six materials: linen, cotton, silk, wool, coarse hemp, and canvas (Vinaya I.280). But the Buddha kept the option of wearing rag-robes open, and they would continue to be worn by some throughout Theravāda history. This does not mean, however, that other materials were seen as luxuries (Dhīrasekere

1984, 184). Here, as so often, we see the Buddha aiming for a middle ground, in this case between the roughest and softest of materials. This approach also comes out at Vinaya II.196, which has the Buddha's rival Devadatta demanding that the Buddha make rag-robes obligatory for his monks, but the Buddha rejects this on grounds of concerns for the monks' comfort. We even find the Buddha making an exception to the rule that allowed monks to possess only three robes, in his allowance of two additional cloths, one for wiping sweat from the face and one functioning as an "itch cloth" for those suffering from any scabbing disease. Discomfort was seen by the Buddha as an obstacle to the life of renunciation, and on several occasions the Buddha indicated that it can actually hinder inner progress (Wijayaratna 1990, 42).

The Kaṭhina Ritual

The most important annual ritual that involves meaningful interaction between monks and laity is the *kaṭhina* ritual. In the Vinaya's Mahāvagga and Pārivāra sections, entire chapters are devoted to its practice. The word "*kaṭhina*" means the frame upon which robe-material is made into an actual robe, and it refers to the cotton cloth offered to *bhikkhus* yearly after the conclusion of the monks' "rains retreat" (P. *vassāvāsa;* S. *vas*) during monsoon season. In theory the lay donors (*dāyakas*) give the gift of robe-material to the whole *saṅgha,* but in practice, each robe will eventually end up going to a particular monk. The monks work out how the robes will be allotted among themselves. Only those who have properly lived out the rules of the rains retreat are entitled to *kaṭhina* cloth. Usually priority is given to those with old, worn robes, with senior monks receiving offerings before junior monks. But it is usually the case that laypersons, in their zeal to gain karmic reward or merit, offer more than enough robes to supply every monk living within the boundaries of a particular monastery during rains retreat with a new robe.

The *kaṭhina* ritual, known as the *Kaṭhina Cīvara Pūjā* ("Offering of the Kaṭhina Robe"), is a traditional and long-standing one among Sinhalese Buddhists. The month of the ritual is known as *cīvara mase* or the "month of the robe" (Disanayaka 1993, 52) The Buddha gives sanction to the rite in the Vinaya (Vinaya I.254), where two chapters are devoted to its practice. In the early Buddhist community, the rains retreat, when monks settled in one location for several months, offered the best opportunity for monks and laypersons to interact, with the monks giving regular sermons to the laity and the laity supporting the monks with alms-food as long as the monks showed their worthiness through purity (*parisuddhi*) of conduct. Through the ceremony, the laity can show their respect for *bhikkhus'* purity, and new, clean cloth is a way for inwardly pure monks to show outer purity (Holt 1983, 135). The rains retreat would have been a very advantageous time for laypeople, who would have gotten to know the monks during the season and at its end, to offer cloth for robes out of respect and in the spirit of generosity (*dāna*). The monks, being gathered together during this season, and the laity, coming back to them again at the end for this ritual, were thus afforded the opportunity to be mutually beneficial to each other.

The *Kaṭhina Cīvara Pūjā* remains largely unchanged today in the South Asian Theravāda world. In a sense, the offering ritual of the *kaṭhina* robes begins early on in the monsoon season, as local people begin preparing them, led by a chief donor (*dāyaka*). The chief *dāyaka* collects money for robes and assigns people to prepare dishes for almsgiving on the *pūjā* day. The ritual comes at the end of the rains retreat, after the ritual of *Pavāraṇā*, in which monks purify themselves by confessing any monastic offences committed during the retreat. Normally, the *kaṭhina pūjā* is preceded by an entire day of the monks chanting protective verses (P. *paritta;* S. *pirit*) for the people. During the chanting, some lay supporters, led by the chief benefactor (*dāyaka mahāttaya*), leave the temple and begin to form the *kaṭhina* procession (S. *perahera*). Carrying torches and moving to the beat of the accompanying drums, the procession goes forth with the *dāyakas* holding the *kaṭhina* cloth respectfully upon their heads. Others carry other material objects to be donated, such as umbrellas, brooms, pillows, coverlets, foodstuffs, and so forth. Those who are not able to make any offering line the sides of the procession to touch the gifts, thus taking part in the merit earned from giving. The procession reaches the temple at dawn, and the *kaṭhina* cloth is offered officially to the *saṅgha*. A worthy *bhikkhu* (one who has kept all the rains retreat rules) says:

> This *kaṭhina* cloth has become the property of the Saṅgha. If the Saṅgha is ready, hand over the *kaṭhina* cloth to such and such a *bhikkhu* to spread out the *kaṭhina*.
> (Vinaya IV.353)[6]

In response, the chief *dāyaka* utters:

> Venerable sirs, we present this *kaṭhina* cloth, together with its accessories, to the monastic community. It would be good if the monastic community would accept this *kaṭhina*

> cloth together with its accessories, and having accepted it, would spread out the *kaṭhina*[7] for our long-term welfare and happiness.[8]

At the conclusion of the ritual, there is still much to be done, as each monk must sew the *kaṭhina* cloth into a robe upon the very day of receiving it. A *kaṭhina* cloth (*kaṭhina-dussa*) becomes a *kaṭhina* robe (*kaṭhina-cīvara*) when it is cleaned, sewed, and dyed correctly. To prepare the robe out of *kaṭhina* cloth requires several monks working together. Thus, the *kaṭhina* robe is the product of collective action of both the monks and laity. This process serves to maintain harmony in the *saṅgha*, and the resulting monastic-lay relationship could be thought of as a communal "middle way" in which monks are neither too familiar with the laity nor at any odds with them.

In the evening of this day, one of the resident monks, dressed in one of the newly fashioned *kaṭhina* robes, gives a special sermon (*kaṭhinānisaṅsa dēsanā*) on the benefits accrued by monks who observe the rains retreat rules properly and the merits of the *dāyakas* who support the monks during the three-month period that culminates in the *Kaṭhina Cīvara Pūjā* (Saddhasena 1999, 161). As is well known, the life of the fourfold *saṅgha* of monastics (monks and nuns) and laypersons (male and female) centers around a mutually supportive, symbiotic relationship between the monks and the laity, whereby the laity materially holds up the monastic way of life by supplying robes and food, and the monks reciprocate spiritually with the "gift of doctrine" (*dhamma-dāna*) that ideally serves to further the laity in their practices. There is no better example of this essential relationship than the *kaṭhina* ritual, where the interdependency and symbiosis between laity and monks is performed through both sides' engagement with the material object that is the robe.

The Purposes of the Robes

There seems to be a conflict between the desires of the monk, who is expected to possess the minimum of material possessions, and the layperson, who wants to give as much as possible to the monks in order to make as much merit as possible. Merit can be seen as a kind of treasury of good karma, meaning that one is destined for greater good fortune later, both in this and in future lives. In the Vinaya, this conflict of desires was ameliorated by a procedure for the distribution of robe-materials among all *saṅgha* members (Vinaya I.285). The giving and receiving of robe material seems to be an area where the Buddha's message of living without greed gets conveyed. To encourage greedlessness, rules were made that forbade a monk both from diverting for personal use what was intended for the whole *saṅgha* and possessing an extra set of robes for more than ten days. If a monk was given any extra robes, he was to share them among those with worn-out robes or donate them to the monastery store. Rules such as these encouraged the spirit of renouncing material objects and practicing selfless generosity. Related to the issue of greediness was instilling and conveying a sense of contentment with and detachment from one's few material possessions. The issue of the monk being contented with what he has is of great significance. As it is put in DN I.71:

> And how is a *bhikkhu* content? Just as a bird takes wings with it wherever it flies, so the monk takes his robes and his begging bowl with him wherever he goes. He is content with robes for his body and a begging bowl for his stomach. Wherever he goes he only takes only the barest necessities along. This is how a *bhikkhu* is content.

Not only does the emphasis on renunciation come again to the surface here, but clearly the importance of being content does as well, demonstrating a crucially important aspect of the middle way: cultivation of the quality of *upekkhā,* or "equanimity." Being content with whatever arises in one's experience is a good definition of equanimity and characterizes a mind that is equipoised in the midst of the "eight worldly conditions" that usually disturb the even-mindedness of individuals: pleasure and pain, gain and loss, success and failure, and fame and disrepute. Equanimity could well be thought of as a middle way of the mind.

Even with the emphasis on greedlessness and contentment with simplicity, the Buddha still insisted on the use of cloth material to protect the physical well-being of his monks. Far from being a form of penance, clothes were meant to "protect the body against cold, heat, mosquitoes, insects, and the wind" (MN I.102). As it is put in MN 2, "A *bhikkhu,* reflecting properly, uses robe-cloth simply to counteract cold, to counteract heat, to counteract the touch of flies, mosquitoes, wind, sun, and reptiles, and simply for the purpose of covering the parts of the body that cause shame." This also typifies the Buddha's middle way approach: there is to be no greed or attachment with regard to material possessions like robes; but a good set of robes was valued as essential to minimizing bodily suffering (Wijayaratna 1990, 41). Furthermore, it is well known from the stories of the Buddha's life that physical well-being must be established in order for inner mental transformation to take place. It is presupposed that physical health is a necessary gift that promotes spiritual progress on the path to liberation from suffering.

The giving of robes has been a major way for laity to gain merit in the community. The following gives us a good picture of the early community's fervor in this area:

> When the people of Rājagaha heard that the Buddha had allowed monks to accept robes given by householders, they were overcome with joy and excitement: 'now we will give robes, and we will gain merit!' . . . In a single day, several thousand robes were given to the *saṅgha* in the town of Rājagaha. (Vinaya I.280)

Merit-making is the result of generosity, which is one of the cardinal Buddhist virtues, especially for laypeople. Ideally, all giving should be selfless, but the desire to improve one's future situation by accumulating merit is hardly frowned upon. Monks have always been regarded by laypersons as "fields of merit" (*puññakkheta*), and as such they are the most common recipients of lay generosity (MN III.81; AN IV.406). Robes may be donated to these "fields of merit" at any time of year, but giving them at the end of the rains retreat is especially powerful because the *kaṭhina* robe is offered to the whole community of monks. The literal meaning of *kaṭhina* is "hard," and the Vinaya commentary tells us that the robes were called this because the gift of robe cloth is an act of merit as indestructible as a diamond (Wijayaratna 1990, 38). Furthermore, the merit gained from giving *kaṭhina* cloth is said to be as great and firm as the immovable Mount Meru (Saddhasena 1999, 161). The *Cūḷavaṃsa* describes how the still much revered medieval monarch King Parākrambāhu joyfully and faithfully gave eighty *kaṭhina* robes on behalf of the whole population in honor of the eighty "greatly glorious" main disciples of the Buddha. It is said that "in this way he increased his merit" (Cūḷvaṃsa 81, 99–108). Many similar royal offerings are recorded in the *Mahāvaṃsa*, and it may well be that the great social and religious meaning that the robe-offering ritual has had for Sinhalese Buddhists over time at least partly stems from knowing about these earlier events when Sinhalese Buddhists' most revered kings made similar offerings with such devotion (Kariyawasam 1995, 48).

The completed *Kaṭhina-cīvara* is said to resemble a paddy field. This metaphoric reference is full of religious meaning. The paddy field

(S. *kuṁbara*) is where the peasants sow their grain. The robe is likened to the *pin kuṁbara*, a "merit paddy field" that is gifted to a local temple and worked on by the villagers for free. The idea is that the *kaṭhina* is not literally a paddy field, but is *like* the *pin kuṁbara*, in that it provides the peasants with great fruitfulness or great merit. In the *kuṃbara*, one reaps what one sows. So it is with the donation of a *kaṭhina* robe and the rest of life: whenever one does good deeds, good merit (*pin*) will follow (Disanayaka 1993, 54).

Other Important Rules Regarding Robes and Their Significance

As is so often the case with rules regarding the robes and bowl, elimination of greed has been a major concern in Theravāda Buddhism. As the merit-making laity gave more and more robes, it became necessary to establish rules about communal ownership of them. The story of how the rules came to be begins with lay dissatisfaction about not being able to give as many robes as they wanted, because all monks were limited to one set of three robes. The Buddha then appointed a monk to look after the robes so damage to unattended robes would not occur. The Buddha demanded that a room inside the monastery be assigned to store the robes so they would not be destroyed by vermin. The Buddha next named a monk to be in charge of the store, but the robes piled up because there was no one to distribute them. Hence, the Buddha appointed a robe distributor. In order to ensure that Buddhist principles were not violated by monks with these special responsibilities, the Buddha declared that they must possess certain qualities: they must not distribute robes incorrectly, or through partiality, hatred, fear, or ignorance (Vinaya I.283–85, as summarized in Wijayaratna 1990, 49).

This account is instructive when we consider one of the main social processes that took place within the fourfold *saṅgha* of monks, nuns, laymen, and laywomen. When it was a new religion with missionary aspirations, Buddhism was very concerned with how the monastic *saṅgha* presented itself to lay communities, many of which they were encountering for the first time. We see this concern in the Vinaya in the repeated refrain of the Buddha to a monk who has committed an offence: "It is not pleasing those who are not yet pleased, nor is it increasing those who are pleased" (Vinaya, Mahāvagga IV.25). Thus, we see here that the Buddha went out of his way to acquiesce to certain lay demands. We also see here that the monks should openly demonstrate their self-discipline to the laity, in this case with respect to donated robes. As we have just seen, the robe officers were expected to maintain a very high standard of discipline and propriety. It may have been only those far advanced on the path to *nibbāna* (Sanskrit: *nirvāṇa*) who could be counted on to handle material objects like robes without partiality, hatred, fear, and ignorance, all of which are major obstacles to the attainment of *nibbāna*.

There is a thoroughness of thought that the Theravāda tradition has applied to the proper use and potential abuses of the robes and other material requisites. It seems to have considered and moved to prevent all of the ways in which greed could enter in to the process of lay donation of robes to the *saṅgha*. At the same time, the tradition, despite its emphasis on an attitude of renunciation within the monastic ranks, affirms at many points why the possession of certain material objects like the robe are essential to the way of life of the *bhikkhu*.

The Bowl, Alms-food, and the Middle Way

> Just as a bee, having gathered nectar
> From a flower, flies away,
> Without harming its color and scent,
> So should a wise man wander through a village.
> (*Dhammapada* 49)

The Bowl: Introduction

The monks' main use for the bowl (*patta* or *patta-dhātu*) was and continues to be as a receptacle to collect alms-food gained by begging from the laity. The common name for alms-food is *piṇḍa-pāta,* which literally means the "food-morsel's fall" into the begging bowl (Khantipalo 1980). The practice of begging for alms has fallen out of fashion in many Asian Buddhist regions, but it strongly persists in Theravāda countries. The authority of the Vinaya ensures that the practice today probably differs minimally from the practice of early Buddhism. In cultures where Theravāda Buddhism remains a dominant influence, food is generally considered the most important of all the material offerings that can be given as regular demonstrations of generosity by the laity. Even children are trained to give alms to the monks so that they too can accumulate *kusala kamma,* or wholesome deeds (Witanachchi 1999, 21). Along with the robe, the begging bowl is the most prized of the eight requisite material objects that a monk may possess. Hence the monk takes great care of it, cleaning it daily to keep it from rusting, and always placing it, when not in use, on a tin or lead stand so that it will not fall and be damaged (Witanachchi 1999, 21). Bowls can be made out of iron or clay; gold, silver, bronze, glass, other metals, and gems were not allowed by the Vinaya. The bowl may not be painted or incised with writing or other decorations (Thanissaro 1996b). Clearly there is a utilitarian emphasis here. When on alms-begging rounds, a monk usually carries the bowl in a sling, for it becomes heavy when full of food and may be dropped by tired hands (Khantipalo 1980). When one's begging bowl wore out, the community could supply another one, but only if the bowl was worn in five different places (Vinaya III.242). To prevent greed, a monk may possess only one bowl at a time. This is based on a case in Kapilavatthu where a group of monks greedily asked a potter to make all sorts of bowls. Observing this, laypeople questioned the moderation of these monks and criticized the hardship that they imposed on the potter (Vinaya II.243–244). The Buddha thus ruled it an offense of wrongdoing (*dukkata*) to possess extra bowls. We see here again how the Buddha responded to how, in the use of material objects, things appeared to lay folk, who were potential converts to Buddhism or recent converts that needed to be retained.

Although not all renouncers did so, and the Pāli texts show *brāhmaṇas* denouncing the practice, the Buddha declared to his followers that it was right livelihood (*sammā ājīva*) to beg for alms. For the consumption of another material, food, monks were always to use their begging bowls, whether they were begging for food or eating at a home at the request of a private householder. Since the time of the Buddha's allowance of begging, the begging bowl has been a symbol and mainstay of Buddhist monks' special mendicancy (Wijayaratna 1990, 63). Like the Buddha, monks in Theravāda countries have received their food in bowls only, and they have eaten from bowls alone as well. In ancient India, this use of the bowl set Buddhists apart from other renouncers, who received food in their hands, on the ground, and in jugs and skulls (Vinaya II.112–114).

The main reception of food into an alms bowl takes place during the monk's begging rounds among the homes of the village nearest to his temple or monastery. Also common is a layperson's hosting a group of monks at his home for a meal. The usual form of religious exchange has the monks chanting protective verses. Alms are given in the home on special occasions such as a housewarming, setting out on a long journey, birth, marriage, and death anniversaries. Almsgiving in the home to at least four fully-ordained monks is called *saṅghika-dāna* or "giving [alms] to the monastic community" (Kariyawasam 1995, 42).

The Ritual of Alms-Begging[9]

Having to eat before noon as the monastic precepts dictate, monks go on begging rounds fairly early in the morning after giving laywomen (*upāsika*) enough time to prepare food. Only after having robed himself properly can a monk go on alms-rounds. In keeping with Buddhist teaching's expectations of modesty and humility, a monk must have his body covered from the neck to below the knees when going "among the homes" (Khantipalo 1980). This conduct is in keeping with the self-discipline and control that a monk must have throughout begging rounds. As *Dhammapada* 308 puts it,

> It would be better to swallow an iron ball,
> Red-hot as a blaze of fire,
> Than to eat the alms of the people
> As an immoral and uncontrolled man.

In keeping with this good conduct and self-discipline, the *bhikkhus* follow each other carefully and quietly as they embark upon alms rounds. At homes, they are not to speak unless spoken to, silence being considered part of the training during a monk's round. The monk also does not let his eyes gaze about, but keeps them fixed on the ground, thereby practicing "restraint of eye" (*cakkhu-saṁvara*) (Khantipalo 1980). The monks do not rush on their rounds, but rather walk in a dignified way with a mindfulness that is steady. Monks are told to think of Buddha's disciple Assaji, whose equipoised demeanor played a large role in the conversion of the Buddha's two chief disciples, Sāriputta and Moggallāna (Khantipalo 1980). That monks should carry themselves with equipoise and mindfulness shows us that alms-rounds are used as opportunities for meditation.

A monk "may enter a village carefully and unhurriedly" (Vinaya, Cullavagga VIII.2–4). Furthermore, he should

> not go ahead of monks who are elders; he should go among the homes properly clad; well-controlled should he go among the homes; with eyes cast down he should go among the homes; not lifiting up robes . . . ; not with loud laughter . . . ; with little noise . . . ; not swaying the body . . . ; not swaying the arms . . . ; not swaying the head . . . ; not with arms

> akimbo . . . ; not muffled up should he go among the homes; he should not go among the homes crouching on his heels; he should not go among the homes lolling; he should not go among the homes encroaching [on space intended] for monks who are elders; newly ordained monks should not be kept from a seat; and he should not sit down among the homes, having spread out his outer cloak. (Vinaya, Cullavagga VIII.2–4)

As is clear here, the Vinaya sets out very precise rules for the disciplined demeanor of monks during begging rounds. The begging round is the central ritual in which monks interact with laity on a regular basis. These carefully delineated rules must have been especially important in early Indian Buddhism as a way for the monastic *saṅgha* to demonstrate its decorum and propriety while carrying the bowl on begging rounds and went about trying to improve the public perception of their order and convert laypeople. Indeed, in the Vinaya's narrative of the life of the early *saṅgha,* we find laypersons and conscientious monks objecting to begging monks who were wrongly dressed and ate in a crude fashion. In order to establish self-restraint and discipline, the Buddha was always quick to disallow such behavior (Vinaya, Mahāvagga I.24–25). That self-restraint and discipline were important to the early community (and still are today) is seen in the Vinaya's further instructions, which amount to what could be considered a middle way of decorum:

> When he is going among the homes . . . he should not enter [the home's property] too hastily, he should not leave too hastily. He should not stand too far away, he should not stand too close. He should not stand too long, he should not turn away too soon. (Vinaya, Cullavagga VIII.506)

By not staying too long, a monk does not succumb to greed or craving, and by not leaving too soon, a monk does not deny laypersons an opportunity to make merit. This monk should also reflect on why he is going out for food. A monk does not use alms-food for intoxication, putting on bulk, or beautification. He begs simply for the survival and continuance of the body, for ending its afflictions, and supporting the holy life (Thanissaro 1996). The monk is to think, "Thus I will destroy my old feelings [of hunger] and not create new feelings [from overeating]. I will maintain myself, be blameless, and live in comfort" (MN 2, as translated in Thanissaro 1996). It is clear that the emphasis here on moderation and eating just enough to survive in comfort is also in line with the idea of the middle way.

When he finds a donor's home and food is about to be given, the bowl-carrying monk is to raise the outer robe with his left hand and uncover the bowl with his right hand. Grasping the bowl with both hands, the monk should receive alms, but he should not look upon the face of the donor of alms. Once the alms have been given and he has completely covered the bowl again with his outer robe, the monk should turn away carefully and unhurriedly (Thanissaro 1996).

Monks usually know which houses to stop at, as there is often a table with food on it placed outside a home. Sometimes certain lay supporters offer to give food on a daily basis. Sometimes the monks hear an invitation (*nimantana*) called out to them (Thanissaro 1996). Still, monks are to stop by every house so as to give everyone the opportunity to make merit. Waiting outside a home in complete silence is also seen by the monks as an opportunity to practice the virtue of patience (*khanti*), which is one of the ten "perfections" (*pāramī* or *pāramitā*) that are to be cultivated for advancement along the path. If a home did not provide any alms, monks are not to feel displeasure, according to the Vinaya (Wijayaratna 1990, 60). Here again, this time with regard to the bowl, we see the tradition encouraging equanimity in the use of material objects (as well as equanimity towards the material contents of the bowl, the food). If a home does provide alms, any member of the family (and often several members at once) may give to the monks (Witanachchi 1999, 60).

The monks follow what is called the "bowl-food-eater's practice" of gathering all donated food in a single bowl. This practice is good for limiting craving, it is said, because it lessens the desire for the "five flavors and textures" (Visuddhimagga [hereafter VM] II.92). Food is simply taken as a medicine for the disease of hunger; it is not for the satisfaction of sensual desires (Khantipalo 1980). This practice is said to be the most applicable to those whose main obstructing defilement is greed or craving (VM II.92).

In accepting foodstuffs from all, monks are following the example of the Buddha, who taught that all have the right to practice generosity should they wish and reap the merits that result from it. The Vinaya teaches that any food is to be accepted, except for certain kinds of forbidden flesh (humans, dogs, tigers, and bears) or a dish that is suspected of having been cooked especially for a group of monks or an individual monk (Khantipalo 1980). As with robes, we again have an example here of being content with what one receives:

> Even though the *bhikkhu* receives but little,
> He does not treat his gift with disdain.
> He whose livelihood is pure and rigorous,
> Him, indeed, the gods praise. (*Dhammapada* 366)

If a home is going to give alms, the householders, prior to doling out the food, are to greet the monks with a show of respect, raising their joined hands above their heads. The monk is to be revered because of his purity of conduct (Khantipalo 1980). The *Dhammapada*, playing with the literal meaning of *bhikkhu* as "beggar," reminds Buddhists:

> One is not a *bhikkhu*
> Merely because he begs from others.
> By not adopting the outward form,
> Does one become a *bhikkhu*.
>
> He who subdues evil,
> Both great and small,
> Is called a *bhikkhu*,
> Because he has overcome evil. (*Dhammapada* 266, 267)

Taking a bowl that is to receive alms-food, the lay donors raise it above their heads and hold it there for about thirty seconds, during which time some fervent wish or vow is made that hopes for some particular blessing to come from their subsequent act of merit, whether that be a mundane desire for better health or material gain or a super-mundane desire such as attainment of *nibbāna* itself (Khantipalo 1980). While the food is given, the monk fixes his eyes on the bowl so as not to see anything that would arouse desire, such as donors of the opposite sex. This is known as *indriya-samvara* or "control of the senses" (Khantipalo 1980). Upon receiving food, Theravāda monks—in Sri Lanka, at least—briefly break their silence to utter *sukhi hotu* or "may you be happy" in a quiet voice.

Back at the monastery for the lone large meal of the day, which is to be had before noon, the monks share the food gathered by all. All gathered food is meant for the *saṅgha* as a whole, and it is an offense involving expiation and forfeiture to take such food for oneself without sharing.[10] Despite hierarchy within the *saṅgha* based on seniority, this is a demonstration of the basic egalitarian ethos of the *saṅgha*. It is not unusual to see pupils giving their teachers something choice, or a monk making sure that those who collected little food (this is often the case with novice or *sāmaṇera* monks) get a good portion (Khantipalo 1980). Such acts are known as "sharing the contents of the almsbowl" and represent a good opportunity to display loving-kindness within the monastic *saṅgha* (Khantipalo 1980). Moreover, monastery workers (*bhikkhu-bhatikas*) and guests are fed as well. Food is eaten in silence so all the monks can maintain mindfulness of just eating itself, in the present moment. The Vinaya instructs monks to fix their minds solely on the food being eaten, the bowl, and how one is eating (Vinaya, Cullavagga VIII.4.5–5.1). The process of eating in this way cultivates meditative concentration (*samādhi*) and mindfulness (*sati*).

The practice of eating at a layperson's home is allowed by the Vinaya and has been practiced since the community's beginnings as well. Throughout the canon the Buddha and his disciples accept invitations to eat at laypersons' homes. Inviting monks to one's home functions as both a sign of respect and a great opportunity to gain merit. To avoid conflict, a special dispenser of food is designated in the Vinaya, one of his roles being to decide which monks will attend an invited meal (Wijayaratna 1990, 64). As with the distributor of robes, the dispenser of food must be advanced enough in the Dhamma to not follow any wrong courses out of partiality, hatred, fear, or confusion (Vinaya III.328).

The ritual of eating at a home begins with monks being led from the monastery or temple in a procession. The lay head of the household holds on his head a relic casket (*dhātu-karaṇḍuva*), which represents the Buddha. As the monks step into the home, the hosts wash the monks' feet in an act of humility. The monks are then led to cushioned seats on the floor, up against the wall. Alms are first offered to the Buddha in a separate bowl and placed on a table along with the relic casket. A senior monk then administers the three refuges and the five precepts, followed by a sermon on the significance of the occasion. The food is then formally presented, with the chief householder reciting the phrase, "These alms, along with other requisites, we offer to the whole community of monks" (Kariyawasam 1995, 42).

Once the meal is over, another monk administers the *puññānu modanā* or "merit-rejoicing," wherein all those who participated in the ceremony are requested to partake of the merits for their future welfare. The participants are also called upon to transfer the merit gained toward the well-being of deceased relatives, friends, and inhabitants of the *deva*-worlds, who are expected to protect the donors out of gratitude (Kariyawasam 1995, 43).

The Benefits of Almsgiving

> Whoever, much delighted, endowed with virtue, having overcome avarice, gives food and drinks to a disciple of the Sugata, the gift is divine, dispelling sorrow [and] bringing happiness. Such a one gains a deva's life-span, owing to the faultless, stainless way. Desiring merit, at ease [and] healthy, such a one delights long in divine company. (Vinaya, Mahāvagga VIII.15)

The act of *dāna* or generosity is regarded highly as the first of ten "perfections to be cultivated and as one of a triad of practices (generosity [*dāna*], virtue [*sīla*], and meditation [*bhāvanā*]) often recommended for Buddhist laypersons (Khantipalo 1980). Although almsgiving is often seen by lay folk as purely a means to earn merit, ideally *dāna* is not simply about merit gained toward a better material life in this rebirth and better conditions in the next, but is also about changing the heart and mind, such that a donor rejoices in performing such wholesome acts (Vinaya, Mahāvagga VIII.15).

Earning merit may seem a selfish motivation for filling monks' bowls until one sees how frequently donors selflessly "tranfer merit" for the welfare of others.[11] Motivation is a crucial factor in the ethics of *kamma* (Sanskrit: *karma*), and so it is popularly believed that one who gives alms simply out of convention or mechanically rarely earns much merit. Giving grudgingly or for some form of self-advancement in the world earns even less (Khantipalo 1980). But in predominantly Buddhist countries like Sri Lanka, most know how to give properly with a sense of joyousness, happily gaining and then transferring merit. As the *Dhammapada* puts it:

> Verily, no misers get to the divine worlds.
> Nor, indeed do fools ever praise generosity.
> But the wise one rejoices in generosity;
> And by that *alone* (my emphasis) is he happy in the hereafter.
> (Dhammapada 177)

This is a significant verse, with its emphasis on generosity as *the* main activity of the layperson through which one may spiritually advance, even to the point of gaining rebirth as a god.

The gathering of food with the bowl and the consumption of that food also embody the middle way. One of the great events of the Buddha's life is when he chose to end his practice of stark asceticism, which he did by taking food. This marks the beginning of the Buddha's establishment of the middle way, since he abandons the life of self-mortification with this act but does not go on to eat self-indulgently, as he had as a pampered youth. The Vinaya rules concerning the use of bowls keep to this middle way as they are designed to promote the physical and mental wellbeing of monks while disallowing overeating and keeping them from going into a life of extreme austerity. The following passage sums up well the moderation required in food consumption, while not denying the importance of maintaining physical and mental wellbeing, in order to have the strength to pursue the demands of the religious life. It also emphasizes the meditative aspect of receiving alms:

> Brahmin, as soon as a monk is able to control his senses, the Tathāgata leads him further still towards moderation in your eating. Concentrate and be attentive when you eat; do not eat for pleasure or enjoyment, nor in order to become handsome and attractive; eat only to keep your body going, to protect it from harm, for the benefit of the pure life. (MN II.2; AN II.40 and III.388)

Monks were also kept on the middle way by rules designed to prevent gluttony on their part. For example, it is forbidden in the Vinaya for a monk to ask for delicacies or any special type of food (Vinaya II.88). And as noted earlier, a monk is not allowed to accept any food that he thinks was specially prepared for him. Furthermore, it has been an offense for a monk to specifically request finer foods such as ghee, fresh butter, oil, honey, molasses, fish, meat, and curds. Such rules have not only compelled monks to be content with what they received and to eat with sobriety, but they also spared laypersons any difficulties with respect to expenses (Wijayaratna 1990, 69).

The interaction between monks and laity during almsgiving is clearly crucial for coherence and harmony within the fourfold *saṅgha*. It is probably for this reason that the Buddha disallowed eating stored up food. As Bhikkhu Khantipalo notes, if monks grew accustomed to stored up food, they would lose motivation for alms-begging, thus depriving themselves of great opportunities to reflect upon their dependence on others as well as the human condition in general, and depriving lay people the benefits that come with daily contact with monks and the chance to practice generosity of the most basic kind every day (Khantipalo 1980).

Conclusion

In closing, it is important to note that even with respect to the monk who possesses few material objects, such as the robes and bowl, the tradition sees these as possibly causing as much craving, greed, and attachment in a monk as other material possessions can do in the lives of laypersons who possess more. This explains the plethora of rules in the Vinaya regarding uses of and attitudes toward the robes and bowl.

In order to breed non-attachment and eliminate craving and greed, it is clear that the Theravāda tradition in South Asia has allowed its monks to possess a minimal number of material objects. While it is clear that Buddhism aims at overcoming possessiveness, it is also clear that the material objects that monks are allowed to possess have taken on great meaning and go a long way toward defining what a monk is. As the quotation that opens this chapter indicates, the robes and bowl are two major constants in a *bhikkhu*'s life. The giving and taking of the robes and bowl are also central to the social processes of conversion and maintenance of ongoing harmony between the monks and laity within Buddhist communities. As Thanissaro Bhikkhu has observed, a *bhikkhu* lives in an economy of gifts, entrusting his life to the generosity and material support of the lay faithful. To maintain the purity of this situation, the monk must not try to influence their faith for his own material gain through inappropriate means or for the sake of items inappropriate for his use (Thanissaro 1996).

In the giving of material gifts of the robes and alms-food in the bowl, the layperson is afforded opportunities to practice the central aim of lay life, which is cultivation of generosity. We have noted how generosity leads to the creation of much-desired karmic merit, but the importance of generosity does not end here. As Witanacchchi has observed, every act of generosity gradually weakens one's greed and strengthens one's love and compassion for living beings (Witanachchi 1999, 60).

In addition to refraining from greed, making merit out of generosity, and cultivating loving-kindness, other significant Buddhist values also merge in canonical discussions of the robes, bowl, and other requisites, as we have seen. One representative passage can be found at AN IV.28, where the Buddha speaks of the *bhikkhu* who never does anything unseemly for the sake of robes, alms-food, or lodging. Such a *bhikkhu* also does not become agitated when these requisites cannot be obtained. Obtaining them, he does not become infatuated with them, for he sees the faults if there is attachment to them. Here we see equanimity, or the mental middle way, as an ideal monk exercises it. Furthermore, being content with any old robe, alms-food, or lodging, he also keeps to a middle way, neither exalting himself nor disparaging others. On the whole, the *bhikkhu* should be "diligent, deft, alert, and mindful." Here we see again the meditative dimension of the use of the robes and bowl. This same passage, AN IV.28, concludes by stating that the ideal monk "stands firm in the ancient tradition of the noble ones" (*ariya-puggala*). A passage such as this is crucial to our understanding of the Buddhist significance of these material objects and their proper use. Just as much as other Buddhist activities, and perhaps more than most, their proper usage can breed important Buddhist qualities like humility, equanimity, selflessness, and mindfulness. Ultimately, their proper use does nothing less than firmly establish one in the path of the noble ones (*ariya-magga*).

Notes

1. Terms, unless otherwise noted, are in the Pāli language, indicated by "P" when necessary. The other language in which terms sometimes appear is the vernacular of Sri Lanka's Buddhists, Sinhala, indicated by "S."

2. Unless otherwise indicated, what is said about a monk in this chapter also pertains to a *bhikkhuni* or nun. Most of the monastic literature referred to here has the same application to nuns as it does to monks, especially where early Buddhism is concerned. I use the term "monk" to avoid excessive wordage.

3. It is very important to note that I am well aware of current arguments, particularly those made in the body of work of Gregory Schopen, that say that Vinaya only represents an ideal of monastic living that is far away from the actual lived realities on the ground. While keeping this in mind, it is also important to consider that there is ample evidence to show that regulations concerning robes and bowls have been followed by Theravāda monks and laity, and when it has become clear that they were not being heeded, concrete measures have been taken to rectify such situations. Furthermore, I would argue that even to the extent that the Vinaya presents "mere" ideals, such ideals are important for students of religion to consider, because they reflect the highest concerns and aspirations for which members of religious traditions aim. My position here tends to agree with that put forward by Charles Hallisey, who has said, "An important historical value of the canonical Vinaya lies in its being a coherent representation of a particular Buddhist *mentalité*." (Hallisey 1990, 208). I am also aware of scholarship that argues that the principles and precepts of the community were subject to elaboration during the first few centuries of its existence. Still, I feel comfortable in seeing the Vinaya as reflective of Theravāda Buddhism's—to use Hallisey's word—*mentalité*.

4. The general term for a monk's apparel or robe is *cīvara*. In Theravāda Buddhism, there is, more specifically, what is known as the *tivīcara* or "three robes." The first is the inner robe (*antaravāsaka*), which is worn to below the

knee held in position by a belt or girdle tied at the waist (*kāyabhandana*). The second is the upper robe (*uttarāsaṅgha*), which is draped over the upper body, covering both shoulders. The third is the double robe or *saṅghāṭi*, which is a cloak or over-garment. This was deemed necessary for the sake of propriety and as a protection in inclement weather. Mohan Wijayaratna has asserted that symbolically, this outfit is related to the rag-robe, in that both were made from cut pieces. He further speculates that cutting up a cloth into three pieces was a way of reducing the value of the cloth to a minimum, as would befit the monks' status as renouncers (Wijayaratna 1990, 36).

5. Vinaya I.305 shows the Buddha prohibiting other ascetic modes of dress, namely clothing made from *kusa*-grass, bark, wood shavings, hair blanket, horse-hair blanket, owl's wings, antelope hides, swallow-stalks, and fiber. Also banned were robes of different colors and decorated borders, jackets, and turbans.

6. To spread out the *kaṭhina* is to make new robes out of the cloth.

7. That is, cut, sew, and dye the cloth into a robe.

8. *Imaṃ bhante sapparivāraṃ kaṭhina-dussaṃ saṅghassa oṇojayyāma. Sādhu no bhante saṅgho, imaṃ sapparivāraṃ kaṭhina-dussaṃ paṭigaṅhata, paṭiggahetvā ca iminā dussena kaṭinaṃ attaratu, amhākaṃ dīgharattam hitāya sukhāya*. Translated by Thanissaro 1996a.

9. The basic outline of the more detailed description that follows here adheres to Bhikkhu Khantipalo's (1980) rendering of his experiences of alms-begging as a Theravāda monk.

10. Vinaya II, 264–265. The same rule applies for robes: one cannot take for oneself what is meant for the whole *saṅgha*.

11. The paradox here is that it is meritorious to selflessly transfer merit!

References

Ahir, D. C. 1996. *The Status of Laity in Buddhism*. Delhi: Sri Satguru Publications.

Carrithers, Michael. 1983. *The Forest Monks of Sri Lanka: An Anthropological and Historical Study*. Oxford: Oxford University Press.

Dhīrasekere, Jotiya. 1984. "Cīvara." In *Encyclopedia of Buddhism*, edited by Jotiya Dhīrasekere, vol. 4, Fascicle 2, 183–86. Colombo: Department of Government Printing.

Disanayaka, J. D. 1993. *The Monk and the Peasant: A Study of the Traditional Sinhalese Village*. Colombo: State Printing Company.

Geiger, W., ed. 1908. *Mahāvaṃsa*. London: Pali Text Society.

———. 1925–1927. *Cūḷavaṃsa*. London: Pali Text Society.

Hallisey, Charles. 1990. "Apropos the Pāli Vinaya as a Historical Document: A Reply to Gregory Schopen." *Journal of the Pali Text Society* XV: 197–208.

Holt, John C. 1983. *Discipline: The Canonical Buddhism of the Vinayapiṭaka*. Delhi: Motilal Banarsidass.

Kariyawasam, A. G. S. 1995. *Buddhist Ceremonies and Rituals of Sri Lanka*. Kandy: Buddhist Publication Society.

Khantipalo, Bhikkhu. 1980. *The Blessings of Pindapata.* http://www.accesstoinsight.org/lib/authors/khantipalo/wheel1073.html.

Khantipalo, Bhikkhu. 1995. *Lay Buddhist Practice.* http://accesstoinsight.org/lib/authors/khantipalo/wheel1206/rain.html.

Morris, R., and Hardy, E., eds. 1885–1900. *Aṅguttara Nikāya.* London: Pali Text Society.

Oldenburg, H., ed. 1879–1883. *Vinaya Piṭaka.* London: Pali Text Society.

Rhys-Davids, C. A. F., ed. 1920–1921. *Visuddhimagga.* London: Pali Text Society.

Rhys-Davids, T. W., and Carpenter, J. E., eds. 1890–1911. *Dīgha Nikāya.* London: Pali Text Society.

Saddhasena, D. 1999. "Kaṭhina." In *Encyclopedia of Buddhism,* edited by W. G. Weeraratne, vol. 6, Fascicle 2, 160–62. Colombo: Government of Sri Lanka.

Takakusa, J., and Nagi, M., eds. 1947. *Samantapasadika (Vinaya-aṭṭhakathā).* London: Pali Text Society.

Thanissaro, Bhikkhu. 1996. *The Buddhist Monastic Code II.* http://www.accesstoinsight.org/lib/authors/thanissaro/bmc2.

Thera, S. Sukmangala, ed. 1932–1936. *Dhammapada.* London: Pali Text Society.

Trenckner, V., and Chalmers, R., eds. 1888–1889. *Majjhima Nikāya.* London: Pali Text Society.

Vijayaratna, Mohan. 1990. *Buddhist Monastic Life.* Cambridge: Cambridge University Press.

Witanachchi, Lalitha Karalliadde. 1999. *Customs and Rituals of Sinhala Buddhists.* Nedimale, Sri Lanka: Srideva Printers.

9

Letting Holy Water and Coconuts Speak for Themselves

Tamil Catholicism and the Work of Selva Raj

Selva Raj and Corinne Dempsey

It is plain to see that material religiosity does not always receive the credit or attention it deserves. Most generally, material religion often contends with normative presumptions that proper religion involves immaterial, spiritual realms and is best conveyed by words, doctrines, and beliefs. Such prejudice carries a certain weight within all major religious traditions yet seems particularly insistent within Christian contexts. As Colleen McDannell describes it, scholars of religion have resisted the study of material Christianity for a variety of reasons, one of which is that it requires us to take seriously the practices of theologically uninformed non-specialists, perceived as "weak" or, worse, superstitious Christians (McDannell 1999, 8–11). In South Asian contexts, it may be easier to take material practices and their practitioners seriously, as religion and materiality are so often intertwined; yet, as this volume attests, not all are equally comfortable with material religious expression in its various forms. Among the least comfortable, I argue, are Tamil Catholic clergy who have been trained in post-Enlightenment theology and whose rural parishes tend to celebrate material religiosity with aplomb and in ways that challenge priestly training. This tension between experts and lay practitioners, between suspicion and celebration of material religiosity—and the championing of the latter—lies at the heart of Selva J. Raj's scholarly career.

Selva Raj was originally meant to co-edit this volume with Tracy Pintchman and was also charted to write a chapter. Tragically, he died of a heart attack in March of 2008 before he had the chance. He nonetheless has left us with a long list of publications focusing on the material practices of Tamil lay Catholics that is breathtaking in its scope and depth. In these publications Selva recounts ritual events such as hair-shaving rites, cattle processions, chicken and goat sacrifices, and fake baby auctions, all of which take place at remote, rural Tamil pilgrimage sites. He describes them in earthy terms, as "grassroots" religiosity, expressing interreligious dialogue "on-the-ground," and as reflecting an "organic" or "bottom up" theological authenticity that challenges "top down" institutional frameworks. In spite of his penchant for material religiosity, Selva Raj was no stranger to institutionally prescribed, "top-down" religion. His "first career," as he liked to put it, was as a Catholic priest, trained in philosophy and theology. Before beginning his studies at the University of Chicago in 1985, he taught philosophy to seminarians at Morning Star College in Calcutta. During this period of seminary training and teaching, Selva was nonetheless drawn to earthy realities endured on the streets of Calcutta, reflected in his work with Mother Teresa and the Sisters of Charity. Such inclinations, as this chapter later describes, can be traced back to a no-nonsense logic that Selva recalls from his boyhood days.

Selva's post-1985 career, focusing on material, performative religiosity, represents not only a departure from his earlier seminary training; his critique of normative theology's limitations is a constant theme. Although this theme coincides with scholarship on material religiosity, rarely does Selva explore the function of materiality itself, thereby using it as an explicit category of investigation. It is my intention here to do just that, to revisit Selva's work, highlighting how items such as holy water and coconuts, sandalwood paste and saint medals, give life and meaning to Tamil Catholicism. Using Selva's writings as my guide, we explore how Tamil Catholicism finds expression not simply through the presence of these articles but through their absence. We view how these items enliven and are enlivened by their mode of use, those who use them, and the ritual setting. I approach this as a co-written paper, brimming with Selva's descriptively rich insights with bits of navigation, offered by me, on the side.

Leading us off will be the few available reflections, lightly edited, that Selva Raj explicitly proposed about material religion, delivered in a paper for the Conference on the Study of Religions of India in 2006. Here Selva touches upon one of his favorite themes: interreligious exchange in the formation of Tamil Catholic identity, a process that emerges in satisfyingly complex ways when viewed "on the ground," seen through the lens of material religion. Keeping this lens affixed, I draw from some of Selva's other writings to further elaborate on this theme. We then shift the conversation to explore contrasting religious worldviews of Tamil Catholic clergy, expressed in the orchestrated presence and absence of ritual items and bodies. Aided by his recently published autobiographical musings, we conclude by reflecting on the ways Selva, as a Tamil Catholic, forged his approach to and respect for material religiosity at an early age, bucking trends and resisting elitist presumptions in the process.[1]

Materiality in Lay Tamil Catholicism: Identity and Interreligious Exchange

Selva's paper, "'Material Dialogue' in Lay Catholic Religion in South India," delivered at the 2006 Conference on the Study of Religion, takes us to the annual festival at the Shrine of St. Antony at Puliampatti, fifteen miles southwest of Tirunelveli.[2] Here Selva describes his arrival in 2003, painting a picture of rural Tamil Nadu.

> As I made my way through a narrow bumpy road, for miles and miles I saw nothing but thorn trees, tamarin trees, and palmyra trees. The land is parched and arid. Having been to this village twice before, I was aware that Puliampatti and its vicinity are some of the most backward and depressed regions of southeast Tamil Nadu. But the thirteen-day February festival transforms this otherwise sleepy, nondescript village into a site of intense ritual activity, social interaction, monetary exchange, and competition for display of economic wealth and religious devotion.
>
> While an imposing twin-towered Gothic structure dominates the otherwise dull and dry local landscape, demographically Puliampatti has a mixed religious population of sixty-five households or 350 residents with an overwhelming Hindu majority and a tiny Catholic minority of thirteen households. Nadars, Pallars, and dalits constitute the three principal caste groups in the village with the Nadars forming a distinct majority.

The event begins, typical of Tamil Hindu and Catholic festivals, with a flag-raising ceremony. Yet, as Selva Raj describes it, the first twelve days of the thirteen-day festival proceed as a dry, institutional prelude to the "real" festival, experienced during the final day:

> As is customary in south Indian temple festivals, a flag-hoisting ceremony sets the thirteen-day festival season in motion. The entire village wears a festive look. Special liturgical, para-liturgical, and secular events are scheduled for the season. Daily devotional activities at the shrine include, among others, morning and evening Masses, a lengthy sermon by guest preachers gifted in oratory, evening vespers, Benediction of the Blessed Sacrament, and a healing service, with an additional noon Mass on the last three days. On the Sunday preceding the festival, pilgrims participate in a solemn Eucharistic procession presided by the local bishop. This solemn but sparsely attended procession where the clergy and nuns play a prominent role is in sharp contrast to the religious fervor, intensity, ecstasy, and enthusiasm characteristic of the chariot procession the next day. On Tuesday, the actual day of the festival, Masses are celebrated round the clock until mid-day when the local bishop celebrates a Pontifical Mass. The festival celebrations conclude the next day, the thirteenth day, with the ceremonial lowering of the flag.
>
> A continuous stream of pilgrims flocks to the shrine during the festival. Typically, those dedicating vows in hopes of obtaining specific favors from St. Antony and those offering thanksgiving rituals for favors already received tend to stay for the entire festival, while others come for the last three days. The vast majority, however, attends only the final day celebrations that include the colorful *chaparam* procession.

Selva then describes final day of the festival, rich in sights, sounds, and emotions:

> All day there is a continuous flow of pilgrims arriving in trucks, mini buses, cars, taxis, two-wheelers, bullock-carts, public buses, and on foot. Over five hundred mini buses, countless cars, and taxis are parked in rice fields. The spacious church compound is teeming with pilgrims. Outside the church, vendors who have set up scores of temporary stalls make brisk business. Among the various wares on sale are a wide assortment of votive objects and ritual paraphernalia such as coconut, coconut sapling, fruits, flowers, garlands, sandal

paste, kumkum (*sindur*), lime, incense sticks (*agarbattis*), and body facsimiles in silver, aluminum, and gold as well as common cosmetic items like bangles, jewelry, saris, textiles. [. . .] Attached to the priest's residence inside the church compound is the shrine's official gift shop where various religious wares including trinkets, souvenirs, medals, pictures, rosaries, holy water, holy oil (*anthoniar ennai*), and devotional literature are on sale.

By nightfall, the pilgrim community has swollen greatly. The air is charged with palpable religious fervor and spiritual energy reaching a fever pitch. Throngs of devotees—some dressed in St. Antony's signature monastic habit—gather in front of two brightly illuminated and richly ornamented *chaparams* readied for procession. Two drummers and two pipers play religious music as lay leaders put final touches on the palanquins (*chaparams*), one containing the statue of St. Antony and the other of Mary. Of the two, St. Antony's *chaparam* gains special attention and prominence in terms of decorations and illuminations. Standing on either side of the processional route are young boys and girls with baskets of salt mixed with black pepper and bright orange marigold flower petals known locally as "*uppu malai*" (literally, "salt garland"), the common votive offering of the very poor.

In sharp contrast to the previous day's somber Eucharistic procession presided by the local bishop, the *chaparam* procession is loud and boisterous. Priests and nuns who were prominently visible the previous day are conspicuously absent. A lone cleric is hustled through the milling crowds before the *chaparams* to offer a few prayers and a quick blessing. His inaudible prayers get drowned in the din and bustle. After he sprinkles the holy water on the *chaparams*, the priest is whisked away to his residence. At this time, Mr Ranjit—the patron [who financially sponsored] the procession—places garlands and gold chains on the statues, officially setting it in motion. The festival is now entirely under lay control and leadership. A sudden burst of energy fills the crowd that surges toward the *chaparams* yearning to touch them. The hundred plus police officers deployed on crowd control appear baffled and helpless. The mood among devotees is at once electric, festive, feverish, and frantic, bordering on the chaotic.

As the *chaparams* are lifted in the sky to the accompaniment of fervent cries and loud chanting of Antony's name, dozens of boys and girls throw baskets of salt, pepper, and marigold petals at Antony's statue. Caught totally off guard, I am completely drenched in the "shower of salt." As the procession inches its way through worshiping crowds, there are periodic and designated stops along the route. At each stop, a select number of devotees offer garlands, gold chains, and other votive offerings to the saints. Each time the *chaparam* is lifted above the ground, the "salt shower" is repeated with abandon as cries of "*uppu malai*" reverberate.

The procession slowly moves past the shrine with Mr Ranjit leading the way as drummers and pipers play religious music. Immediately behind the *chaparam*s are a hundred plus devotees. Walking five abreast, these devotees prostrate on gravel streets for a few seconds—unmindful of the filth and dirt on the streets—stand up and walk about ten yards, and repeat the prostration every five minutes. This pattern continues for the entire four-hour procession. [. . .], Leading this prostration ritual, known as *kumpidusevai,* are female devotees suffering from various types of mental illnesses including demonic possession and psychosomatic disorders, screaming aloud St. Antony's name as they prostrate on the ground. Next in line are *pada-yatri*s (pilgrims who have undertaken foot-pilgrimage to the shrine) sporting Antony's signature brown habit, followed by children, and other male and female devotees. Devotees assert that the *kumpidusevai* is one of the most auspicious ways of demonstrating the urgency of their petition and the earnestness of their devotion to Antony. Unlike other events, *kumpidusevai* is accessible to people of all economic and social status. Almost always it is a spontaneous display of piety, requiring no prior bid or approval. [. . .]

Using one's body as a site and vehicle of religious devotion and piety is an enduring pattern in popular, folk Hinduism. While *kumpidusevai* is not as spectacular or colorful as the *kavati* or hook-swinging rituals, it too reflects the pervasive Hindu, indeed South Asian, religious assumption that one's physical body can serve, with proper training, motivation, and preparation, as a medium and platform for expressing devotees' religious devotion, resolve, and fervor. Devotees highlight the religious significance—however temporary—of their physical bodies by accessorizing them with certain material objects like sandal paste, neem leaves, garlands, medals, and specific clothing so that their physical bodies serve simultaneously as

> sacred terrain and devotional vehicle. The *kumpidusevai* ritual where devotees subject themselves both before and during the festival procession to a series of bodily deprivations and humiliations is one compelling instance where the material body is used to attain mundane and spiritual rewards.
>
> Of special significance in St. Antony's cult and festival at Puliampatti are salt and neem leaves, two popular ritual items in the cult of Mariamman, the Hindu goddess of disease and healing. While salt mingled with marigold flowers are thrown at the processing statue of St. Antony by all Catholic devotees, neem leaves and neem paste are used especially by those devotees said to be suffering from various psychological afflictions and demonic possession. In addition to the medicinal qualities attributed to neem leaves by the indigenous curative system in Tamil Nadu, neem leaves have special religious significance as these are believed to be particularly efficacious in warding off the ill effects of black magic and sorcery, and the psychological distress caused by wrathful malevolent spirits. Devotees suffering from these maladies either apply neem paste on their heads or consume balls of neem paste in an effort to ward off the ill-effects of black magic, sorcery, and demonic possession. It is not uncommon to find scores of Catholic devotees in other reputed popular pilgrimage sites like Velankanni, and Uvari apply neem paste on their heads. Another material element used by this particular cultic constituency is the blessed oil locally known as "*Anthoniar puthumai ennai*" (literally, the miraculous oil of St. Antony). Though blessed by a Catholic priest, the use of oil as a curative instrument is pervasive in popular Hindu religious practice.

Selva notes how the material items used during the festival, drawn from a ritual repertoire that is both Catholic and Hindu, produce a ritual blending across religious boundaries that he identifies as a form of ongoing, authentic interreligious dialogue, arising organically from lived experiences rather than abstracted theologies.

> Elsewhere I have discussed the complex negotiations and complicated identities, or what Julius Lipner calls, "the ambivalent minority status" of Tamil Catholics that predicate periodic excursions into the religious culture and ritual terrain of their religious others, especially, their Hindu neighbors. More concretely, this suggests that Tamil Hindus and Catholics not

> only share a common physical and cultural geography, but also draw from common religious assumptions, worldviews, conceptual frameworks, ritual sources, and material culture. The festival tradition at Puliampatti offers an illustrative micro case-study for the multiple exchanges occurring at the grassroots level that accounts for the family resemblances and striking uniformity in the votive objects used by Hindu and Catholic devotees. This phenomenon of shared systems serves as a metaphor for the culture of dialogue that defines south Indian religious praxis.

In his article, "Being Catholic the Tamil Way: Assimilation and Differentiation," Selva reflects further on Tamil Catholic strategies of identity formation in relation to both Hindu and Christian material culture, viewed most dramatically within the festival context:

> Put simply, the Catholic festival tradition involves a wide assortment of devotional rituals and votive offerings including, though not limited to, goat or chicken sacrifices, the offering of coconut saplings, circumambulations, flag-hoisting, colorful *chaparam* processions, ritual tonsures, ceremonial auctions, possessions, bodily prostrations, and spectacular displays of piety and devotion (Raj 2002, 2004). And the material objects deployed to accentuate and accessorize these votive ritual performances include such common votive items as coconuts, fruits, sandalpaste, salt, pepper, neem leaves, and body facsimiles in silver, aluminum, and gold. Even a cursory look at these material objects reveals the striking family resemblance between these votive objects and those used by other South Asian religious practitioners, whether Hindu, Muslim, or Buddhist.
>
> What is notable about Tamil Catholic festival traditions is that in addition to these common South Asian votive items drawn from the indigenous—some might argue, Hindu—ritual databank, Tamil Catholics also use traditional Catholic ritual objects like candles, holy water, rosaries, saints' medals, crucifix, and scapulars. Thus, the material objects and religious symbols which Tamil Catholic devotees use to accessorize their ritual performance at festivals and pilgrimages are drawn from multiple religious sources—Tamil, Hindu, South Asian, and Catholic—making way not merely for the juxtaposition but for the organic blending or synthesis of diverse ritual traditions. By drawing on multiple ritual sources, Tamil Catholics freely assimilate the indigenous religious culture into their

Figure 9.1. Coconut sapling carried in St. Antony festival procession in Puliampatti. Photo courtesy of Amanda Randhawa.

> ritual praxis while consciously differentiating themselves from non-Catholic pilgrims. Such a strategy enables them to simultaneously express their attachment to indigenous religious heritage and loyalty to their new-found Catholic identity (53).

Selva finishes his article by shifting his gaze from public to domestic space, to a context that again articulates strategies of Tamil Catholic assimilation and differentiation amid material and ritual exchange.

> Let me turn to one final autobiographical anecdote. When my elder brother began constructing a new home in 1990, his

Hindu contractor and mason demanded that a special *pūjā* involving chicken sacrifice be offered to ensure the wellbeing of both construction workers and future residents of the home. Though life-long and devout Catholics, my brother and his family acceded to the demand and provided the prescribed ritual items and paraphernalia that included fruits, banana leaf, flowers, incense sticks, coconuts, camphor, betel leaves, and a live chicken. On an auspicious day determined by a Hindu astrologer, in the presence of my brother and his family, the mason—acting now as a ritual specialist—killed a chicken at the construction site, sprinkled its blood on its corners as well as on the foundation stone, and offered fruits and coconuts intended to placate some unknown malevolent spirits that are said to occupy and hover over open, uninhabited space. When he finished sprinkling the chicken blood, the mason spread a banana leaf on which he placed some fruits and a broken coconut, lit some incense sticks and camphor, performed *arati*, and carried the burning camphor (*chutam*) and incense sticks around the site, warding off evil spirits. Following this, the mason poured the water into a pit he had dug in the middle of the site. My sister-in-law later explained to me that the water ritual was to ensure good drinking water for the new home. After the mason completed the water ceremony, my brother and his family also poured a jug of water into the pit. As the mason conducted the *pūjā*, my brother and his family stood there along with other construction workers and witnessed the entire ritual sequence—sometimes taking active part, but for the most passively observing it.

While the mason was performing the *pūjā* and offering Hindu prayers, my sister-in-law—she later confided—was silently praying to St. Antony and other Catholic saints. When he completed the *pūjā*, my sister-in-law who is a pious Catholic lady pulled out a bottle of blessed holy water that she had obtained from the parish priest and proceeded to bless the four corners of the site by sprinkling them with holy water and placing an assortment of votive items (a holy picture, a Christian medal, and a crucifix) on each of the four corners of the site so that—she later told me—"Jesus might guard our family and protect our new home." (Interview with Ruby Amaladoss on August 1, 1990)

Evidently, both assimilation and differentiation are at work in this domestic ritual performance. Assimilation is

> amply evident in my brother's and sister-in-law's ritual behavior. Even though they did not take active part in the ritual, their physical presence, their willingness to have this ritual performed at their site and on their behalf, their endorsement of the ritual, and their material contributions to the ritual suggest that they assimilated, or at least endorsed, the ideology behind this ritual performance and prescription. Differentiation is prominent when my sister-in-law performed her "Catholic thing" in the presence of Hindu masons and workers. By her ritual actions, she was letting her Hindu workers know that while she shares Hindu religious ideas and ritual idiom, she also has a different religious identity and a distinct ritual tradition. Neither my brother's family who consider themselves devout Catholics in good standing nor their Catholic friends and neighbors view their ritual performance as a sign of dysfunctional faith. They deem such assimilation as not only inevitable but religiously salutary. As in public devotional rituals like festivals and pilgrimages, in the domestic realm too, the assimilation/differentiation or both/and dynamic enables Tamil Catholics like my sister-in-law to draw from multiple and different—even disparate—religious sources and ritual streams that help "cover all bases." (54–55)

This domestic example of interreligious mixing is decidedly more nuanced than the dramatic convergences that Selva Raj describes at rural Catholic festivals. Here, ritual performers adhere more strictly to their respective religious frameworks, witnessed by their choice and employment of ritual objects: Hindu workers ignite camphor and break coconuts to perform a *pūjā* and a Catholic homeowner seals a Hindu blessing with explicitly Christian prayers aided by holy water blessed by her parish priest, a saint medal, and a crucifix. As Selva intimates, we can best see the flexibility of religious boundaries in this instance when we step back a few paces and view intersecting practical and religious realities on the ground, desires and beliefs bound together through material expressions that help, as Selva puts it, "cover all bases."

A View of Materiality from Above: Clerical Ambivalence and Orchestration

Stepping back a few more paces, we bring into our frame the counter discourse of institutional Catholicism. Far from endorsing the organic exchange of ritual objects across established boundaries, institutional frameworks, promulgated "from above," are often more interested in reining in boundary lines or asserting (against the evidence) their impenetrability. Selva Raj's work often gives voice to this counter discourse implicitly, as the backdrop against which he terms lay Catholic rituals "transgressive" or as acts of dramatic defiance. True to his focus on material religiosity, he rarely conveys the clerical perspective in the form of words, surely not in short supply in sermons during key festival moments or sparsely attended masses. Instead, he illustrates the admittedly uneasy position of the shrine priest by calling attention to his body, its conspicuous absence and begrudging presence, often with a vial of holy water, at festival events. Also of interest to Selva are progressive clergy at urban Catholic ashrams who consciously orchestrate Hindu-Christian exchange by integrating Hindu symbols and implements into liturgical settings. While the religious objects these clergy adopt may be similar to those found in lay ritual contexts, the manner and meaning of their employment differ significantly.

This section explores these two modes of clerical material expression, the presence and absence of priestly bodies and water at lay-led festival rituals and the orchestration of Hindu objects at Catholic ashrams. Although these strategies—one resisting and the other supporting Hindu-Christian exchange—seem at odds, their view of material exchange performed "on the ground," championed by Selva, is similarly at a remove, if not dismissive.

I introduce the subject of clerical bodily expression at festivals by recalling Selva's rather comical depiction of the Puliampatti priest, related above, who seems propelled, and unwittingly so, by the force of lay devotion. He finds himself at the *chaparam* procession, constituting for many the "real" festival event, occurring after twelve days of somber masses and Eucharistic processions. His seemingly half-hearted and half-heard blessings provide a subtle endorsement and bridge between officially mandated activities and this spectacular concluding event: "Priests and nuns who were prominently visible the previous day are conspicuously absent. A lone cleric is hustled through the milling crowds before the *chaparams* to offer a few prayers and a quick blessing. His inaudible prayers get drowned in the din and bustle. After he sprinkles the holy water on the *chaparams*, the priest is whisked away to his residence."

In "Transgressing Boundaries, Transcending Turner: The Pilgrimage Tradition at the Shrine of St. John de Britto," Selva mentions priestly absence and minimal presence—and shifting trends of presence and absence—witnessed at four lay-centered ritual events performed at the shrine.[3] The hair-shaving rite, the most popular vow activity at Britto's shrine, is also the least supported by current clergy. Although the rite can take place at any time, throngs of pilgrims visit the shrine for this purpose during the annual September festival:

> [S]everal professional barbers—many of them Hindu—are pressed into service. On the last day of the festival, an average of 600–700 devotees have their heads shaved. The rite itself is simple and straightforward, devoid of any religious or liturgical components. Conspicuous by his absence is the shrine priest who has no part or function in this rite. However, according to an elderly catechist of the shrine, in the past the priest used to cut off a few plaits of hair prior to the actual hair-shaving. Today the shrine priests have no such symbolic roles. In fact, many shrine priests deliberately distance themselves from these popular practices, even though the vast majority of devotees who take tonsure at Oriyur are Catholics. [. . .] Following the hair-removal, pilgrims bathe, apply sandal paste on their head, circumambulate the shrine, and offer prayers, candles, flowers, fruits, grains, and other offerings at the altar of Britto. (97)

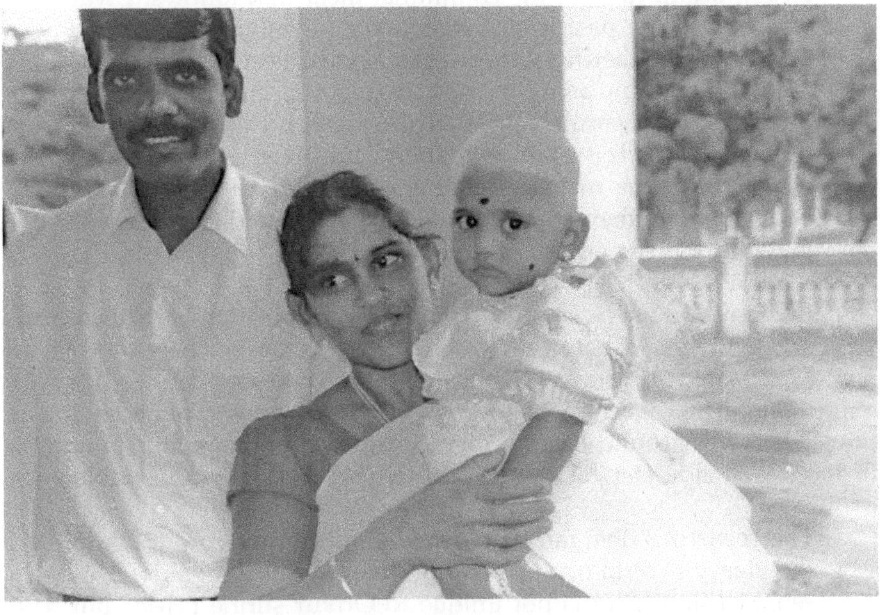

Figure 9.2. Sandalwood paste is applied to a newly shaved head at St. John de Britto Shrine in Oriyur. Photo courtesy of Amanda Randhawa.

The cattle procession, likewise taking place on the final day of Britto's festival, includes a begrudging priestly blessing with holy water (100) as does the goat and chicken sacrifice described below, replete with instances of material exchange:

> Adorned with garlands, vermilion powder, and other ornaments, the sacrificial animal is led by the pilgrim family to the martyr's shrine, where the priest blesses it with holy water, often reluctantly. Pilgrims solicit this blessing not to insure the efficacy of the rite but primarily for psychological satisfaction, as it gives some semblance of official validation for *their* ritual. The animal is then led to the slaughter area—located behind the shrine of Britto's martyrdom—where family elders bless it by tracing the sign of the cross on its forehead. [. . .] A senior member of the family then pours holy water on the animal, blesses and venerates it, followed by the actual slaughter witnessed only by men and children. A notable feature of the slaughter rites is the prominence of the laity in the performance of the ritual functions and the exclusion of ordained priests. The carefully collected blood is an important item in the communal meal that follows. I was told that in the past it was customary for pilgrims to offer a portion of the sacrificial meat—usually the best portion of the animal—some measure of rice, vegetables, and other cereal offerings to the shrine's priest. This practice was discontinued due to a Church prohibition. Today, however, pilgrims leave a portion of the meat and the animal's skin at the "priests' booth," where they are auctioned off quickly and the proceeds given to the shrine priest. (90–91)

In many ways sympathetic to the awkward position of shrine priests who are sandwiched between conflicting expectations, Selva recalls an anecdote related to him in Oriyur. Here we find clerical acquiescence amid blatant lay rejection of institutional restrictions. This parrying of power revolves around a ritual item considered perhaps too "Hindu"—or too far outside clerical control—to be institutionally acceptable.

> The recurring demand of pastoral compromises produces in the clergy a certain personal and theological liminality. This sense of liminality is not unique to Oriyur shrine priests but is widespread among many Catholic priests in Tamil Nadu. The following incident well illustrates this fact. A Catholic

> bishop in Tamil Nadu issued a decree in December 1974 banning all *tēr* (chariot) processions during Catholic festivals. A few days later, the bishop presided over festival celebrations in one of his parishes and reiterated the ban he had issued earlier. As the bishop came out of the church after the service, a group of local parishioners asked him to bless the *tēr* that was kept ready to be taken out in procession. Despite his condemnatory sermon against such practices minutes before, the bishop blessed the *tēr*. When one of his priests sought an explanation for his quick turnaround, the bishop said: "We have no choice but to respect the traditions and sentiments of our people." (105)

This clash between understandings of the propriety, efficacy, and ownership of religious materials finds interesting expression through the use of holy water. An essential component of Catholic ritual and staple of priestly blessing, holy water is also quite flexible, witnessed at Britto's shrine when a senior family member performs an apparently necessary post-priestly blessing over the sacrificial animal and when Selva's sis-

Figure 9.3. St. Antony festival procession on the beach. Photo courtesy of Amanda Randhawa.

ter-in-law seals the Hindu builders' ritual with a sprinkling rite of her own. Since a vial of holy water is a moveable object it can—unlike holy orders—theoretically end up in the hands of anyone, not just ordained men. And although water is made sacred through priestly blessings, giving it a certain institutional weight, it regularly flows outside priestly comfort zones, often in the absence of clerical bodies. As a result, as Selva's excerpts demonstrate, holy water can assist lay Catholics in widening and endorsing the realms of interreligious exchange available to them.[4] Indeed, the power and flexibility of a range of ritual objects, whether traditionally Hindu or Catholic, potentially used by an array of practitioners, is foundational to the interreligious exchanges—and intra-religious tensions—that structure lay Catholic rituals at rural shrines.

We now turn to instances where institutional Catholicism engages in interreligious ritual exchange while maintaining its grip on sacred objects. The difference between the following and the previous examples of ritual exchange is marked not so much by the materials put to use but in the way they are used and by whom. In "Adapting Hindu Imagery: A Critical Look at Ritual Experiments in an Indian Catholic Ashram," Selva outlines attempts by Catholic clergy to adopt Hindu paraphernalia beginning with Robert de Nobili, a seventeenth-century Italian missionary priest who went native, donning the sannyasin's ochre robes and adhering to Brahmanical rules of purity. His article then focuses on a recent example of clerical borrowing represented by Bede Griffiths's Catholic ashram movement in Tamil Nadu. Griffiths's Saccidananda Ashram is the permanent residence of monks and nuns who live simply and wear the robes of Hindu renunciates like de Nobili before them. The mixing of Hindu and Christian images and materials in the ashram setting, described by Selva, is extensive:

> The chapel is built in the style of a typical South Indian Shaivite Hindu temple. Statues of Mary, Benedict, and Paul adorn the chapel *gopuram* (towers). The inner sanctum of the chapel is darkened to resemble the *mula sthanan* (inner sanctum) of a Hindu temple. An inverted lotus serves as the altar of sacrifice on which the Mass is offered. The eucharistic liturgy is suffused with various Hindu symbols and gestures. The sanctuary walls are dotted with dark triangular niches for little oil lamps (*deepa*). The tabernacle in the sanctuary is built in the shape of a lingam. Over the door of the sanctuary is an inscription in Sanskrit. In the courtyard of the chapel is a prominent stone cross in an enclosed circle with the

> symbol "OM" inscribed in the middle. Sanskrit *slokas* from the Vedas and Upanishads, as well as readings from other Hindu scriptures and the Bible, are incorporated into the morning, noon, and evening prayers. These prayer services also include popular Hindu rituals such as prostrations; the *arati* (waving of the lamp in front of the tabernacle); and the distribution of sandal paste in the morning as the symbol of grace and divinity, *kumkum* (auspicious red powder) at noon as the symbol of the third eye of wisdom, and ashes in the evening as the symbol of the impurities burned away. [. . .]
>
> After each community prayer meeting, the residents, guests, and visitors gather in a simple dining room for community meals. Two large pictures of Griffiths and Ramana Maharishi adorn the refectory walls. An invocatory *bhajan* in praise of the name of Jesus—often sung in Sanskrit or Hindi—sets the mood and atmosphere for these communal exercises. All sit on the floor and eat simple vegetarian meals in prayerful silence and depart quietly. In the adjoining octagonal meditation/lecture hall, there is a wooden statue of Jesus in a lotus position, which has four faces pointing in four directions. Thus, while preserving its Catholic identity, the Saccidananda Ashram has assumed Hindu forms in architecture, style of life, dietary practices, and worship. It is both Hindu and Christian. (343–344)

Selva cites a variety of reactions to this Hindu-Christian mix, some positive but mostly negative, published in the Madras edition of *The Indian Express* between March 1987 and April 1989. Among the negative Hindu reactions was an indignant physician who wonders "what authority the Vatican or the Pope has to accord approval or give permission to misuse or abuse Hindu symbolism and spiritualism. Would they dare to conduct this type of experiment with Islam by building mosque-type churches, nailing the crescent on the cross [. . .]?" Another Hindu gentleman felt the Catholic ashram movement was simply a ploy for tricking Hindus into conversion: ". . . it is obvious that a common man can very easily be deceived by the usage of Hindu symbols and rituals by the Christian Missionary. [. . .] The cheating of illiterate masses is clearly unethical, illegal and should be stopped forthwith" (345–346).

Selva also reports Christian critiques, including the following: "Griffiths, by superimposing the sacred word Om on a Cross imagines that he has created a new spiritual phenomenon. On the contrary he confuses and insults both Hinduism and Christianity. . . . One has to respect the unique rites and rituals of each religion, which placed in another context will be meaningless and confusing" (347).

Rebuttals to these critiques include ones from Griffiths and his followers who consider the borrowing of Hindu symbols a theological imperative since, as Selva paraphrases, "they believe Hinduism can open up in the Christian tradition new levels of meaning whose organic and dynamic nature facilitates the assimilation of new insights." Selva goes on to explain that "Griffiths' perspective on adaptation is related to his understanding of the nature of dialogue. For him, true dialogue occurs within onself, in 'the cave of the heart,' and at the point where the two halves of the soul (the rational and the intuitive) meet. [. . .] Given this mystical emphasis, implicit here is the claim that the adapting of Hindu imagery is an outward sign of the interior dialogue with Hinduism occurring within the heart and the soul." Since this theology places meaning and power in an interior, mystical venue it seemingly dodges critiques that focus on the material consequences of interreligious adaptation including, at worst, as Selva puts it, "a new phase in Christian missionary imperialism" (348–349).

Selva then describes interreligious borrowing that thrives at Catholic parishes across rural Tamil Nadu and that incorporate an array of Hindu practices and items, many similar to those adopted by Catholic ashrams. He notes that these organically grown rituals not only avoid critique by lay Catholics and Hindus, but also enjoy the enthusiastic support—in the form of participation—of both communities. Selva identifies the crossfire of critique leveled by clergy and laity at the respective other's style of interreligious adaptation to be rooted in clerical elitism and the laity's resulting mistrust:

> While the church hierarchy that promotes institutional inculturation views the various expressions of popular inculturation as unhealthy and unreflective borrowing of Hindu practices and rituals, the Catholic laity have been critical of and indifferent to institutional inculturation modeled by Catholic ashrams because of its leaning and bias toward the mystical, philosophical, and ritual traditions of Sanskritic or brahminic Hinduism. From de Nobili to Griffiths, inculturation has meant adapting Sanskritic patterns of life and worship. However, many Indian Catholics, who freely borrow from popular Hinduism, view the Sanskritic tradition not only as a system of the elite but also, in the words of a liberation theologian, as "a primary source of the oppression of dalits, tribals, and

> women." Hence, they consciously distance themselves. [. . .] Thus, the Church elites and the laity are at odds with each other's adaptive techniques and, hence, are indifferent, if not disdainful, of the other's inculturative efforts. While the former is preoccupied with the proper, the latter is concerned with the efficacious. (352)

Viewed from the perspective of material religiosity, the divide between proper versus efficacious ritual seems to reflect different understandings of the nature and locus of power. In the ashram setting, as Selva notes, religious efficacy is spiritualized; materials borrowed from the Hindu ritual repertoire are meant to express and enhance an internalized religiosity that, for the most part, is institutionally contained and ordained. In popular practice, ritual objects themselves are considered powerful—those who mix and exchange items across normative boundaries do so in order to increase the power of the rites and of those who perform them. Put another way, the ashram adapts Hindu objects because they are considered theologically appropriate and symbolically potent while popular practices experience them as containing their own, intrinsic efficacy. For critics of the ashram movement, the nature and locus of power between these two settings are also significantly different. Ashram adaptation of Hindu imagery appears institutionally manipulative, widening the scope of clerical power, while popular adaptation potentially widens the scope of sacred power in a very different direction: due to the placement of power in tangible and portable objects, as we have seen, it has the capacity to land in the hands of lay Catholics and Hindus, beyond the grasp of the institution.

Selva concludes his article by encouraging those who engage in Catholic ashram experiments to "shed their inherent clerical elitism and institutional character and become truly inclusive in perspective, membership, and rituals." Possibilities for entering into interreligious dialogue "that is neither arrogant nor one-sided" are demonstrated by popular inculturation that arises not over concerns about the theologically proper, but from the lived experience of its participants (353).

Smashing Coconuts and Clashing Theologies

In "Being Catholic the Tamil Way," Selva Raj offers a view into his own lived encounter, at an early age, of clashing priorities between the proper and the efficacious. This episode—centering, not incidentally, on a potent ritual object—illustrates Selva's natural inclination to support, with palpable enthusiasm, interreligious exchanges that transgress institutional boundaries:

> When I was a high school teenager, my parents lived in a small south Indian town and our house was directly opposite a tiny Hindu shrine that had no roof, side walls, or door. Placed against the compound wall of the local king's palace were a simple iron trident and a large stone. It was known as "Muniandi kovil," a shrine dedicated to the local Hindu deity Muniandi. Daily after sundown, I would sit on the steps of our house and watch people go by. Some would stop at the shrine, stand with folded hands for a moment, place a few limes on the trident, and apply some *kumkum* on it while others would break coconuts on the stone causing a stampede as neighborhood kids and adults scrambled for the coconut pieces. Week after week I used to watch this ritual with certain youthful fascination and curiosity. Every time I saw a devotee break a coconut, I wanted to try my chances at the holy slivers. But I was too shy and too self-conscious.
>
> One evening, as I sat in my favorite spot, I saw a couple ready to do the coconut thing. "This is it; I'm going to do it, come what may," I said to myself, and ran to the shrine. As luck would have it, there were not too many young scramblers on that day and I was lucky to get a few slivers. With no second thought, I delightfully consumed the pieces. When I shared my adventure with my mother, being a pious Catholic, she was visibly upset and angry and scolded me: "Don't you know that you shouldn't eat food offered to idols?" From my catechism lessons I knew that I shouldn't have but I didn't care about normative guidelines. Three decades and two careers later, I recognize that I had instinctively responded to the situation in the way most of my cultural peers routinely respond, particularly during crisis moments. In the process, I had absorbed, as one absorbs one's mother tongue, the interactive and assimilative spirit—some might say transgressive spirit—and religious pragmatism of the land. Ironically, while my mother had absorbed the "either/or" spirit in which she was firmly grounded—thanks to catechetical indoctrination—I had absorbed not my mother's spirit but the "both/and" spirit of my mother-land. (48)

Clearly the disagreement between Selva and his mother has nothing to do with resisting the merits or possibilities of material religiosity;

the coconut shards represent religious potency for both parties. The difference resides in the perceived nature of this power and, more to the point, in the merits and limits of religious inclusivity. Looking at another site of contention for Selva, the Catholic ashram movement where religious inclusivity is celebrated in material splendor, we find a different issue at stake. Here the problem for Selva is clerical elitism, one that potentially leads to irrelevance at best or, at worst, religious, social, and political domination.

Selva Raj's lifelong insistence that religion be inclusive and relevant to lived experience—and the far-flung worlds he bridged to hone this position—finds fitting material expression in the gleeful propulsion of his boyhood body across the street to partake in sacred coconut slivers. This portends a future in world-bridging body propulsions for Selva. As a Calcutta seminary student and teacher, mentioned at the start of this chapter, Selva regularly sojourned to the other side of the city to serve the destitute; as a scholar of religion he beat a well-worn path to the remotest of Tamil villages to experience grassroots religious exchange; as a field researcher he may have slept at the shrine priest's house—thanks to his "first career" connections—but spent his waking hours engulfed in pilgrims' lay-centered practices. Where other priests were conspicuous in their absence at these shrine events, Selva, the ex-priest with camera and tape recorder must have been conspicuously present.

Figure 9.4 . Selva Raj interviewing pilgrims outside St. John de Britto shrine. Photo courtesy of Amanda Randhawa.

Now that he has been propelled conspicuously out of material existence, I know I speak for many in my gratitude for the legacy of Selva Raj's life-long propulsions, his tireless dedication to inclusivity of all kinds, and for the resulting priceless writings on material religiosity left in his wake.

Notes

1. Helping me to honor Selva Raj's contributions is a former student of mine, Amanda Randhawa. In 2003, Amanda traveled with Selva to the remote St. Antony and St. John de Britto sites and worked, for one month, as his research assistant. The photos featured in this chapter were taken by her.

2. St. Antony's coastal shrine at Uvari at the tip of the Indian peninsula is also the subject of many of Selva's writings. For a comparison and description of the caste makeup of both shrines, see Raj 2004.

3. For other descriptions of similar practices, see Raj 2006b.

4. As mentioned in the above description of the Puliampatti chaparam festival, another material element used by this particular cultic constituency is the blessed oil locally known as "*Anthoniar puthumai ennai*" (literally, the miraculous oil of St. Antony), known for its curative properties. Like holy water, this sacred oil, blessed initially by a Catholic priest, often ends up in the hands of the laity who apply it to those in need of cures.

References

Lipner, Julius. 1999. *Brahmabandhab Upadhyay: The Life and Thought of a Revolutionary.* New York, Delhi: Oxford University Press.

McDannell, Colleen. 1998. *Material Christianity: Religion and Popular Culture in America.* New Haven, CT: Yale University Press.

Raj, Selva J. 2000. "Adapting Hindu Imagery: A Critical Look at Ritual Experiments in an Indian Catholic Ashram" *Journal of Ecumenical Studies,* vol. 37, issue 3/4: 333–353.

———. 2002. "Transgressing Boundaries, Transcending Turner: The Pilgrimage Tradition at the Shrine of St. John de Britto." In *Popular Christianity in India: Riting between the Lines,* edited by. Selva Raj and Corinne Dempsey, 88–111. Albany: State University of New York Press.

———. 2004. "Dialogue 'On the Ground': The Complicated Identities and the Complex Negotiations of Catholics and Hindus in South India." *Journal of Hindu-Christian Studies* vol.17: 33–44.

———. 2006a. "'Material Dialogue' in Lay Catholic Religion in South India," paper delivered at the *Conference on the Study of Religions of India.* Paper. Albion, Michigan.

———. 2006b. "Shared Space, Shared Deities, Shared Vows." In *Dealing With Deities: The Ritual Vow in South Asia,* edited by Selva J. Raj and William P. Harman, 43–64. Albany, NY: State University of New York Press.

———. 2008. "Being Catholic the Tamil Way: Assimilation and Differentiation." *Journal for the Society of Hindu-Christian Studies* 21: 48–55.

Turner, Victor. 1969. *The Ritual Process: Structure and Ant-structure.* Ithaca, NY: Cornell University Press.

Contributors

Bradley Clough is an associate professor of liberal studies and Asian religions at The University of Montana. His research interests include early Indian Buddhism and the ongoing Theravada tradition in Sri Lanka. In these areas he has published many articles and book chapters along with a book titled *Early Indian and Theravada Buddhism: Soteriological Controversy and Diversity* (2013).

John E. Cort is a professor of Asian and comparative religions at Denison University, Granville, Ohio. His research focuses on the Jains, and on religion and culture more generally in western India. He is the author of *Jains in the World: Religious Values and Ideology in India* (2001), *Framing the Jina: Narratives of Icons and Idols in Jain History* (2010), and, with Lawrence A. Babb and Michael W. Meister, *Desert Temples: Sacred Centers of Rajasthan in Historical, Art-Historical and Social Contexts* (2008).

Corinne Dempsey is an associate professor of religious studies at Nazareth College of Rochester, New York. Her research interests include Hindu-Christian popular exchange in south India, North American Hinduism, and Icelandic spirit work (*andleg mál*). Her publications include numerous articles and book chapters, three co-edited volumes, and three monographs: *Kerala Christian Sainthood: Collisions of Culture and Worldview in South India* (2001), *The Goddess Lives in Upstate New York: Breaking Convention and Making Home at a North American Hindu Temple* (2006), and *Bringing the Sacred Down to Earth: Adventures in Comparative Religion* (2012).

James McHugh is an associate professor of South Asian religions at the University of Southern California, Los Angeles. His teaching and research interests include the material culture of South Asian religions, the senses and religion, and the history of alcohol. He is the author of *Sandalwood and Carrion: Smell in Indian Religion and Culture* (2012). He is now working on a second book, titled *An Unholy Brew: Alcohol in Indian History and Religion,* under contract with Oxford University Press.

Afsar Mohammad is a lecturer in the Department of Asian Studies at the University of Texas at Austin. His research interests include Sufism and popular Islam in South Asia, Sufi literature in South India, and Telugu and Hindi literatures. His scholarly publications include more than twelve articles and book chapters and one monograph, *The Festival of Pirs: Popular Islam and Shared Devotion in South India* (2013).

Tracy Pintchman is a professor of religious studies and director of the International Studies Program at Loyola University Chicago. Her research interests include Hindu goddess traditions, women and religion, and transnational Hinduism. Her scholarly publications include more than twenty articles and book chapters as well as four edited and coedited volumes and two monographs, *The Rise of the Goddess in the Hindu Tradition* (1994) and *Guests at God's Wedding: Celebrating Kartik Among the Women of Benares* (2005).

Selva J. Raj (1952–2008) was chair and Stanley S. Kresge Professor of religious studies at Albion College in Albion, Michigan. His research interests included popular Catholic practices and Hindu-Christian ritual dialogue in Tamil Nadu as well as Indian Christianity in the United States. He published numerous articles and book chapters as well as six co-edited books, *Popular Christianity in India: Riting between the Lines* (2002), *Dealing with Deities: The Ritual Vow in South Asia* (2006), *Miracle as Modern Conundrum in South Asian Religious Traditions* (2008), *South Asian Christian Diaspora in Europe and North America* (2009), *Sacred Play: Ritual Levity and Humor in South Asian Religions* (2010), and *South Asian Religions: Tradition and Today* (2013).

Stuart Ray Sarbacker is an associate professor of comparative religion and Indian philosophy in the School of History, Philosophy, and Religion at Oregon State University. His work is centered on the relationships between the religious and philosophical traditions of Hinduism, Buddhism, and Jainism. He has written extensively on topics related to the theory and practice of yoga (both contemplative practices and bodily disciplines) in traditional, modern, and contemporary contexts, including a book entitled *Samādhi: The Numinous and Cessative in Indo-Tibetan Yoga* (2005).

Mathew Schmalz is an associate professor of religious studies at the College of the Holy Cross. His areas of scholarly interest are global Catholicisms, Hinduism, and modern religious movements. He co-edited (with Peter Gottschalk) *Engaging South Asian Religions: Boundaries, Appropriations, and Resistances*. He also writes regularly for the website "Crux."

Neelima Shukla-Bhatt is an associate professor of South Asian studies at Wellesley College. Her work focuses on devotional literature of medieval north India, goddess traditions in Gujarat, Gandhi's thought and work, and South Asian religions in the context of globalization, especially as they traverse popular media. She is the author of *Narasinha Mehta of Gujarat: A Legacy of Bhakti in Songs and Stories* (2015), and, with Surendra Bhana, *A Fire that Blazed in the Ocean: Gandhi and the Poems of Satyagraha in South Africa, 1909–1911* (2011). She has published several articles and book chapters on a female poet Mira of Rajasthan, saint-poet Narasinha Mehta, women in Hindu traditions, and commercials for faith healers on South Asian television channels in the diaspora.

Index

Note: Pages containing images are indicated with **bold** type.

abhiṣekam (ritual bathing), 115, 128
Abhyudaysāgar, Muni, 58–59
Acala Gaccha (Śvetāmbara mendicant lineage), 51
"Adapting Hindu Imagery: A Critical Look at Ritual Experiments in an Indian Catholic Ashram" (Raj), 210–13
Ādeśvara. *See* Ādinātha (Ādeśvara)
Ādinātha (Ādeśvara), **41, 52,** 53
Ādiśeṣa. *See* Ananta (Śeṣa, Ādiśeṣa)
aesthetic critique, of external eyes, 52–56
agency of objects, 4–5, 85–86, 137, 167–68
alms-food, 182–90
Ambika (goddess manifestation), 94, 99
Amṛtsūri, Ācārya Vijay, 50
Āṇandjī Kalyāṇjī (Śvetāmbara Jain temple trust), 55
Ananta (Śeṣa, Ādiśeṣa), 5, 16, 23–24, 27, 28, 30–31, 34n3
animals, sacrifice of, 204, 208
ANI News, 106
Antony, Saint: festival of at Puliampatti, 197–201, **203, 209**
Appadurai, Arjun, 3
āratī (ritual of waving lamp before altar), 75, 141, 142, 204, 211
archetypes, 80–82
architecture, 53, 55, 74, 79–80, 210–11
artisans, 96, 99–100, 105, 158–59
Arweck, Elisabeth, 3
asceticism: Buddha's abandoning of, 189–90; *faqīri* and, 155, 163; *nāga* associated with, 24–25; Patañjali and, 26, 29, 30. *See also* renunciation
ashrams, Catholic, 70, 74–79, 206, 210–13, 215. *See also* temples
assimilation, 202–203, 204–205, 214. *See also* inculturation
aṣṭāṅgayoga (eight-limbed yoga), 18, 19–20, 26, 30
Ātmārāmjī, 57

Baba Fakhruddin, 164–65
Babb, L. A., 77
Batley, Claude, 55
battle of Karbala, 154–55, 156–57, 162
battle standards, 155, 156–59, **157, 160,** 167–68
"Being Catholic the Tamil Way: Assimilation and Differentiation" (Raj), 202–205, 213–15
Benjamin, Walter, 146
Berger, Arthur Asa, 5
Besley, Catherine, 91
betel, 139–40, 148n13
Bhandas, 92, 95
Bhatt, Vallabh, 98
bhikkhus. See monks, Buddhist
Bindhu, 121
biographies, of objects, 11–12, 137–38
bodies, female, 7, 97, 104–105, 106, 200–201

bodies, mastery over, 31
bodies, religious devotion and, 200–201
borneol camphor, 138–39, 140, 144
bowls, 182–90; centrality of to Buddhist monks, 173–74, 191–92; materials of, 183; rules about, 183, 190
bronze icons, 46–47
Brown, W. Norman, 47
Buddhism, 9, 173–92; bowls in, 182–90; *nāga* traditions in, 23, 24–25; robes in, 174–82; sectarian division in, 39
Burgess, James, 53–54

cakras, on shaligram stones, 124, 126, 127, 128–29
camphor, 8, 135–47; historic uses of, 139–44; as institution, 136, 137–38, 146; as lamp fuel, 140–44; models of how to talk about the substance, 137–38; mode of production of, 135, 145–46; in *pūjā* rites, 204; shifting meanings of, 10, 146–47; sources of, 138–39; synthesis of, 139, 144–47; types of, 138, 144; value of, 145–46
Camphor Flame, The (Fuller), 136
camphor manufacturers, 136–37, 146, 147
Carakapratisaṃskṛta, 27
caste system, 6, 67–68, 73–74, 77, 85, 96, 163, 197
Cathedral (St. Mary's) at Varanasi, 79–85, 86
Catholicism: inculturation of, 69–70, 74, 75, 81, 212–13; sectarian division in, 39
Catholicism, North Indian, 6–7, 67–86; materiality of, 67–69; in Matridham Ashram, 74–79; in Shantinagar mission, 69–74; in St. Mary's Cathedral, 79–85
Catholicism, South Indian (Tamil), 9, 195–216; clergy of in North Indian cities, 67; clerical perspective in, 205–13; identity in, 197–205; in Raj's life, 213–15
Ceiyavandana Mahābhāsa (Śāntisūri), 45
celebrities, yoga and, 31, 32, 35n5
celluloid, 144, 146
Chakrabarty, Dipesh, 145
Chamar caste, 68, 85
chaparam processions, 199–201, 202, 206
chariots, 122, 209
charismatic movement, 6, 74, 75, 77–79
Chidambaram. *See* Cidambaram temple
Chidester, David, 91, 98, 109
China, camphor from, 138, 139
Chopra, R. N., 139
Christianity: sectarian division in, 39. *See also under* Catholicism; Jesus, images of
Cidambaram temple, 28–29, 30, 34, 119
cinema, 83, 85
Citamparamāhātmya, 28
clergy, Catholic, 205–13; at Catholic ashrams, 70, 78; laypeople and, 195, 206–207, 208–209, 212; in North Indian cities, 67; Selva Raj as, 196; in St. Antony festival, 198, 199. *See also under* monks; priests, Hindu
clothing: in *garbo* ritual, 104, 107; in Jeevan-Darshan exhibition, 83; monks' robes, 174–82, 192–93n4, 193n5; in Muharram performances, 158
cloths, 48–50, 51, 52, 176–78
Clough, Bradley, 9, 11, 12
coconuts: in goddess image, 93; as offerings to Mary, 70; in Tamil Catholicism, 198, 202, **203**, 204, 214
Colas, Gérard, 141
color: in external eyes of icons, 44; of *faqīri* threads, 162; in Jeevan-Darshan exhibition, 83; of robes, 175; in Sanskrit poetry, 140; skin color of Jesus images, 72, 78, 84

conservation critique, of external eyes, 51–52
continuity/discontinuity of discursive meaning, 10
conversion: to Buddhism, 174, 175, 183, 184, 185, 191; to Catholicism, 67, 68, 211
coolness, of camphor, 140
Cort, John E., 6, 11, 12
cosmic Christ, 80–81
Cozad, Laurie, 25
cradles, offering of, 155, 156, 163–64
craftspeople. *See* artisans
crystal, eyes of, 44, 45, 53
Csikszentmihaly, Mihaly, 3
Csordas, Thomas, 2
Cūḷavaṃsa, 180
"Cultural Biography of Things, The" (Kopytoff), 11
cultural exchange, 10–11, 19. *See also* interreligious exchange
cultural flow, multidimensionality of, 12, 17, 33–34

Dalits ("crushed ones"; Untouchable caste), 6, 67–68, 73–74, 85
dargāhs. See *pīr*-houses (Sufi shrines)
darśana (devotional gaze), 40–42, 56–57, 62n29, 76–77
Darśan: Seeing the Divine Image in India (Eck), 4
Dasgupta, Surendranath, 26
Davis, Richard, 4, 57
dāyakas (lay donors), 176, 177–78
DeMichelis, Elizabeth, 18
Dempsey, Corinne, 9–10, 11, 116, 146–47
Deshpande, Madhav, 27–28
Desikachar, T. K. V., 18, 20
Devī Māhātmya, 92–93
devotional gaze, 40–42, 56–57, 62n29, 76–77
Dhammapada, 182, 184, 187, 189
diaspora, 107, 116–17, 130
Diaspora of the Gods (Waghorne), 130
differentiation, 202–203, 204–205
Digambara (Sky Clad) branch of Jainism: critique of external eyes by, 42, 56; icons of, 40, **41**, 56; offering of ornaments in, 48; sectarian division of, 39–40, 59–60
Dīkṣita, Rāmabhadra, 28
Dīkṣitar, V. V. Svarnavenkateśa, 119
Divine Mother: Karumariamman as, at Parashakthi Temple, 117; protective power of, 123–24, 131; revelations from, 121; temple to, 120. *See also* goddess/divine mother; Karumariamman (goddess)
dreams, 118, 120, 132n6, 158, 164
DuPont Company, 145
Durham, Walter, 144

Eck, Diana, 4, 76
Eco, Umberto, 91, 109
Elias, Jamal, 167
Elucidation of Pūjā (Pūjāprakāśa), The (Mitramiśra), 141, 143
enamel, eyes of, **44**–45, 52
equanimity, 179, 186, 191
eyes, external (on Jina icons), 6, 39–60; aesthetic critique of, 52–56; conservational critique of, 51–52; devotional gaze and, 56–59; history of, 45–51; production of, 42–45; sectarian division and, 40; theological critique of, 56
eyes, on image of Jesus, 76–77

faqīri (ritual practice), 154, 155, 160–63
Fatima (mother of martyrs), 157–58, 162
feet, 72–73, 188
fertility symbolism, 93, 94, 97, 164
flag-raising ceremonies, 197–98, 202
flags, offering of, 155, 156, 163–64, 165
flowers: in Muharram performances, 158; offering of to Jina icons, 48; Sufi saints and, 164; in Tamil Catholicism, 199, 200, 201, 204, 207

food: alms-food, 182–90; eaten at laypersons' homes, 188; in *garbo* songs, 101; ghee (clarified butter), 101, 142–43, 147, 190; North Indian Catholicism and, 68; offering of at Sufi shrines, 165; purpose of, 185–86. *See also* coconuts; fruit, offering of
forehead-mark *(nāmam)*, 140, 143
fossils. *See* shaligram stones
fruit, offering of: to Jesus image, 75, 77; to Jina icons, 48; in Tamil Catholicism, 198, 202, 204, 207; at yoga studios, 32. *See also* coconuts
Fuller, Christopher, 136
funding (patronage) of worship, 122, 141–42, 143–44, 199

garbo dance, 7, 89; meanings of, 10; at organized events, 105–107; origins of, 92; ritual elements of, 103–105; in secular contexts, 90, 107–109
garbo image (clay pot with lamp inside), 7; meanings of, 89–90, 93–98, 109–10; at organized events, 106; in secular performances, 107
garbo songs, 7, 89, 98–103, 106, 107
generosity: alms-giving and, 182, 186, 189, 190; cultivation of, 191; *kaṭhina* and, 177, 179, 180
George, Kenneth, 159
ghee (clarified butter), 101, 142–43, 147, 190
Ghura Master, 71–73
glass, eyes of, **43, 44,** 45, 47, 54
globalization, 19, 31–32, 130
goddess/divine mother, 89, 92–93, 93–94, 95, 96, 106. *See also* Divine Mother; Karumariamman (goddess)
goldsmiths, 158–59
Gotama Buddha, 24–25
Gramsci, Antonio, 68
greed, 178–79, 181, 182, 183, 185–86, 191. *See also* renunciation
Griffiths, Bede, 80, 210, 211–12
Gūgūḍu, India, 158–59

hair. *See* head-shaving
hands/arms, 16, 28, 57, 78–79, 82, 84, 156
Haracaritacintāmaṇi (Jayaratha), 28
Harivamsha, 92
Hazrat, Kallolini, 105
heads, metal, 156–58
head-shaving, 175, 202, 206–207, **207**
Hindu (newspaper), 136–37
Hinduism: dividuality in, 73; inculturation of Catholicism in, 69–70, 74, 75, 81, 212–13; in interreligious exchange with Catholicism, 11, 196–97, 201–202, 206, 210, 212–13, 213; materiality of, 69; *nāga* traditions in, 23–24, 25; Śaiva tradition, 28; Vaiṣṇava tradition, 27, 28, 30–31, 42, 110n2, 125, 163; wearing of sacred threads in, 162–63; yoga as central to, 17–18. *See also* priests, Hindu
holy water, 199, 202, 204, 205, 206, 208, 209–10
homam (ritual fire sacrifice), 115, 127–28, 131
Hoskins, Janet, 97
Houtman, Dick, 1, 3, 5
Hyatt, John Wesley, 144

icons: at Parashakthi Temple, 117; of Venkateśvara, 140, 143; in yoga studios, 15. *See also* Jesus, images of; Jina icons, external eyes on; Patañjali icon
identity, sectarian: in Jainism, 6, 59–60; Jesus images and, 69, 73; in Shi'i Islam, 155, 156; in Tamil Catholicism, 197–205; in Theravāda Buddhism, 173; in yoga traditions, 30, 32
identity, social, 11, 23
Imaging Wisdom: Seeing and Knowing in the Art of Indian Buddhism (Kinnard), 4
Impact of Buddhism on Chinese Material Culture, The (Kieschnick), 4

inauspiciousness, 77
incarnation *(avatāra)* doctrine, 27, 30–31
incense, 32, 48, 75, 140, 199, 204
inculturation, 69–70, 74, 75, 81, 212–13
Indian Express (Madras), 211
indigo, 139
industrialization, 144–47
interaction (engagement, exchange): between Buddhist monks and laity, 174, 175, 176–78, 180–81, 182, 184–87, 188, 190, 191; between Catholic clergy and laity, 195, 206–207, 208–209, 212; with images of Jesus, 69, 70, 72–73, 76–77, 78, 86
interreligious exchange, 11, 196–97, 201–202, 206, 210, 212–13
invocations, 20, 27, 34n3
Islam: materiality in, 166–69; metal battle standards in, 155, 156–59; ritual objects in, 8–9, 153–69; sacred threads in, 159–63; sectarian division in, 39; wish fulfillment in, 163–65. *See also* Muslims
Iyengar, B. K. S., 18, 19, 20, 21, 30, 31, 33

Jainism: Digambara branch, 42, 48, 56; *nāga* traditions in, 24, 25; sectarian division in, 39–40, 59–60; Śvetāmbara branch, 40, 51. *See also* Jina icons
jajmānī system, 68, 77
jālīs (aluminum grilles), 80, **81**–82
Japan, 145
Jayaratha, Rājānaka, 28
Jeevan-Darshan ("Life Vision") exhibition, 80, 82–85, 86
Jesus, images of, 6–7, 67–86; as archetype, 80–82; as charismatic, 77–**79**; as child, 71–73; as contemplative, 74–77; functions of, 10–11; as guru, 70–**71**, 73; as hero, 82–85; in Matridham Ashram, 74–79; in St. Mary's Cathedral, 79–85; in Shantinagar mission, 69–74
jewelry: in *garbo* ritual, 104, 106; in *garbo* songs, 99, 101; in goddess images, 93; offering of to Jina icons, 48; at St. Antony festival, 199
Jina icons, external eyes on, 6, 39–60; aesthetic critique of, 52–56; conservational critique of, 51–52; devotional gaze and, 56–59; history of, 45–51; production of, 42–45; sectarian division and, 40, 59–60; theological critique of, 56
Jin Pūjā Paddhati (Jin Pūjā Vidhi Saṅgrah) (Kalyāṇvijay), 51
Jinpūjā Paddhati kī Samālocnā (Abhyudaysāgar), 58–59
Jois, K. Pattabhi, 18, 19, 20, 30, 31

Kalyāṇ Kalikā (Kalyāṇvijay), 51
Kalyāṇvijaygaṇi, Paṅnyās, 48, 51–52, 54, 55, 58
karma. *See* merit, earned from giving donations
Karumariamman (goddess), 7–8, 115, 118–19, 121, 122, 130
kaṭhina ritual, 176–78, 180–81
Keane, Webb, 91, 103, 109, 130
Keenen, William, 3
Kelting, Whitney, 57
Khantipalo, Bhikkhu, 190
Kharatara Gaccha (Śvetāmbara mendicant lineage), 51
Kieschnick, John, 4
Kinnard, Jacob, 4
Kopytoff, Igor, 11, 137
Korom, Frank, 167
Krishna, *garbo* dance and, 92, 110n5
Krishnamacharya, Tirumalai, 18–19, 20, 30, 31
Krishnamacharya Yoga Mandiram, 19, 20, 30
Kuḷḷāyappa, 158
Kumar, G. Krishna, 8; on building of Rājāgopuram, 132; chariot vision and, 122; on Divine Mother, 121,

Kumar, G. Krishna *(continued)* 130; founding of Parashakthi Temple by, 117–19, 120; on protection by Divine Mother, 123; on shaligram stones, 116, 126–28, 129; shaligram stones brought from India by, 115
Kumar, Lalit, 47–48
kumkum, 199, 211, 214
kumpidusevai (female devotees in prostration ritual), 200, 201

laity. *See* laypeople
Lalbhai, Kasturbhai, 55
lamps: *āratī* (ritual of waving lamp before altar), 75, 141, 142, 204, 211; camphor burned in, 140–44, 147; symbolism of in *garbo* image, 93–94
land, as power spot, 119–20, 122
Larson, Gerald, 26, 27
Latour, Bruno, 85, 135–36, 137, 147n2
laypeople: Buddhist monks and, 174, 175, 180–81, 182, 184–87, 190, 191; Catholic clergy and, 195, 206–207, 208–209, 212; giving of alms-food by, 187–89; *kaṭhina* ritual and, 176–78; in St. Antony festival, 198, 199–200
light: symbolism of in *garbo* image, 93–94. *See also* lamps
Lipner, Julius, 201
Lives of Indian Images, The (Davis), 4, 57
local economies, 137, 146, 147
localism, 130, 131
locks, 164–65

Maas, Phillip, 27, 34n2
Madurai, India, 120
Mahābhārata, 24, 142
Mahābhāṣya, 27
Mahāmayī, 121
Mahāvaṃsa, 180
mantras, 20, 93, 129
Mariamman (goddess), 130, 201. *See also* Karumariamman (goddess)
Marriott, McKim, 73
martyrdom, commemoration of: with *faqīri*, 160–62; at Muharram, 154, 155, 156–58, 159; at Saida shrine, 163–64
Marx, Karl, 68, 86, 145
Mary, 70, 83, 120, 199, 210
masterpieces, 85
Material Christianity (McDannell), 3
material culture, definitions of, 5
material culture studies, 3–4, 91
"'Material Dialogue' in Lay Catholic Religion in South India" (Raj), 197, 198–201, 201–202
materiality: academic interest in, 2–4, 166–67; meaning-making and, 90–91, 130; objectification and, 85–86; spirituality in opposition to, 1–2
materialization, 166–67
Materializing Religion (Arweck and Keenen), 3
Material Religion (journal), 3
Matridham Ashram, 74–79
McDannell, Colleen, 3, 32, 195
McHugh, James, 8, 10, 11, 12
Meaning of Things, The: Domestic Symbols and the Self (Csikszentmihaly and Rochberg-Halton), 3
meat, 68, 208
Meghani, Jhaverchand, 104
Meghrājmuni, 51
Menon, A. G., 79
merit, earned from giving donations, 177, 178, 180–81, 186, 188–89
Meyer, Birgit, 1, 3, 5, 166–67
middle way, the, 9, 174, 191–92; bowls and, 185–86, 189–90; robes and, 175, 178, 179
Miller, Daniel, 85
Mīnākṣī Temple, 119, 120
missions, Catholic, 67–68
Mitramiśra, 141
Mohammad, Afsar, 8, 11, 12
money, 78, 163. *See also* funding (patronage) of worship

monks, Buddhist, 173–92; bowls of, 182–90; robes of, 174–82
monks, Jain: garb of, 39, 40
moon, the, 95, 98, 128–29, 140
More Than Belief: A Materialist Theory of Religion (Vasquez), 3
Morgan, David, 3, 91, 109, 130
Muharram, 154–55, 156–59, 160–61
mūrti (icon), 15
music, 129. See also *garbo* songs
musk, 72, 73, 140, 144
Muslims: production of icons/icon eyes by, 43, 61n5; as vendors in *garbo* arena, 96; worship of material objects by, 168–69. *See also* Islam
Mysore Palace, 19

Nāgarāja (King of the Serpents): Ananta as, 23–24; asceticism and, 24–25; Patañjali as, 5, **16**, 20–**21**, **22**, 27–**29**, 32–33
nāga (mythical half-serpent) traditions, 5, 23–25, 30–31
nakṣatras (minor constellations), 128–29
Narayanan, Kirin, 124
Native Americans, 120
nature, *nāga* and, 23, 25. *See also* trees
Navarātri festival, 7, 89, 92–93, 94, 105–107
neem leaves/paste, 200, 201, 202
neem trees, 165
Nevrin, Klas, 30
nīrājanam (rite), 141
Nirguṇa Brahman, 121
de Nobili, Robert, 210
Notes on Modern Jainism (Stevenson), 54
numbers, meaningful, 118, 128–29

objectification, 85–86
oil, holy, 199, 201, 216n4
On Wings of Diesel: Trucks, Identity and Culture in Pakistan (Elias), 167

paintings, eyes on, 47
paṁsukūla (rag-robes), 175, 176
Panchal, Govardhan, 92
Pandyan Empire, 119
Parā-Brahman, 121
Parashakthi Temple, 7–8, 115; founding of, 116–20; matter/materiality at, 121–24; mission of, 123, 131–32; Rājāgopuram at, 131–32
Parkes, Alexander, 144
Parmar, Khodidas, 94
Pārśva (Pārśvanātha), 24, **46**–47
Patañjali: institutional authority of, 15, 30–31, 33; *nāga* and, 31; narratives of, 28–29; texts and, 25–27. *See also* Patañjali icon
Patañjalicarita (Dīkṣita), 28
Patañjali icon, 5–6, **16**, **21**, **22**, **29**; description of, 15–16; exoteric/esoteric dynamic of, 32–33; meanings of, 10; modern yoga traditions and, 17–22; *nāga* traditions and, 23–25
Pathak, R. V., 92
perfume, 72, 73, 140, 144, 146–47, 147–48n5
Pia, Secundo, 76
Piety: A History and Theory of Popular Religious Images (Morgan), 3
Pintchman, Tracy, 7–8, 105
pīr-houses (Sufi shrines), 155, 158, 160, 164, **165**
plastics industry, 144, 145
Pontiac, Michigan, 119
potters, 96, 98, 100, 183
prakriti (matter), 104
priests, Hindu: at Karumariamman temple, 122; receiving of divine energy by, 127; unimportance of in *garbo*, 90, 94, 96, 98, 100, 104. *See also* clergy, Catholic; monks
prostration rituals, 200, 202, 211
protective power, 123–24, 131
pūjā rites: chicken sacrifice in, 204; *kaṭhina* ritual, 176–78, 180–81; offerings to Jesus image and, 77;

pūjā rites *(continued)*
offering to Jina icons in, 48–50, 57; showing of camphor flame in, 136, 141–42
Puliampatti, Tamil Nadu, India, 197
Purāṇa literature, 16, 23, 124

rag-robes *(paṁsukūla),* 175, 176
rags, offering of, 155, 163–64, 165
Raheja, Gloria Goodwin, 77
Raj, Selva J., 9–10, 11, **215**; "Adapting Hindu Imagery," 210–13; autobiographical anecdote by, 213–14; "Being Catholic the Tamil Way," 202–205, 213–15; career of, 196–97, 215; "'Material Dialogue' in Lay Catholic Religion in South India," 197, 198–201, 201–202; "Transgressing Boundaries, Transcending Turner," 206–207, 208–209
Rāja Yoga (Vivekananda), 18
Ramdas (priest), 122
Ratnaśekharasūri, Ācaryā, 48, 52
reciprocity, 77, 78, 178
regionalism, 146, 147
relics, of saints, 155, 156, 157, 164, 165–66, 168
religious objects: biographies of, 11–12; functions of, 10–11; meanings of, 10
religious studies (academic discipline), 1–4
renunciation: Buddhist robes and, 175–76, 179; charismatic prayer services and, 78; Jesus image and, 73; yoga and, 25. *See also* asceticism
rice Christians, 67, 68
rituals: *abhiṣekam* (ritual bathing), 115, 128; *āratī* (ritual of waving lamp before altar), 75, 141, 142, 204, 211; *faqīri* (ritual practice), 154, 155, 160–63; in *garbo* dance, 103–105; *homam* (ritual fire sacrifice), 115, 127–28, 131; *kaṭhina* ritual, 176–78, 180–81; prostration rituals, 200, 202, 211; sacred space in, 103–104; in Theravāda Buddhism, 174; *'urs* (ritual practice), 154, 155–56, 159–60, 163–64. See also *pūjā* rites
robes, 174–82, 192–93n4; centrality of to Buddhist monks, 173–74, 174–75, 191–92; colors of, 175; giving of *kaṭhina* cloth, 176–78; materials of, 175–76; purposes of, 178–81; rules about, 181–82
Rochberg-Halton, Eugene, 3
Rodrigues, Hillary, 93

Saccidananda Ashram, 210–11
sacred space, 103–104
Sage Patañjali Temple, 20–21, 22
Saguṇa Brahman, 121
Sahi, Jyoti, 80, 81, 82
Saida shrine, 163–64
Saint Mary's Cathedral, Varanasi, 79–85, 86
Śaiva tradition (branch of Hinduism), 28
Sakalacandragaṇi, Upādhyāya, 48–50, 57
Śakti (goddess), 121
śālagrāma. See shaligram stones
salt, 199, 200, 201, 202
sandalwood, 140; incense, 75; paste, 198–99, 200, 202, **207**, 211; powder, 48
Sangīt Ratnākar, 92
Śankhacuda (demon), 124–25
Śaṅkheśvar Pārśvanātha (Jina icon), 58
Śāntisūri, 45–46
Sarbacker, Stuart Ray, 5–6, 10, 11, 12
saris, 83, 93, 99, 100, 104
Sattar Saheb, 153–54
Schmalz, Mathew N., 6, 10–11
sectarian divisions: in Jainism, 39–40, 42; study of, 39–40
sectarian identity: in Jainism, 6, 59–60; in yoga traditions, 30, 32
Serpent King. *See* Nāgarāja (King of the Serpents)

Śeṣa. *See* Ananta (Śeṣa, Ādiśeṣa)
Shah, Ambalal Premchand, 54–55
shaligram stones, 7–8, 124–29; description of, 115–16; of Parashakthi Temple, 126–**29**; shifting meanings of, 10; Viṣṇu and, 124–25
Shantinagar mission, 69–74
Shapiro, Allen Aaron, 124, 125
Shi'i Islam, 155, 156
shrines: of Muniandi, 214; of St. John de Britto, 206–207; Sufi (*pīr*-houses), 155–56, 158, 160, 163–66, 164, **165**
Shroud of Turin, 6, 76
Shukla-Bhatt, Neelima, 7, 10
sin, materiality of, 77
Singleton, Mark, 18, 19
Śiva, 24, 28, 82, 121, 125
skin color, of Jesus images, 72, 78, 84
snakes. See *nāga* (mythical half-serpent) traditions
Social Life of Things, The: Commodities in Cultural Perspective (Appadurai), 3
spirituality: materiality in opposition to, 1–2
Śrāddhavidhi (Ratnaśekharasūri), 48, 52
state government, of Tamil Nadu, 136–37
Stevenson, Margaret, 54
stone icons, 46, 47
Sudarśana *cakras*, 126, 127
Sufi shrines, 155–56, 163–66
sugar, 165
Surya (deity), 94, 110n6
Śvetāmbara (White Clad) branch of Jainism: icons of, 40, **41, 46, 52,** 56, **58**; mendicant lineages of, 51; sectarian division of, 39–40, 59–60
Swamy, A. N. K., 117, 118, 119, 126, 127

Tamil Nadu. *See* Catholicism, South Indian (Tamil)
Tapā Gaccha (Śvetāmbara mendicant lineage), 48, 49, 50, 51, 58
temples: ashrams, Catholic, 70, 74–79, 206, 210–13, 215; Cidambaram temple, 28–29, 30, 34, 119; Mīnākṣī Temple, 119, 120; Sage Patañjali Temple, 20–21, 22; Saint Mary's Cathedral, Varanasi, 79–85, 86; Tulsi Manas Mandir (temple), 83. *See also* Parashakthi Temple; shrines
Temples of Śatruñjay, The (Burgess), 53–54
texts, meanings of, 91
textualism, 2, 40
Thanissaro, Bhikkhu, 191
theological critique, of external eyes, 56
Theravāda Buddhism. *See* Buddhism
Things: Religion and the Question of Materiality (Houtman and Meyer), 3
Thiruverkadu, India, 122
threads, sacred, 155, 159–63
Tirupatayya, 159
Tod, James, 53
tourism, advertising for, 31
Trainor, Kevin, 168
"Transgressing Boundaries, Transcending Turner: The Pilgrimage Tradition at the Shrine of St. John de Britto" (Raj), 206–207, 208–209
trees, 25, 138, 155, 164, 165
Tulsī (goddess), 124–25
Tulsi Manas Mandir (temple), 83

Untouchable castes, 6, 67–68, 73–74, 85
upekkhā (equanimity), 179
uppu malai ("salt garland"; marigold petals and salt mixture), 199, 200, 201
'urs (ritual practice), 154, 155–56, 159–60, 163–64

Vaiṣṇava tradition (branch of Hinduism), 27, 28, 30–31, 42, 110n2, 125, 163
Vasquez, Manuel, 3, 166

Venkateśvara, icon of, 140, 143
Vijayānandsūri, Ācārya (Ātmārāmjī), 50
Vijñānabhikṣu, 27
Vinaya Piṭaka (monastic code), 173, 174, 192n3; bowls in, 182–83, 184–85, 186–87, 188, 190; robes in, 175–76, 178, 180, 181
visions, 118–19, 122, 132n6, also dreams
Viṣṇu: camphor and, 141, 142; Nāgarāja's association with, 16, 24, 28, 29, 30–31; shaligram stones' association with, 8, 116, 124–25
Vivekananda, 17–18
Vyāsa, 26, 27

Waghorne, Joanne, 130
Waqil Saheb, 78
water: in *garbo* songs, 102; in goddess images, 93; *nāga* and, 23; in *pūjā* rites, 204; in Sufi shrine ritual, 165. *See also* holy water
Whicher, Ian, 26
whiteness, of camphor, 140
Williams, Raymond, 162
Witanacchchi, 191
wombs, symbolic, 7, 89, 93–94, 96
women: *garbo* dance and, 7, 104–105, 106, 108; *garbo* image and, 97, 98; in *garbo* songs, 100–103; *kumpidusevai* (female devotees in prostration ritual), 200, 201
Woods, James Haughton, 27
Woodward, Ian, 3
"The Work of Art in the Age of Mechanical: Reproduction" (Benjamin), 146

yantras (geometric diagrams), 92, 93, 119
Yaśovijaya, Mahopādhyāya, 48
Yogabhāṣya (Vyāsa), 26, 27
Yogasūtra: appeal to authority of, 17, 30; Patañjali as compiler of, 15, 25–27; as source of modern yoga, 18, 33
yoga traditions, modern, 5–6, 15, 17–22, 31–33

zikr (remembering the name of God), 161